FIRST NATIONS
CRYSTAL HEALING

FIRST NATIONS
CRYSTAL HEALING

Working with the Teachers of the Mineral Kingdom

LUKE BLUE EAGLE

Bear & Company
Rochester, Vermont

Bear & Company
One Park Street
Rochester, Vermont 05767
www.BearandCompanyBooks.com

Text stock is SFI certified

Bear & Company is a division of Inner Traditions International

Cataloging-in-Publication Data for this title is available from the Library of Congress

ISBN 978-1-59143-427-6 (print)
ISBN 978-1-59143-428-3 (ebook)

Printed and bound in the United States by Lake Book Manufacturing, Inc. The text stock is SFI certified. The Sustainable Forestry Initiative® program promotes sustainable forest management.

10 9 8 7 6 5 4 3 2 1

Text design and layout by Priscilla H. Baker
This book was typeset in Garamond Premier Pro with Futura, Gotham, Legacy Sans, and Southwest used as display typefaces

To send correspondence to the author of this book, mail a first-class letter to the author c/o Inner Traditions • Bear & Company, One Park Street, Rochester, VT 05767, and we will forward the communication, or contact the author directly at **info@savoirancestral.com** or **ancestralwisdomtoday.com**.

Contents

Introduction: Establishing Context   1

 **Part 1** ◄◄

Preparing for a Healing Practice
1. A Holistic Understanding of Healing   14
2. Three Preliminaries to Working with Crystals   20
3. Foundational Native American Teachings and Practices   40
4. The Fundamental Laws of Healing   66

 **Part 2** ◄◄

Crystal Attributes and Correspondences
5. Crystal Form and Structure   74
6. Working with the Five Elements   79
7. The Colors, or Rays, and Their Properties   94

 **Part 3** ◄◄

Principal Practices for Crystal Use and Care
8. Creating Sacred Space   102
9. Caring for Crystals   126
10. Establishing Right Relationship   134
11. Using Crystals to Help and Heal   143

▶ ▶ **Part 4** ◀ ◀

Advanced Healing Practices

12. Preparing for Hands–On Energy Healing   158

13. Laying–On of Hands   166

14. Healing Practices Using Quartz Crystal   173

▶ ▶ **Part 5** ◀ ◀

The Stones and Their Properties

CLEAR LIGHT CRYSTALS   189

Clear Quartz Crystal, Diamond, Herkimer Diamond

CRYSTALS OF THE RED RAY   198

Garnet, Red Coral, Rose Quartz, Ruby

CRYSTALS OF THE ORANGE RAY   203

Carnelian, Citrine

CRYSTAL OF THE YELLOW RAY   207

Topaz

CRYSTALS OF THE GREEN RAY   209

Amazonite, Bloodstone/Heliotrope, Chrysocolla, Malachite, Turquoise, Chrysoprase, Emerald, Green Jasper, Green Tourmaline, Jade, Peridot

CRYSTALS OF THE BLUE RAY   216

Aquamarine, Azurite, Celestite, Dioptase

CRYSTAL OF THE INDIGO RAY   223
Sapphire

CRYSTAL OF THE VIOLET RAY   224
Amethyst

WHITE CRYSTALS   229
Moonstone, Opal, Pearl

BLACK CRYSTALS   234
Black Tourmaline, Obsidian, Smoky Quartz

MULTICOLORED CRYSTALS   236
Agate, Labradorite, Watermelon Tourmaline

OTHER STONES   237
Amber, Fool's Gold/Pyrite

Conclusion   239
Index   241

INTRODUCTION

Establishing Context

In Native American teachings, context is everything. Traditionally, the teachings contained in this book would take many years to transmit to those in the tribe who have demonstrated "the gift." The human soul and mind are capable of vast depths of understanding that only ritual and ceremonial environments can instill. As I've taught these sacred teachings for more than forty years now, I've always used ritual and ceremony to begin these teachings. This allows the two hemispheres of the brain to synchronize. I call this *self-focusing* or *centering*. These and other traditional teaching tools are conducive to a full, in-depth understanding of what is being conveyed. We always begin with an opening ceremony where all participants share ritual purification, offerings, and the ancestors' chant to welcome all good energies. It would therefore be very beneficial for those who really wish to acquire the wisdom of right relationship with crystals to do a small centering exercise or purification ritual as you begin reading this book. Such exercises are given in the beginning chapters.

I have sought to render the poetic and energetic impact of traditional oral teachings in this book. Reading can thus bring a more holistic transmission of these teachings. The oral teachings are like a multifaceted jewel. Thus, another traditional teaching technique used here is that of repetition. As we look upon the multifaceted wisdom jewel from different perspectives, more and more aspects of the teachings are revealed. By hearing the same information but in a different context, one can grasp it as a whole, thus encouraging a more comprehensive and holistic understanding. All teachers have experienced the usefulness of repetition. We are delving into important, life-changing teachings. For this reason there are many repetitions in this book; this is intentional.

We might wonder why such a book, the contents of which are based on oral tradition, would be written. There are several reasons for this. We are living in different times today. The urgency of finding ways to heal humanity, nature, and the earth is very compelling. We are living in a globalized civilization that is destroying that which supports life. Everything is polluted today—the oceans, the air, the lands, even the snow and ice of the Arctic and Antarctic show signs of pollution. The number of diseases humans experience has exploded and new ones appear every month. Thus we need to find solutions, and all traditional knowledge becomes very important to preserve at this critical juncture. As nature is being destroyed, so have aboriginal nations all over the earth endured genocidal attitudes and policies. Many Native peoples have completely disappeared. They all hold or have held wisdom about humankind's relationship with nature and the planet; that traditional knowledge is now paramount if we are to find our way back into harmony and healthy living today.

A crystal, contrary to what some New Age books state, does not produce healing by itself, in an isolated way. Crystals are amplifiers or transformers of existing energy. Proof of this is our electronic virtual world today. These information technologies are all powered by crystals. What allows electrical energy to be put to so many different uses are very small pieces of different kinds of crystals arranged in different types of arrays. And very often they are used to convey messages like *buy this* or *buy that,* or they are sometimes used to horrific, violent, or abusive ends. So crystals, in and of themselves, do not decide what they project; rather, they amplify what we give them.

Thus it is the person working with the crystal who determines what healing energy is available. Spiritual practice, purification, clarification, perception, working with energy—these are all part of the training of a crystal healing practitioner. We would not want to use crystals in a way that would be harmful. Thus, training oneself is essential before working with crystals.

This is why this hands-on instruction on healing with crystals is now offered. Of course, training under an experienced practitioner would be really helpful in mastering these techniques. All true traditional training requires what is called *transmission*. This is where the teacher bestows on the student not only his or her knowledge, but also the proper context in which the teachings can be understood as well as the energetics behind those teachings. The notion of person-to-person transmission, from teacher to apprentice or student, is basic to many of the world's spiritual traditions.

The way we approach crystals in this book is very different from all the other books on crystals you'll find. This is because we have created context, what we call *sacred space.* This context is extensive, and some readers have commented that it takes quite a while before we begin to talk about the crystals themselves. This is very true, but there are important reasons and a history around this way of approaching crystals.

In some Native mystery schools, when a person is chosen for their gifts, for their ability to work with crystals, there would be twelve years of spiritual practice before they even touched a crystal. Yes, twelve years! When we come to the crystal, all that we are is amplified by the crystalline being. Thus important inner work must be accomplished so that the multiple dimensions and aspects of what a person needs to understand and to *be* is acquired, before doing effective healing work with crystals. This is why I have prepared an extensive background of the teachings, exercises, and meditations here that will attempt to re-create this preliminary context. Anyone who sincerely wants to follow the path of crystal healing will find here the food and thoughts to train with. We need powerful healers today, and my aim is to give as many tools as possible for this to happen. Therefore, it would be a good idea to refrain from using crystals until you have read the chapter on purification and care of the crystals. Don't jump ahead! Honor the path that has been laid out by tradition. Wisdom is in scarce supply in today's world, and it's the most precious of all our gifts, as it leads to peace, love, and harmony in all our relationships. Honor this wisdom by following this path.

When I began training with Native elders I soon understood that crystals would be a part of this training. Because of my fondness for these flowers of the mineral kingdom I was anxious and eager to learn. Yet it would be a long time before the elders would teach me anything about crystals. So I started reading a lot of New Age books on the subject. I even developed a small methodology to be able to use crystals. However, when I did begin the training with crystals, especially that taught by OhShinnàh Fastwolf, I took all of this New Age stuff and put it in the trashcan. I started anew from scratch. None of it stayed with me. When discussing this with my teachers I even realized that some of what is in these books is harmful!

So, let's begin by giving a human context to these teachings. The best way for me to do that is to introduce myself. This is the Native way, as teachings emanate from stories and examples, of which you will find many here. As my life is very atypical and stems from a will to follow Spirit from a very young age, this will give us the context we need to better understand the pertinence of the teachings shared here.

I was born a French Canadian in Canada, in Saskatchewan Province. Our Native ancestry was never mentioned. When at seventeen I left home to go study in another city, that first night a Native ancestor came to me in a dream, calling me to this work, what is called the *Red Road*. I embarked on that path and have stayed on it ever since. Many years later, a family member finally did the research, and we found three Native ancestors, and I suspect another one who was hidden. They come from both sides of my family. Our research has revealed Abenaki, Algonquin, and Pawnee ancestry.

Thus, after searching and finding Native elders who taught me and trained me over a period of eight years, I myself began to teach and have been doing so for over forty years now. I have never stopped learning and seeking more and more teachings, thus I've acquired some insight into Native healing arts.

Yet my spiritual training, and in particular my training with crystals, actually started much earlier, at a very young age. My experiences with crystals began in childhood. I began to be interested in them one day when I was returning home from kindergarten, when I came across a special stone in a back alley. It was of clear quartz and as big as my father's fist. I found it very beautiful, a translucent rock through which one could see. I brought it to my bedroom and placed it on a small stool. The light from the sun shone on the crystal. I sat down so as to be able to gaze at it comfortably. After a short time, my surroundings became indistinct; it seemed as if the crystal and I were beyond time and space. I no longer felt as though I were in my room. It was blissful and very peaceful. The whole experience felt very natural. Then I decided to go out to play. Yet maybe some thirty minutes later, as I was playing outside, I had the distinct impression that I was being pulled up, as if someone was pulling my hair toward the sky. I broke into a run and rushed upstairs to my room. The crystal was gone! The sun was still shining on the small stool, everything else seemed the same, yet no crystal. I looked around, asked my mother, but never saw that stone again. That really provoked my interest in stones, and from that day on whenever I would see white or other interesting stones I would pick them up and bring them to my room.

In this way I collected all the interesting stones I could find. One day, when I was about seven or eight, I decided that I would try to sell some. I gathered the small white stones I had in my collection, as I thought they were the most precious. Only now do I realize that it was because they were quartz, the most important of all mineral substances for us humans. So there I was, going from door to door selling rocks! I only did this once, but what I found interesting was that when the person didn't want to exchange a penny for a rock, I would lift my hand and look at them through the rock and say, "you really need this rock," or something similar. Invariably they would buy my pebbles. I made sixteen cents that day.

Another story that describes my early interest in crystals happened when I was nine. Accompanied by my father, I went to several meetings of the Lapidary Club at Saskatoon University in Saskatoon, Saskatchewan. Needless to say, I was the youngest one in the room. The stones and crystals I saw there were very beautiful and surprising, so many colors and different geometrical shapes. Yet the feeling of wonder and bliss I had experienced once before with my first crystal was nowhere to be found. I soon realized that this was not what I was looking for, despite the fascinating mineral specimens I saw there.

When my family moved to Quebec many years later, I had to leave my boxes of rocks behind. Not a problem for me at that time, as girls had suddenly become a lot more interesting than boxes of rocks! It was when my ancestors came to call me back to my roots, with my dream at age seventeen, that I subsequently found the elders who would teach me and they were using crystals to help and to heal! I'd finally found what I had felt with the crystals when I was a child. This is when everything fell into place for me.

The elders who have taught me are from Native American nations that have what is called a *priestcraft tradition*. These nations are known as Temple Builders, those who have a more organized spiritual society and thus have special permanent buildings for spiritual practice and ceremony—mounds with underground chambers, kivas, and pyramids. In these tribes, children who are recognized as having the gift are chosen to become healers, guardians of traditions and ceremonialists. Many teachers will assist them in learning how to pray, meditate, and perform healings and lead ceremonies. It's not a coincidence that these are the tribes that developed the most advanced therapeutic use of crystals. We will speak more about this when we describe the training called *spiritual practice* and how this is essential when working with crystals. What's most important to understand is that these ways have been handed down through generation upon generation of Native healers. Elders teach what works, thus these techniques have passed the test of time. They are efficient and trustworthy.

Over the years I have worked with this knowledge and have found it to be invaluable in helping people work their way back to health and happiness. I have verified its efficacy in many different situations and with many different kinds of pathologies. Empirically tested techniques of crystal healing have revealed that our mineral friends can be very helpful. I have trained many people in these techniques, in several countries, and over the years many have written to say they are grateful and most important, that these techniques work!

It's important today to always verify and test the techniques and methods that we are taught. All of us need to go beyond blind faith to acquire solid knowledge and wisdom in our healing modalities. Too often we have given our power over to people in authority or in academia, thinking that since they hold high positions they are truthful in their words. A reality check will find that a lot of what's being held as high ground is actually meant to control and manipulate humanity for financial gain, thus holding us in bondage. For this reason I would advise that we develop discernment and critically evaluate all the information we receive, especially when it pertains to our spirituality and our health. This is fundamental to having a balanced and powerful methodology for helping others. Thus, knowledge must always be balanced and verified by experience.

In working with crystals over the years I have combined different techniques that come from different Native traditions and nations. I've found this to be helpful, giving more power to my work. We are truly entering the time described in the prophecies where the Rainbow Nation, the mix of different races and traditions from all colors of humanity, will produce Rainbow Warriors, those who are ready and able to protect and defend the Earth Mother and all primordial traditions that are healthy and helpful. As I have worked with many different nations and have been to the Rainbow Gatherings from the very beginning, I consider myself a Rainbow Elder, one who does not belong to any one specific nation but ready to help all of humanity. Genocidal policies have been instrumental in destroying the people's traditions and teachings. Although many have survived, there are holes in the tradition where information is missing. When possible I've gathered the missing information from other ancient ways that have survived.

One of the particularities of Native spirituality is the use of humor and laughter as a teaching tool. You will not find this very often in other religious or spiritual traditions, yet in all Native nations with whom I have worked I have found this to be a most important trait. Humor is very important in the teaching methods of many of the Native elders I've trained with. It's an integral part of the Native way of life. Laughter is very important for dissolving tension in the solar plexus, which is the energy center of the emotional body. Laughter has allowed many Native nations to survive despite the horrifying conditions under which they were put by the invading European colonizers. It has allowed them to endure incredible hardships and to maintain a positive outlook on life even in the direst circumstances. There are holy people who are among the strongest of all the shamanic practitioners, who in Native culture are called *heyokas* or *contraries*. Their first mission is to make people laugh. This is considered a very important spiritual responsibility, for if you take yourself too seriously, life will be strenuous and heavy, and will often lead to an inflated ego.

One example of the use of laughter is in education. Native people do not punish for wrongdoing except in very extreme cases. It's counterproductive. A person who is punished will have a tendency to retreat into themselves or revolt. It's only natural, as we are each an emanation of Great Spirit's mind, and thus our basic freedom as human beings is sacred. What is used to correct minor character traits is teasing.

We need to understand the basics of the indigenous way of life common to all aboriginal peoples. The people live in communities. They need to get along. They need harmony on a daily basis, so they have a very strict code of conduct to ensure that everybody works together in harmony. As human beings, we all have things to work on, and minor character traits that are abrasive to others must be corrected. This is a lot different from what happens in modern society, where people don't need to enter into right relationship with one another. All they need is a lot of money or power, and then they can impose their will on others. We see this daily with many of our government officials, bureaucrats, and corporate executives.

Thus, when confronted with individual behavior that needs to be adjusted to the needs of the community, Native peoples use teasing, ribbing, taunting, and kidding, with the expected result of laughter. If you can laugh at yourself, you can transform easily, and although it's not as harmful as punishment, it is extremely uncomfortable! Thus the incentive to change said behavior is strong, yet still respectful of the person, and this adds movement, grace, and laughter to daily life. One of the techniques of correcting bad behavior is to perform sketches in the evening or on special occasions in which we recognize the funny or annoying traits of others without pointing a finger at the person, and this is often quite hilarious—and so much better than punishing children. In fact, Native peoples of America were horrified to see how white Europeans punished their children with physical force. Such brutal, barbaric behavior was incomprehensible to them.

I must confess, it's quite difficult to use humor in a book on crystals. I haven't been able to put much in here. I'm not a very funny person naturally, although I love to laugh. So this is just a reminder that we need to laugh as often as possible. It's very therapeutic. The stones don't laugh at all . . . so sad!

There are certain references to science in this book, and these are mostly to things I know or to affirmations that come from some of my teachers. I want to stress two things here: First, I'm not a particularly scientifically minded person, so if you're looking for pure science, this is probably not the best source. Second, I consider modern science to be more in the way of a sectarian religion than an actual search for truth and reality. Many claims are made by scientists because they are paid by companies to say these things. As an example, for many years it was said that tobacco did not harm one's health. Many scientific discoveries were pushed under the rug as they clashed with the established authorities of the academic and corporate elite. And finally and most importantly, science has often not served life, but rather, death. The best examples are the terrible radioactive waste produced by nuclear power and the constant threat of annihilation by nuclear warfare.

In reality, technology is a dead science. A machine does not reproduce itself and will always one day need to be repaired or replaced. That's because it's not a living organism. Using a horse might take a bit longer to get to where you need to go, but there's no pollution, it repairs itself, it gives birth to the future generations of transportation vehicles, and only uses renewable resources like grass that are then reinjected into the environment as fertilizer. I could go on and on in this vein, and if this subject is of interest to you, then my book *The Philosophy of Nature* might be something you'd like to read.* Nature has all the wisdom and resources we need to lead happy and healthy lives.

Also, in an effort to create context, I want to mention the power of symbols. Everything originates in the mind. All things are interrelated. As we explore our world and its symbols, our understanding becomes multidimensional. The vaster the mind, the more powerful the intention and thus the more power for creating health and harmony. Symbols are vast; some say that they are infinite. Thus we will dwell on symbols to nourish our minds, to create vastness of thought and references. Colors and structures are important symbols that have a direct relationship with the crystal world. So we will begin our study of crystals by creating a detailed description of these symbols. Meditating on these symbols can be a spiritual practice that helps us integrate a depth of understanding and vision. This will enhance our work with the mineral kingdom.

Finally, we need to explain the word *medicine*, which has a very different meaning in an indigenous context than it does in the general vocabulary. In this book, *medicine* means something that acts as a

---

*Available at ancestralwisdomtoday.com in the Member Area under Add On/Blue Eagle's Books.

conduit between the spirit world and our physical world here on earth. Medicine can be an object, a person, or a ceremony. It's anything that helps us incarnate in a more perfect way the original instructions that are held in the archetypal world of ideal form, what we call the *spirit world*. The word *medicine* means someone, something, or some circumstance that creates a doorway for sacred energy to flow through for the good of the people. This can be for healing, but it can also be for finding food, for predicting or influencing the weather, and for any number of functions that help us.

It's impossible to give the flavor of the voice, the singing, and the energies that come through ceremonies when these teachings are given in a book. Thus some of the teachings have been filmed and are available at www.ancestralwisdomtoday.com. There, with a free membership, you can learn the chants and also some of the more advanced meditations, as I did not feel comfortable writing them down. Our traditions stem from oral transmission, including stories that teach. This method has proven its worth, as our history is alive and is a lot older than modern "civilized" cultures.* We Native peoples consider books to be somewhat dead compared to the oral transmission of teachings, which are given in a carefully prepared context involving ceremony and the community's commitment to hold them for future generations. Ethical behavior, morality, and compassion is easily taught by sharing the incredibly rich lore found in the myths, legends, and stories of all indigenous cultures—so much better than trying to impose these virtues using punishment and reward.

May we all find our way back to the Great Tree of Peace. May we find harmony and unity with the earth, with nature, and with all people. And may those most evolved beings of the mineral world, the crystals, accompany us on this path to health, happiness, and harmony.

---

*We trace our roots back to the First World, 127,500 years ago. We are currently at the beginning of the Fourth World purification before entering into the Fifth World. Modern history goes back 12,000 years, although some traditions remember the Third World purification, the Great Flood described in the Bible, and Noah's ark.

Part 1

Preparing for a
Healing Practice

1

A Holistic Understanding of Healing

As we study crystal healing, it's important to know that the methods that are explained here come from a holistic understanding of what healing really involves. The human being is a very complex entity that has different "bodies" working synergistically to create the experience of life. We each have a physical body, the temporary vehicle of our soul. We have an emotional body, which is all those feelings that have great impact on who we are and on our health. We have a mental body, which is one of the higher aspects of our being that brings understanding to what we experience and helps us create and invent our life. And we have a spiritual body, which is the eternal, immortal soul as it journeys through the many lifetimes and physical bodies that it uses to experience life and to evolve and grow.

When you meet somebody in order to help and to heal, it's important that you consider the whole human being. Take time to listen to the feelings and emotions that person is experiencing. Often that's the most important thing that a healing person need do. Our relationships are the most important aspect of our lives. These emotional and relationship dynamics and how to work with them exceed the scope of this book. I mention this, however, as no healing approach is truly valid unless the whole person is considered, and this is probably the most important aspect in our times. I say this because our current modern lifestyles

14

rarely take the emotional body into account. We live in a dry, asphalt, justice-blind world. Thus the first thing a person will sometimes need to do is express all that their heart is carrying. If we can listen without giving any advice (unless requested), this alone can be intensely healing.

We also have to give careful consideration to the person's understanding of life. What does he or she know about health? How does he or she consider life? What's true and real for the person?

We also need to consider what the person's spirituality or religion is all about. Usually this can give us an indication of the person's life mission. We come to earth to learn, to train our souls. If we are not following our life path, the path that our soul has come here to experience, we can have serious health problems. These health problems or life challenges are there to redirect us onto the correct path. Understanding one's passions, goals, and associated talents and their love of life is very important. The ability of a person to reflect on their life mission has a great influence on everything they will experience. A person's religion and/or spirituality is an important aspect in this regard, as it can influence one's ethics and moral behavior, and this has a great impact on what happens in one's life.

Then, we come to the physical body: all the aforementioned aspects of our being have an impact on the physical body.

I use many crystals in my work, on all levels of being. Yet with time I have found that I'm using fewer crystals as I become one with my crystals. I usually start by visualizing emerald and go from there as the person seeking help expresses him- or herself and I get a clearer picture of their needs. I use dialogue, wisdom, shamanic energies through sound and music, and totems and guides to harmonize the spiritual, mental, and emotional aspects of the person's being. When I come to the physical being, to any illness of the body, that's when I start using the quartz crystal healing method described later in this book. But as you read this, *please do not skip ahead;* this is a step-by-step process that requires spiritual practice. To be effective as healers, we need to integrate many aspects of being and understanding.

The method using the healing quartz crystal we describe later in this book is very effective, yet it needs to be repeated again and again as a medicine that takes time to fully integrate in a person's life. My experience is that a person feels better almost immediately, but as they return to their lifestyle, the old habits and energies kick in, and they return to the discomfort they were experiencing previously. If you repeat the method, the person can experience relief for more hours or days, but the pain will come back. But if you persist in keeping at it, at some point you will attain a level where the body of the person fully integrates the energies that accomplish the healing, and they will finally be relieved of that for which you have been treating them. This can take time, and we need to persevere.

We also need to look at all aspects of a person's lifestyle. Eating habits are important. Family relationships, workplace experience, all of a person's life is important, as all can have an impact on one's health. What we are treating is not the disease. The disease or discomfort is but a symptom of what's really ailing the person. As the wise elder Sun Bear used to say, "Ninety percent of all disease starts in a person's head." Even our emotions are stimulated by our thoughts. We often invent many scenarios in our mind about what others are thinking, and this can give us great anguish until we find out that it's all an illusion, that those people are not at all thinking that way. I think we can all relate to our inner folly and self-inflicted stress. It's okay, that's life. The point is, you cannot really help someone if you don't consider all that they are, and that includes the physical, the emotional, the mental, and the spiritual aspects of the person's being. Looking at the whole person rather than just the disease is what is called *holistic healing*. As another wise elder, J. T. Garrett, said (in my words, from what I remember): "When a person comes to you for healing, they need to leave you having become a better person, or you're not doing your job right."

Another important understanding that's essential in creating a context where these teachings can have coherence and be holistic involves shamanism. Shamanism is practiced by Native, aboriginal, indigenous people all over the world. It's a universal methodology that has proven itself in an infinite number of healings and demonstrations of power since the beginning of our evolution as humankind.

What is shamanism? What does a shaman do? We can boil it down to one thing, as all shamans practice the same thing: they communicate with the invisible realms.

It's a general understanding among all shamans that there is an invisible counterpart to all things, and those "spirits" exist in the spiritual world. This is a world of ideal forms, where the spirits of all manifest things reside. Each person also has a spirit counterpart, as do the trees, the animals, the plants, the stones, the crystals, the wind, the fire, the earth, and the water. There is a lot more in the invisible realms than there is in the dense, physical, material world. As there are many specifics involved, we will just give a general overview here of some aspects of shamanism that relate to crystal healing.

Because one of the attributes of crystals is their capacity for interdimensional travel, they are very often used to communicate with the invisible. Crystals can be portals to other worlds and other dimensions. The most powerful among them in this regard is the Herkimer diamond. We'll talk more about this stone later, in part 5, when we discuss the specific properties of the different types of crystals.

It is also here that we will elaborate on the difference between what I call *initiatory shamanism* and *hard-core shamanism*. As mentioned in the introduction, the people who developed advanced crystal healing methods are the Temple Builder nations. Because they have a more organized spirituality, they have created specific places where the energy called *mana, prana, orneida, ki,* or *chi,* the vital spiritual energy that healers and shamans call on to heal and do their magic, can be accumulated. Because the Temple Builders are not nomads and have built spiritual centers, they have also developed and integrated training methods into their spiritual practices.

Hard-core shamanism is often spontaneous, coming after a near-death experience or very intense, physically difficult rituals designed to separate one's energy or light body from its physical manifestation, the human body. Once the light body's journey into the invisible realms has been experienced, it's easier to re-create it at will. That's when the more experienced shaman will start training the novice in his or her art. Thus while the nomadic tribes rely on experiences in which life itself determines the future shaman, the Temple Builders have ways of reaching the same results by determining which children have the gift, and then training them for years through spiritual practice. The constant in both ways is that ultimately we are spiritual beings who take on different bodies lifetime after lifetime. Yet although in a physical body, we are still able to communicate with our essence, sometimes called the *over-soul,* our spiritual counterpart, as well as with our ancestors and helping spirits, sometimes called *totems,* to live a more balanced, evolved, healthy life.

The existence of the soul and spirit of things is well-documented. Our current explosion in communication technologies has put an incredible wealth of information at our fingertips. Books by shamans, scientists, hypnotherapists, healers, and such have expanded the limits of our empirical knowledge and wisdom a thousandfold. Thus the question is not whether spirits exist, whether we have a soul, and whether we are immortal spiritual beings, but rather this: since we now know that all life forms and all human races are interdependent, linked to one another in all worlds, how do we best learn to live, honoring and developing our bodies, minds, and souls in the best way possible, respectful of all life forms? This is the ultimate question facing humanity today.

We will have to learn fast. We have gone too far, have destroyed too many life forms, and left too little for future generations. There are highly evolved spirits and the four elements that are much more powerful than this now-pitiful humanity, and lessons are going to be served. If we don't honor who we are, what the deep significance of being a human being means, and if we are reduced to serving as cogs in a system that is destroying natural habitats and ecosystems all over the earth, then it's a given that we will suffer. The world is always balancing out and bringing back into equilibrium all things. The elements of wind, earth, fire, and water supersede human control. We need to be in balance with nature, with Mother Earth, and a good way to start is by honoring our human nature. How we survive the cleansing that is coming and whether we can make a harmonious transition depends on whether we can unite in the fundamental understanding of who we truly are. Those who carry the wisdom ways must be honored and heeded. Sadly, we often persecute those who speak the truth about our world; I've had my fair share of this kind of persecution. This is because true knowledge takes power away from those who manipulate humanity for financial gain and power. Instead, we must give this sacred knowledge back to the communities living on the land, as they protect the land and all life.

The time is at hand when humanity is being challenged to take a giant leap forward in its evolution. We can choose the present path, spiraling further downward, or we can absorb the lessons and take advantage of the opportunities on offer at this pivotal time in human history. Our vision is that of a pristine, beautiful planet supporting plentiful life, in which we will live as immortal, eternal spirits who can embody in thousands of different worlds—to learn, to love, to become ever more luminous and powerful for the greater good of all beings.

2

Three Preliminaries to Working with Crystals

There are three principles that anyone who wants to work with crystals must understand and adhere to. These are: 1) having a spiritual practice; 2) having respect for the living nature of crystals; and 3) demonstrating a willingness to protect and help nature and Mother Earth.

FIRST PRELIMINARY: SPIRITUAL PRACTICE

The first crystal with which we work, cleaning, polishing, and purifying, is ourself. Before any healing work with crystals can commence, there must be spiritual preparation.

It's no coincidence that among the Native peoples of America, the nations that developed the most elaborate crystal healing techniques were the Temple Builders. These nations have developed a more organized and formal spiritual structure and methods of transmission, in which spiritual elders met and did ceremony and passed their knowledge along to those chosen to work with crystals. The Temple Builders include the Cherokee, with their great earth mounds; the Hopi, with their kivas; and the Maya, with their pyramids. Those who are destined to become holders of healing crystals are chosen to do so when young and trained for many years to do this work. Thus if one is to be proficient in the use of crystals, training is required to discipline one's thoughts, emotions, and energy. The more organized forms of spirituality, such as those of the Temple Builders, allow for this kind of training.

It's important to understand that the crystals themselves do not decide what they will amplify or restructure. They accept all types of energy, and as this energy passes through them, they modulate these energies following their specific molecular structure and their programming. This can be clearly seen in a simple experiment. If you hit a one-pointed quartz crystal on one of its sides with a hammer, you will see a spark coming out its tip. The crystal has transformed physical energy into electrical energy. This is how microphones work. A tiny piece of crystal is impacted by the movement of air as influenced by the sound of our voice, and the subsequent electrical variations produced are amplified so that the resulting sounds are broadcast through a sound system. Similarly, if you send a tiny electrical current through a crystal, it will start vibrating, transforming electrical energy into physical energy. This is how your quartz watch works. A tiny battery feeds electricity into a small piece of quartz crystal, which then vibrates to an exact pulse that is used to count the seconds, minutes, and hours of the day. The laser is electrical energy becoming coherent photonic (light) rays as it is modulated through a ruby. Another easy image that everyone knows is that of white light or sunlight going through a crystal and becoming the different colors of the rainbow. In short, all energies are amplified or transformed when modulated through a crystal. What is of interest to us here is the way crystals can amplify and/or transform vital energy, human intentions and thoughts, positive emotions, and other healing energies.

Now, for a person to be able to modulate precise energy and clear intentions through a crystal takes practice. Try holding onto a single thought for sixty seconds and you'll see that saying and doing are two different things. For a person to be able to use a crystal efficiently in a healing mode, that person needs to be able to hold clear, focused thoughts, an intelligent intention, and must have a very strong vital energy to support this intention. They also need to know how that can be communicated through the crystal. Such a person must be able to perceive energy and sense how to transform or amplify this energy using a crystal. This takes practice, years of practice.

When we hold a crystal, every thought, emotion, and energy is immediately amplified and/or transformed by the crystal. Therefore it is important that we work on purifying and disciplining ourselves and our energies so that we can achieve the greatest well-being in all our relationships. The crystal awaits whatever energy is channeled through it and amplifies or transforms this energy. It does nothing by itself. We are the ones that must perfect these energies so that they are pure, focused, and beneficial.

What allows us to perfect who we are, to master our thoughts and emotions so we can perceive and modulate energy is called *spiritual practice*. Meditation, prayer, and specific physical and energy exercises are all appropriate means of achieving purification of and mastery over one's thoughts, feelings, words, and energy. These are the three essential aspects of spiritual practice. We will now look at these three dimensions of spiritual practice: prayer; meditation; and taking care of the embodiment of our spirit, our physical body. Let's look at what these practices entail and how to make them a part of our daily lives.

Prayer and Offerings

Prayer is giving thanks, expressing gratitude for life. This stimulates joy and health and initiates a cycle of reciprocity with the world. Saying thank-you for the new day as you awaken will put a very positive spin on the day. It's difficult to be sad when you are thankful. So prayer stimulates your life force, your vital energy, and positive emotions. It also nourishes the land and all beings around you. Prayers of thankfulness have a frequency, a vibration of hope and joy. All beings are nourished by a person's prayers. What we give comes back to us. This is the cycle of reciprocity. By giving prayers and offerings of gratitude, you nourish the world with this positive energy, and in return favorable circumstances and beneficial energies will come your way. By bringing joy and dispelling sadness, you develop your vital energy. This is very important for the person using energy healing tools such as crystals.

Thus, all forms of prayer that are from the heart and express thankfulness for the gift of life are beneficial. Native, indigenous, and aboriginal prayers are in tune with the natural rhythms of the earth. Those prayers that come from your family and from community traditions are in tune with your ancestry. What I have found important is that the prayer must be more than just a silent prayer. Praying out loud has a greater effect, as it manifests sound into the environment, and this sound is imbued with the intention of giving thanks. One example of manifesting physically our gratefulness is the practice of making offerings. All Native, indigenous, aboriginal cultures practice making offerings, and most religions do as well, often in the form of incense.

Here is one way you can practice this. Before your next meal, take a small amount of each aliment on your plate and put it on a small piece of bread or in a small cup. After your meal, go outside, find a tree or natural place, and give this food offering to the spirits of nature who so generously provide the sustenance you just ingested. After offering this token of appreciation, remain a few moments in silence, observing how you feel and what happens around you. Food offerings are universal, as they are found in indigenous traditions worldwide. Smoke offerings are also widely used and will be described later on.

You can also offer a song or a dance. Or you can refrain from one of your more addictive habits for a while as an offering. As you can see, there are many ways to offer thankful prayers. These kinds of offerings should be cultivated as part of one's daily practice. Only through repetition and regularity will we develop those attributes that will enhance our ability to help and to heal.

When people pray together, this is very nourishing on all levels and is a form of offering as long as the feeling and expression of thankfulness is present. Positive energy is always created. Praying with others purifies one's intention and creates a feeling of unity. The ancestors and spirit beings who assist with healing feed on this energy like a battery. Ceremony, ritual, and prayer, accomplished with the right intention, that of giving back to the world through feelings of thankfulness and appreciation, has far-reaching effects. The natural environment will benefit from the heightened frequencies created by these practices.

That is the first practice of the three. We have been speaking to the universe of our appreciativeness and gratitude for the gift of life. Now we need to listen; this is called *meditation.*

Meditation

We need not make this more complicated than it is. What listening to the universe actually is, is simply sitting down once or twice a day and doing nothing. Simple! Yet people have a hard time doing that today in our goal-oriented modern civilization.

We all need time to reflect on our lives. Making time and space for understanding reality and the constant, ever-changing evolution of our existence as individuals and as a collective is a must for all those who would like to help others. To be truly able to help others you must understand what is happening to them, and this is very complex. By "understand" we do not mean trying to master the intricacies of human life, although that is a very useful endeavor; rather, it means to make sense of who we are. The eternal question "Who am I" that all philosophers debate is the starting point of this practice of listening. For a healing practitioner, this does not involve heavy mental and intellectual pursuits, but rather, trying to integrate into one's understanding the essentials of what our heart, body, and mind are trying to convey to us. To do this we must remain still and listen.

Meditation can make you aware of destructive thoughts before they manifest in your life. If you realize, for example, that you are having violent thoughts about someone, you should concentrate on the antidote—that is, the opposite thought, which means looking at the positive aspects of that person. But if you are not attentive and don't realize that the thoughts you harbor are negative and damaging, they will continue and follow their course to conclusion. Much strife and misunderstanding can result, and the end result can sometimes lead to war.

Our mind is like a great lake, and our thoughts are like waves that reach many people before touching the shore and returning to us. Our thoughts, although invisible, have an effect on the world and the people around us. An easy example that many older people have experienced is the youthful desire for some material object that the person no longer wishes for, yet comes into their life. That ardent thought of desire created an energy that eventually brought the object of desire into physical manifestation. For this reason we must be the guardians of our thoughts, as they can break the peace as surely as the sound of gunfire.

The following saying is common in Native American spirituality: "Never judge another man until you have walked a hundred miles in his moccasins." We must be mindful about how we speak of others so as not to amplify their negative traits.

Teaching Story

Here is a story of how some Cherokee elders applied the principle of mindfulness. One day the American government decided to relocate the Cherokee nation from their homes in the southeastern United States. Soldiers arrived without warning, and the people had to abandon their homes and possessions to travel on foot thousands of miles, in the middle of winter, with inadequate food supplies and inadequate clothing. Thousands died. This infamous event in their history is called the Trail of Tears. The Cherokee elders gave these people who forced them to walk a name: "the men who seem to be evil." In the minds of the elders, this would allow them to influence their outer reality by allowing for the possibility that the Americans would one day change.

We are an integrated part of a world equation called Mother Earth. Humanity has its role and utility for the planet. We have what Native peoples call our "original instructions," the mission for the person and the collective in the global living sphere of life that is our planet. All our thoughts, words, and actions reverberate throughout the world and come back to us. If we are in harmony with our original instructions, we'll be happy and healthy. If not, then we suffer. For example, modern people are increasingly afflicted with life-threatening diseases such as cancer. This disease is a condition wherein the cells in the body start growing in ways that are destructive to the whole. This is not a coincidence, because humankind, an integral part of the world's ecology, is also acting in ways that destroy the earth. We humans are literally a cancer on the earth, and thus this vibration resonates in our individual bodies.

It is extremely important, therefore, to be mindful of what we think and say, because these are the threads with which we weave our tomorrows. Our lives are the result of yesterday's thoughts, words, and actions. Thought precedes action, thus the need to be awake and aware, and this, like everything in life, requires practice.

In our Native ways there are visualizations, ways of working with color and geometrical shapes, using sound such as chanting, special movements, breathing exercises, and energy work, all of which are used in various types of meditation to better train our minds and spirits. Further on in this book we will give you some practices that can help you train your mind and spirit.

So meditation is the second aspect of spiritual practice. What will enhance your practice still more is the third aspect, taking care of this vehicle that expresses life, the physical body.

Taking Care of the Vehicle

Our bodies have many channels of energy through which the life force circulates. Keeping these open and flowing increases the body's vital energy, that pervasive energy called *orneida* by the Cherokee, *prana* by the Hindus, *mana* by the Hawaiians, and *qi* or *chi* by the Taoists. This a practice common to spiritual traditions throughout the world. Many Native Americans remained healthy to an incredibly old age by keeping their bodies moving and their energy channels open and clear. They did not become senile in their final years. In fact, right up to their final moments they were still supple, their backs still straight, and they danced every morning. That dance is one of the reasons they stayed so healthy. For energy to move within us we need to move, and if we imitate the movements of nature, the energy channels will remain open.

The healthier your body is, the more energy you will have and therefore the greater potential to effectively help and heal others. Physical exercises are very important for tuning up the body of a healing practitioner. We have a whole series of exercises for stretching and breathing, and the movements of the sacred dances are also very helpful. Here again, all methods can be useful. What you practice is not as important as doing some kind of practice every day. Use what works for you. The most important exercise is walking. We need to move on Mother Earth's body and admire her beauty every day.

Besides exercise there are six other keys to a healthy body. It's important to mention them here as they are essential and not often emphasized by the medical industry. It can be very frustrating to work very hard at helping someone heal from a difficult disease, only to find that when they go back to their daily routine of fast food, tap water, and lack of exercise, it's destroying all your good work. So let's have a brief look at the other basic keys to a healthy body.

Food

Hippocrates, the ancient Greek wise man who is considered the father of modern medicine, said, "Let food be thy medicine and let medicine be thy food." The foundation of health is what we ingest, and the closer we are to nature, the closer we'll be to perfect health. That is why many health professionals recommend a raw vegan diet.

All creatures on earth eat their food raw. Cooking food considerably reduces its content in vitamins, organic minerals, and enzymes. Vitamins are destroyed, minerals become inorganic, and enzymes, which are necessary for digestion as they are the living part of food, are killed by the heat in cooking. A healthy person can eat up to 20 percent of cooked, plant-based food without falling ill, but a person with health challenges should eat all raw if they want to recover.

The food should be plant-based, with as few animal proteins as possible. All animal proteins rapidly decay and putrefy within our extensive digestive system, thus producing a lot of toxins. Our digestive system is simply not geared to digest animal proteins. It's also very important to avoid processed foods. Only organic produce guarantees that we are not ingesting genetically modified organisms (GMOs), pesticides, and herbicides, and the residues of chemical fertilizers used in industrial agriculture. There are plenty of books on this subject and, of course, no one can change their eating habits overnight. Be kind to yourself, but understand what's good for your body and strive to change your eating habits. We also need to adapt our eating habits to the land around us. Some people have no choice and need to eat animal protein, yet as they work hard outside in very cold weather, these conditions will burn up any excess toxins.

Pure Water

Drink a sufficient amount of *pure* water. You might think that's easy, but in fact it's very complicated today. Water from the faucet is not pure water. It may have been treated with chemicals to sterilize it, making it dead water as well as polluted water. Imagine how far this water has traveled in pipes. Ask those who distill tap water what remains in the tub after distillation. The smell is atrocious, and you can find everything, even worms, in what has been purified from tap water.

The best water, second only to that which is naturally filtered by the earth, such as well water, particularly from a deep well, is distilled water. The apparatus to do this is affordable and available. Another method of cleansing water is the inverted osmosis filtering system. You will need to add living minerals to this kind of water. The water thus purified by these two methods does not have any life left, it's dead water, therefore it's important to restructure or reactivate the water. There are several methods for doing this. One requires nothing more than a wide-mouth jar: fill the jar with purified water; expose it for three hours to sunlight; then put it in a dark place for three hours. The natural bacteria will then return to the water, and it will once again become living water.

Many people don't drink enough water. You cannot count tea, herbal drinks, juice, or other liquids as part of your intake of water. Part of the water in those beverages will serve to digest the elements in it, and coffee and alcohol will dehydrate you. Drink a lot of water. People have different needs, but as a general rule if you take half of your body weight in pounds and put the word ounces after it, that's the amount of water that you should drink every day.

Pure Air

Breathe pure air. The air in our houses and buildings is more polluted than the air outside in the city center of a metropolis unless you have a device to purify the pollutants from the air and then circulate it. It is only in nature that we will find pure air. It is thus important, even in winter, to open windows. As well, various environments provide a very vivifying air. Mountains, because of their huge quantity of granite, are natural producers of negative ions. Ancient trees and evergreen forests produce beneficial bacteria, plant essential oils, and negative ions, all of which interact and influence one another, and this synergy has a positive effect on the human gut through inhalation. Seaside environments create iodine-filled air, and waterfalls generate negative ions, uplifting the spirit and just making you feel better. It's a very wholesome activity to take long, brisk walks in such environments. Our breath feeds us more than all other foods. Therefore, taking a daily walk outside is one of the healthiest and most wholesome activities there is.

Exercise

The body needs movement every day, and we also need to improve our muscular capacity and stamina. There are many ways to do this and many spiritually based movement practices like yoga or tai chi are readily available. Of course, if you work on a farm or out in nature, you'll be exercising all day in a healthy environment, as long as the technology you use is not spreading pollutants.

Sleep

It's imperative to get enough rest and sleep. We need seven to nine hours of sleep a night. Working at night and even during the evening can have negative consequences on one's health. And the quality of our sleep also matters. Your room should be cool, dark, and quiet. Electronic devices emit blue light, which has been shown to reduce or delay the natural production of melatonin in the evening, decreasing feelings of sleepiness. Blue light can also reduce the amount of time you spend in slow-wave and rapid-eye movement (REM) sleep, two stages of the sleep cycle that are vital for cognitive functioning. Preserve your bedroom as an electronics-free zone.

Sunshine

We have all felt the incredible benefit that comes from exposing our body to warm sunshine. Numerous scientific studies prove the many benefits directly connected to exposure to the sun's rays. Among these, let us not forget to mention the effect on mood. In winter, among city dwellers of northern countries who remain indoors most of the day, sales of antidepressants increase substantially, amplifying long-term problems and creating dependencies that result in other problems. It would be a lot healthier to mitigate this deficiency by more natural means. Gazing at the sun is also beneficial, but is only possible at sunrise and sunset, when the atmosphere eases the strength of the sun's rays.

Cultivating a Life Mission

A passion for life! A reason to live! Meaning in life! We need profound motivation to stimulate our willingness to be the best we can be. Understanding the meaning of our life and our place within the community and the universe supplies this motivation. From there stems the wisdom of performing the rites of passage that aboriginal peoples everywhere on earth practice. Thus the need to periodically reflect in solitude on our life and what we want to make of it. We need the psychological support found in love and friendship, which we experience within the family, among friends, and within the community or workplace.

Following Our Original Instructions

Prayer, meditation, and taking care of yourself so your body will serve your spirit and soul adequately are the foundations of spiritual practice and are required before you attempt to use crystals for healing and to help others. There are, of course, many more benefits to spiritual practice. Your spiritual practice is what distinguishes you from the other life forms on earth. Beings from the mineral, plant, and animal realms always follow their instincts, their *original instructions,* as Native peoples put it. Their original instructions are encoded as their life mission. As an example, you'll never see a wolf going to the tavern to have a beer; the wolf will always do what it's supposed to do. You'll never see a tree try to plant itself in the ocean; the tree will always do what the tree is supposed to do. They have no choice in the matter. Only human beings have the choice to do otherwise. This is called *free will.*

Since we have free will, it is possible to choose the wrong path. That is one of the most important things that we have come to learn here on earth—how to choose what is of the spirit and not to be taken in by the illusions of a temporary physical form on earth. Our immortal soul has a life span that is eternal, that spans millions of years. One lifetime on earth is like the blink of an eye in our life story. When we are born into this world we temporarily forget our past lives, but before coming here we have encoded in our soul what our lessons are to be this time around, what our mission is. That is encoded in the heart. Our mission in life is what really gives strength, power, love, joy, and peace to all our endeavors. It's when we are following our original instructions that we are the happiest. To be able to hear what the heart is saying, we need to listen. That requires the mind to be silent and that needs practice and training.

Your spiritual path can take you to many places in life. We all need to seek what's essential, what is more than just our physical body, more than our personality, more than our name, more than our financial status, more than all our material possessions.

On the spiritual path you value your relationships. Our souls know one another and meet between lives, in the spiritual world. We meet again and again on earth and in the spirit world.

As we have free will, we may choose a different path that's not a part of our original instructions. We may choose the easy way, the way of pleasure, the way of the body, the many damaging appetites the body can crave. Giving free rein to these appetites can turn into addictions. What trains our body and mind to follow the way of the soul and spirit, what aligns us with our original instructions, is spiritual practice. Without spiritual practice we cannot begin to fathom our mission in life. Without this knowledge, we go astray and are a danger to ourself and others. Other life forms always follow their original instructions. We humans need training so that we can make the right choices and have the courage to follow them. This training is what we mean by spiritual practice.

Those who have no spiritual practice are thus inferior in their relationship to the earth and to nature. Even earthworms accomplish their original instructions. Their work in airing and fertilizing the soil is very important for all beings on earth, as everything is in relationship and interconnected. The human being who does not follow his or her original instructions is a destructive influence, as is evident in the pollution of all ecosystems on earth in these times.

Spiritual practice is the only thing that helps you tame your mind so you can listen to the soul. There are certainly pitfalls, such as putting too much importance on the teacher, the prophet, the sect, the religion, the ritual, rather than the teachings and the personal development that spiritual practice is there to accomplish. So it's important to not get too attached to specific practices. This is why we insist that you must always go for what's useful, what works for you. As Sun Bear once said to me, "Don't talk to me about a philosophy that doesn't teach me how to grow corn." What a wise man he was!

It's good to be aware that when you first put your feet on a spiritual path you will be facing a number of tests and trials. The universe and your own immortal soul will both test you to see if your resolve and intentions are firm and pure. All that you have done that has created disharmonious energies in your past will come up, asking to be resolved. This is the law of cause and effect, what Hindus and Buddhists call *karma*. As you embark on the spiritual path, the Lords of Karma say, "So you're ready to start cleaning up the mess you've created?" And then they dump it all on you and you're faced with major challenges. You might have thought that the going would be easy and harmonious now that you're on the peaceful spiritual path . . . Think again! You'll have to face all that you've created in the past before moving on.

Thus you should be aware that there are multiple levels and dimensions to your evolution and spiritual quest. Layer by layer you will peel away the old to discover more and more treasures of the mind and spirit. This requires diligence and practice. You will find great peace when you dwell in the heart, the divine source that connects you to everything, and where everything is possible. Thus you can see that spiritual practice begins way before you work with crystals. Therefore the first preliminary before working with crystals is to clean, polish, and purify oneself.

Chapter 3 will provide you with specific tools to help you with your spiritual practice.

SECOND PRELIMINARY: A LIVING CRYSTAL

Just as earth is alive, so are her crystals. Thus the second preliminary begins with cultivating an attitude of respect for the crystals as living, sentient beings.

Many advanced crystal practitioners have crystals that actually grow! And not because they are in some sort of mineral solution. Because of the special influence the healer has with crystals, they sometimes have a tendency to evolve and grow. This is proof that crystals are living beings. I have witnessed this phenomenon many times. Some of my crystals have grown in size, others have added numerous additional points to a multipoint cluster, and others have developed a bitermination (or double-termination) where there was none before. On the mountain close to where I live, there is a huge rock where I have grown accustomed to praying in the morning. After a few years I noticed that tiny crystals had started growing on the rock face, which shine in the light of day when I pray.

Crystals are multidimensional beings and sometimes when they have completed major accomplishments and service to the world they will dissolve back into the source of manifestation, or to the group soul of the mineral kingdom. Other times they will go somewhere else and then come back. I had a meditation crystal that would disappear when I was lax in my meditation practice and then reappear in most unexpected places when I had begun practicing with regularity again.

We can learn to communicate with crystals. They don't speak in human languages, but they do communicate. A crystal practitioner who understands the living nature of crystals does not *use* the crystal, she works *with* the crystal! Thus, there are two beings working to help and heal, and the synergy this creates is superior to what either would have been able to do individually. We thus understand that respect must be extended to crystals. This consideration for the crystal as a living, breathing being is what makes it possible to commune and communicate with the crystal. One way traditional First Nations crystal healers have ensured that attitude of respect is by not purchasing a crystal. The healer either finds one in nature or is given a crystal by his teachers or friends. Thus, we don't buy the crystal friend, because it knows when and how to find us when the time is right. This is not meant as a restriction, it's simply a way of understanding the special relationship one must have with crystals. There was a time where I was very strict with the directive to not buy crystals. Times have changed quite a bit, however, and now we do sometimes have to purchase crystals to do the work we are called to do.

Teaching Story

The following is a good teaching story about the time when a crystal friend decided to come to me. This was in Germany many years ago. I was giving a conference on crystals in a large wellness and healing New Age expo. They had let me set up a small booth where I could sell my wares. There was at that time a great fad around crystals. As German people don't do things halfway, they had a lot of crystals in this big fair. I think at least half of the booths must've held crystals. Some were enormous, with many tables full of stones and crystals. So one day I walked around the great conference hall and in a corner I saw a small booth with a glass window counter, behind which were ten or eleven labradorite stones. One flashed me. I needed this one, it was speaking to me. I wanted it so badly! Yet I was strict with this directive not to buy one, so I tried to play a trick on myself. I put my hand out, telling myself that any crystal that would vibrate into my hand I could take, as it was given to me. I could have bought all of them, except the one I wanted. It was really enforcing my directive to not buy crystals. So I completely let go and decided to forget about that labradorite, walking away after sending it a thought from my heart that I would have loved to bring it with me. The next morning I arrived at the convention center early. Sitting alone in the corner of my booth, taking a coffee before the day began, I saw a small box on my booth in front of me. Curious, I opened it and there was my labradorite crystal friend! I was awash with joy. Soon after, the kind young German woman who was helping me with the booth and with translation exclaimed, "You found the gift I bought you!" I told her I had been attracted to that very crystal but had declined purchasing it because of my directive, but that I had communicated with it nevertheless. She could hardly believe me, as there were millions of crystals in that place. But by telling her I knew exactly which booth she had bought it, where it was among the myriad other booths, she finally believed me. I've had that crystal ever since, and it's been with me every time I've taught crystal work.

At the same time, we must not get too attached to our crystals. When the time is right, we may be invited to let them continue on to other places. Sometimes we have to give up our crystals, and that's all part of the game of life.

So it *is* possible to communicate with a crystal. There will be exercises later in this book to help you learn how to do this.

THIRD PRELIMINARY: RESPECT FOR MOTHER EARTH

The third preliminary when working with crystals is respect for Mother Earth. Crystals are a very intimate part of Mother Earth. They act as her ears, eyes, and voice. They channel her energy meridians, and huge deposits of crystalline substance in the earth's body are her energy centers. With these she communicates with other planets, with the sun, and with other celestial beings.

Native peoples consider the earth to be a living being of great evolution, a conscious, living, breathing being who gives us all we need to live healthy, happy lives. Yet humanity today is torturing the earth in so many ways. A crystal healing practitioner needs to be aware of this. All our actions have an influence on the earth, and we must understand what we are doing to the planet if we are to work with crystals. As crystals are an intimate and important part of Mother Earth's being, to be true, efficient, and faithful practitioners we must develop an understanding of our place in the earth's biosystems and our responsibility to the earth. We are the earth's consciousness. Humanity has the intelligence necessary to bring about a positive change in our treatment of the earth, just as we have had the means to bring about the ecological disaster that we face today. Everything is interrelated, connected in some way.

When shamans offer ceremonies and teachings in nature, things happen. Rainbows often appear after ceremonies. Eagles turn overhead. Birds come to see what's happening. Animals come to listen from the cover of the forest, as close as they can come while remaining hidden. The winds dance with us, small gentle rains fall from a blue sky, and so on and so forth. This is in fact normal, nothing special, but for those who live artificial technocratic lifestyles, this is just superstitious nonsense. Yet for those of us who live and breathe within the consciousness of being in harmony with the Earth Mother, these signs are indications that we are in harmony, that we are heard and appreciated. They bring joy, awe, and wonder. When you experience this you understand that living a technocratic lifestyle with no earth magic is indeed a stale, poor way of living.

When one learns to respect nature, share with nature, talk with nature and the elements, one begins to enter into a magical, harmonic resonance with the world. When these synchronicities happen, it's not us doing anything other than praying, making offerings, and humbly making a request. There is spirit in everything and when we are in good relationship with all beings and with the Earth Mother, there is communication, a response, a feeling of interconnectedness, harmony, and beauty.

Crystals are organs of communication for Mother Earth. It's through crystals that the earth shares information with nature and with other worlds and dimensions. Everything we think, say, and do is registered, expressed, and amplified by crystals—including the throes of suffering the earth is going through at this time. Many galactic beings are very concerned with what is happening on the earth at this time, and they reverberate this concern out into the solar system and beyond. Crystals are living beings and an intimate part of the earth.

If you are given the privilege of working with crystals, you also have the responsibility that goes with it, as with any power comes responsibility. You have been given the ability to think, to be conscious, to understand, thus the responsibility that comes with these gifts is knowing who you are in relationship with the earth and with nature. The very best way to protect Mother Earth is to care for your garden, to grow your own food. The only way to truly protect the environment is to gather your sustenance from nature.

Artificial Stones

The crystalline substances created by industry have many of the same qualities in energy transmutation as natural stones. Yet what's missing is the magical, living entity that the mineral kingdom reveals in the most evolved beings of the mineral kingdom, the crystal flowers of the stone world. Nothing is impossible, yet we must refrain from using these artificially created stones, as their creation has a heavy environmental impact. Thus, our third prerequisite to crystal work, earth consciousness, informs us that we should never work with these kinds of materials or with any stone that's been subjected to technological treatment other than cutting and polishing.

Let's consider another type of substance called *crystal*, as in crystal drinking glasses. Although it is called crystal, it is not at all crystal, but a refined form of glass. It is mainly used for costume jewelry, luxury glassware, and decorative ornaments. Sometimes it's used for pendulums, and it is very pretty hanging in front of a window, where it takes sunlight and releases its rainbow reflections. Crystal often contains lead, which makes it transform light into the shining rainbow reflections we see in these ornaments and reflected on surfaces around them. I mention this substance as many people have come to me with shiny pendants saying it was sold to them as crystal but in fact they were wearing glass ornaments, expecting it to have the same energy as quartz crystal. Crystal glass is not used in First Nations crystal healing. It can be used for its beauty, for the rainbows it displays when put in the sunlight. Feng Shui consultants often use this substance to disperse energy in some environments. But crystal glass should not be used as a healing tool, as the lead it contains may have a heavy grounding and deadening effect.

This is the third prerequisite in working with crystals: an intimate and ongoing respectful relationship with the earth and with all of nature. In this way you will enrich your life with a magical understanding of the interrelationship of all things on earth. This will contribute to your ability to work with crystals, as this understanding will open the doors of perception, making it possible to communicate with these crystalline beings.

Thus, there are three prerequisites to working with crystals: The first crystal we work with is ourself, so we must engage in appropriate spiritual practices to prepare for our work with crystals. Then we must approach the crystals themselves as living, breathing, conscious beings. And finally, we must recognize that we are a part of a global planetary web of life that's in relationship with all that exists in the universe.

3

Foundational Native American Teachings and Practices

We need to study certain Native American teachings before we are ready move on to working with the crystals themselves. These are teachings and practices that can nourish your spiritual practice, thus they are important on the path we are taking together. We will speak of centering, the four directions, smoke offerings, electromagnetic purification, and an alternative to purifying with smoke when it's impossible to burn herbs, as in a hospital setting. We will also consider the role of masculine and feminine in our world, the implications for this being out of balance in modern times, and the way Native peoples have traditionally maintained the balance of our polar energies.

CENTERING

We will now describe a method for achieving heightened awareness and concentration. This is very important when working with crystals. We will discuss the brain and how to change the measurable frequencies it emits. These brain waves are classified as beta, the ordinary waking state; alpha, a more relaxed state that can tap into higher frequencies; and theta, as in sleep, yet when achieved in waking consciousness this state allows for better perception and control of a wider array of frequencies.

Controlling our brain waves is done by simply striving for a more holistic experience of life, where the right and left hemispheres of the brain synchronize. This is known as *centering.* Centering is something that you should do before any of the other practices in this book, and should be done before beginning any spiritual practices. It only takes a few minutes, and it is very effective.

To understand the mechanics behind this exercise we must consider how the brain works. We have a left and a right hemisphere to our brain. The left hemisphere is the rational, logical, linear mind that sees things from an objective standpoint. It acts as a memory bank, helping you perfect all mundane tasks and integrate scientific information. It's the doubting Thomas who doubts everything he hasn't seen for himself. The right hemisphere is the imaginative, intuitive, circular mind. It's that part of our intelligence that deals with emotions and sees things from a subjective standpoint. It understands that spirituality and faith are more important than doubt, and it enjoys fantasy.

If one side of the brain works independently of the other, we will be unbalanced. Therefore, to have a clear vision of reality we need both hemispheres to work together so we have a holistic understanding of the world. Most of the teachings that people receive in modern schools are all left-hemisphere thinking. So this can be a challenge for people when they start studying energy work, which requires that we trust our feelings. You need to see the people who come to you for healing as all that they are. If you see them only with the left hemisphere, you will only be interested in their symptoms and prescribing an herb or doing the appropriate treatment. You won't have any bedside manner. All the emotional information that can have a huge impact on a person's health will not be available to you.

If you're thinking only with the right side of your brain you will have a tendency to get caught up in the person's emotions and will not have sufficient objectivity to administer hard advice or establish proper boundaries in the healer-client relationship. As a crystal practitioner working with energy you will only have the heartfelt energy available, in this case that which comes from Mother Earth, and you'll have very little of the mind energy that comes from Father Sky available to you. Thus you'll be working with reduced energy.

We could go on and on in this manner to explain the many difficulties that can be encountered when we're not balanced. This is why we need to synchronize the two hemispheres of the brain to have a holistic outlook on our client and on life in general.

I have found over the years that students have had many different observations before and after doing this centering exercise, but the most consistent comment is that they have more visual acuity, better auditory acuity, and more extrasensory perceptions. They report feeling calm and relaxed, with heightened vital energy. They feel "empty" in a good way. This feeling of being empty is very important. A pure, empty mind space in which both hemispheres are synchronized has a totally different perception of reality. A good example is that of a child in contrast to a politician.

When a child begins schooling and has not yet been altered by childhood difficulties or negative experiences in class, he has a very special way of listening to the teacher. His mind is empty, without concepts, so he understands what the teacher says at the very moment the teacher has spoken. There is no need to reflect upon it, to think it over or to evaluate. The two hemispheres work together in a synchronized manner and understanding is immediate, instantaneous.

In contrast, if you listen to politicians speaking nowadays you'll notice they never *really* hear the other person. Everything the other person says evokes their own version of what's being discussed, so they constantly interrupt in order to bring forth *their* version of what they think is right. Yet, if you listen attentively, you might notice that they're often saying the same thing with different words. As they never listen, truly listen, to the other person, they don't really understand what the other person is saying.

To center the two hemispheres of the brain, thus attaining a very open and empty inner receptivity, we will describe a simple breathing technique. This will help to clear and relax the throat. The two hemispheres of the brain will then synchronize and become focused when the throat is open and relaxed. This method of centering and focusing one's body-mind is the quickest and simplest of all those I've been taught over the years. As always, you must check and verify if this technique works for you. To do this, note how you perceive the light and the colors around you, the sounds that are naturally occurring around you, and the smells, and notice how you feel within before doing this exercise. Then compare these four indicators after doing the exercise.

The opposite of what we are striving to achieve with this exercise is when our throat is tight. To feel what it's like to have a contracted throat, take a sudden deep breath and hold it at the top of your breath. Can you feel the contraction at the base of the throat or neck? This is the contraction that you must avoid. Your goal here is to have the throat open and relaxed when you suspend in the middle of the exhalation.

⚡ Centering Exercise

1. Start by taking several deep breaths, breathing in through the nose and breathing out through the mouth. To test to see whether you have a deep breath, put a hand on your stomach and another on your chest. When you breathe in deeply, you should feel your stomach move and then your breast. If you do not feel this, keep practicing until you have a complete breath.

2. After three complete deep breaths, breathe in slowly through your nose and then very slowly exhale through your mouth. In the middle of your exhalation, suspend your breath naturally, visualizing your throat open and relaxed. After a few seconds continue to exhale.

3. Breathe in again through the nose, out slowly through the mouth, again suspending the breath in the middle of the exhalation, but now remaining a bit longer in this suspension of the breath.

4. And now a third time, breathe in deeply through the nose, slowly out of the mouth, this time suspending the breath for as long as you can, but without any tension. As soon as you feel your body calling for air, continue exhaling and then breathe in. That's it!

If you have performed this exercise correctly you should feel focused, and you will remain centered for at least forty-five minutes. You might experience the emptiness I spoke of. You will feel relaxed. You will have a lot more potential abilities available to you. You are once more in the real world. The two hemispheres of your brain have been synchronized. They are both working simultaneously, in collaboration.

If you use this exercise before an exam, you'll have better results. If you do so before giving a concert or a presentation, you'll have a better performance. And so on and so forth. This exercise is a must before all spiritual practice and all the exercises described in this book. It is the first and foremost exercise you will learn here.

An electroencephalogram shows that before centering we habitually demonstrate brain waves in the beta range. After centering we can go from alpha to theta.

You can also obtain a centered mind after actively listening to music for twenty minutes.* Active listening refers to when you really listen without doing any other activity, focusing completely on the music. This will bring you to the same state of a focused and centered mind that emits alpha or theta waves. But the centering exercise, above, is faster.

THE FOUR GRANDFATHERS:
THE CARDINAL DIRECTIONS

To all First Nations peoples of North and South America, the four directions are the great angelic beings who were placed here at the very beginning of the world at the time of the creation of this planet. Their role is to keep the poles, including the North Pole and the South Pole, which are well known, as well as the East Pole and the

---

*Most music has the potential to heighten vital energy. The only exceptions I have found are heavy metal and ritual music intended to harm others. Drumming and rattling music, in particular, work wonders to synchronize the brain. Check out my *Earth Drums* recording at https://aiglebleu.bandcamp.com/album/tambours-de-la-terre-m-re-earth-drums.

West Pole, which are situated on the Tibetan Plateau and between the four great mountains in the American Southwest where the Hopi people live. These sites generate electromagnetic energy and it is no coincidence that some of the most spiritual people on the planet live in these places. You will also find that thunder and lightning are frequent there. The four directions are also guardians of specific wisdom and teachings for the people.

Every First Nations people has its own symbols, its own traditions, and its own culture concerning the Four Grandfathers. So the meanings of each direction and their colors can vary from one nation to another. Here, for example, are the colors attributed to the directions by the nations of the Canadian Northeast: white for the north, yellow for the east, red for the south, and black for the west. Cherokees of the Bear Clan associate their colors in the following way: north, blue; east, gold; south, green; west, red. The Chinese, the Vedic people of India, and the Tibetans also have teachings on the four directions, as do aboriginal people all over the world. This indicates the importance and universality of these teachings.

Just as each cardinal point has a color, each direction has a specific meaning and certain attributes. These also vary from one nation to the next, each being unique, although there are many similarities in the various systems. The teachings that I received from a Bear Clan lineage of the Cherokee people is the one we will study here. Having studied for twenty-five years with the Bear Clan of the Ywahoo lineage, it's the one I know best. I have found many similarities between the Cherokee system and the teachings of the northern Algonquin and Tibetan cultures.

First of all, the directions help us find our way. Everybody knows that. Those who venture into the forest on camping trips often take a compass. Formerly, First Nations peoples, like all other inhabitants of nature, did not need a compass. Migratory birds know exactly where they're going without a compass. What we need to understand here is that there are resonant harmonics of these directions that exist within us. Knowing where the directions are, in the outer world and within, facilitates our finding our way in life. These fundamental principles are encoded in the teachings on the directions and guide us as we find our way in the world and in life.

North

The north represents mirror wisdom, the quiet waters of the sacred lake that reflects things as they are. This picture of the quiet lake where the water reflects the sky is a symbol of our mind. When the mind is quiet and still, all things appear in our consciousness as they are. When the mind is active and agitated, we perceive things as we *think* they are; the world appears to us through our many filters and conditioning, thus not as it is but as we think it is, which is most often far from reality. As soon as the wind stirs the waters of the lake, the waves break the perfect image of the sky, and the waters become cloudy. The truth disappears, giving way to a storm of thoughts and feelings. When peace and quiet returns, the waters settle, giving us once again the perfect image of all that is.

When we understand how our mind works, it becomes easier to recognize what is true and what is untrue, to know what our thoughts are and which thoughts come from others as a result of conditioning and false programming. Meditation is an excellent way of cultivating this understanding as it allows us to harmonize and regulate our thoughts. When the mental body is quiet, it understands immediately and does not require thinking to understand. Indeed, real understanding is immediate and requires no time for reflection. It is this movement of Spirit that sees and understands all in the same moment. It is the internal voice that says, "Ah! It is so!"

The north symbolizes the wisdom to see things as they are, the mind being as still and quiet as the great northern frozen lakes. The north teaches us to relax and understand the mind through the practice of contemplation and meditation so that our thoughts and emotions do not color our perception of reality.

The north symbolizes the unmanifest potential represented by the frozen lakes of the north. The ice is immovable, petrified; nothing seems to live there. Nevertheless, under the ice the potential for life exists, and when spring comes, life is revealed. Another symbol of unmanifest potential is the egg or the seed, symbols of life, yet nothing is yet revealed.

From the north come the strong, cold winds that give us strength and stamina. The north also symbolizes those tests in life that will either break us or strengthen our being, giving us more resolve and stamina.

Thus the north wind, when it blows with its icy cold breath, summons from our core vitality, stamina, and strength. If we have the courage to complete the tests that are sent to us, we stand to grow and become stronger because of them. To make a sword that will not break, one must take iron, plunge it into red-hot coals, beat it repeatedly into its perfect shape, and then plunge it into ice-cold water and then again into the blazing fire, beating it again with a heavy hammer, then back into the ice-cold water, repeating this process again and again until it becomes unbreakable steel. So is the path of the initiate who walks the way of Spirit in our times.

The animal representing the north is the Great White Buffalo. The earth is covered with electromagnetic currents that cross from the north to the south, and also from the east to the west. These electromagnetic currents are the etheric web of the earth, the blueprint of the planet. The energy battery or primary source of these energy flows that support this immense electromagnetic web is represented by the Great White Buffalo. This is an actual spirit being and is for all First Nations a very important being. Many prophecies shared by many nations say that when the pounding of the hooves of the Great White Buffalo will resound again on the earth, it will sound the healing of the earth. Then the great herds of buffalo of former days will reappear from beneath the ground and we shall come again to the joys and freedom of our ancestral way of life.

What Is the Etheric Web?

All living beings, plant and animal, are surrounded by an aura made up of a number of electromagnetic layers. The first layer around the body is the densest layer, a special structure known as the *etheric web*, a web of filaments of etheric material that can be seen by those who are clairvoyant as a fine web formed of thin, light-emanating cords or as a halo of clear or rose colored light. Beyond this layer lies the astral body and mental bodies. The etheric web of the earth corresponds to its magnetosphere, which provides protection against solar flares and deflects the charged particles of solar flares. In the same way a person's etheric web shields her or him from harmful energies or disruptive thoughts forms. In psychically weakened or unwell people the etheric web may be damaged. These damaged parts appear as holes or tears in the etheric web. The etheric web is one of many electromagnetic fields that exist, though sometimes we use these terms interchangeably.

The color of the north is deep blue or white, a white that is so white it contains blue reflections, as often seen on the snow. The north wind speaks of the night, of winter, its strongest moment being midnight on the winter solstice. In the life of a human being it is when we have white hair and are the elders of the nation. We can then contemplate the world and reflect on our lives, distilling the pristine wisdom we can offer the younger generations. The Spirit world is in the north. That's where our ancestors reside, in *Ungawi,* the world of ideal form. Thanks to the clear vision of our still mind we can perceive and understand the teachings of our ancestors.

The crystal associated with the north is the clear quartz crystal.

East

In the east we find the wisdom of inspiration, the wisdom of the sphere of existence and illumination. The east represents inner and outer light. It is also knowledge and the desire to acquire new knowledge. It is birth, the beginning of things. Understandings, revelations, as well as the expression of one's potential are in the east. Between the north and the east, between the old man and the newborn child, we find the period of learning about life, the expression of our individuality. It is also the sweet winds that take care of us, the east zephyr.

The animal totem of this direction is the golden eagle; its season, spring; its moment of day, dawn; and its color is the golden yellow of the rising sun. Its stone is golden topaz. The morning energy is special, and all First Nations gatherings begin with a sunrise ceremony. Morning exercises in front of the rising sun confer a magnificent energy to those who practice them. All traditional peoples have this understanding. The strongest moment of this direction is at sunrise on the day of the spring equinox.

South

The south embodies the wisdom that succeeds, manifesting our dreams and aspirations. This wisdom channels the energy and motivation that allows us to realize our projects. It is the medicine of success and rapid growth. It is the warm period of summer, laughter, joy, innocence, love, and all the qualities that are connected to love.

The totem animal of the south is the coyote. In First Nations mythology this animal is the one who plays tricks on people to teach them life's hard lessons despite their bitter resistance. Citrine is the crystal that serves well to channel the medicine of coyote. We all have in our families people who are creatures of habit who have a rather boring life: they eat, work, eat, TV, sleep, over and over again. We can incite the coyote to come surprise these people and wake them up a bit. There are those people who perhaps once had everything, who knew glory and fortune, but were arrogant about it, and they found themselves poor and on the street, meeting with bankruptcy and humiliation. It's the medicine of coyote teaching them humility and the value of relationships.

To know how to laugh at oneself is a great virtue. Laughter is a natural immune-booster and energy-purifier. When we know how to laugh at ourselves and our errors, integrating life lessons goes much easier. This is one facet of the teachings of coyote medicine.

We have another animal associated with this direction as well, the little mouse. Its role consists of teaching us confidence, trust, and innocence.

Teaching Story

Many years ago I was celebrating a summer solstice ceremony. As the sun rises very early at that time of year, everyone was supposed to wake up at 4:30 a.m. to prepare for the sunrise ceremony. The night before I had shared the story of Jumping Mouse, a beautiful story on the ability to love and trust life completely. The following morning, at 4:15 a.m., a small mouse ran over every single person in that tipi and woke them up. This can show us how nature does in fact participate in our ceremonies.

The color of the south is green, and its time of day is noon. Its highlight is at noon on the summer solstice. One of the symbols of the south are the grandmothers dancing with baskets of seeds to insure a future full of abundance, love, and compassion. If we look closer, we notice that these grandmothers are in fact old warriors who are disguised as grandmothers to avoid forever the madness of war, thereby looking out for future generations.

Carnelian and ruby are the stones that shine of south energy.

West

The west represents the wisdom that understands the specifics without losing sight of the whole situation. It understands the experiences of life and the cause and effect behind our actions. It's the fire that destroys and then restores back to life. It's the fire of autumn that adorns the trees with many fiery colors. It's the door through which we cross to reach the death of the ego. The line is very thin between asserting our individuality and trumpeting our ego. Our personality, which we also call the ego, is the sum of all the perceived experiences since our birth. These recollections, and mostly the way we have reacted to them and the way we have perceived them, will often determine the way we are going to react to events and people in the present. The ego is a temporary creation that dissolves at death. It is the supreme illusion to which we are much attached, but which has in fact no reality other than what we give it.

The wisdom of the west teaches the perpetuity of the soul, the eternal life of the spirit, and nonattachment to the imaginary and passing personality that is the ego. It teaches us to assert our individuality in a healthy and well-balanced way, without falling into the trap of personality. It is thus the way of integration, as well as the dissolution of unhealthy desires. It is the path of medicine, the difficult road that requires renunciation, fasting, and the practice of solitude and introspection.

One of the ways shamans would search for knowledge and personal transformation would be to intentionally inflict certain forms of physical suffering on themselves in order to transcend identification with the physical body and the ego. First Nations who still practice the Sun Dance seek to reduce the suffering of their people by offering their flesh and blood in this ceremony. Some Inuit shamans, when seeking a vision, will rub two stones against each other, sometimes for days on end until they obtain a vision from Spirit and soul. Again, the purpose of these methods is to transmute any attachment to the body, to reach this place inside oneself that is without limit—one's real essence. Of all First Nations peoples, the Inuit have the most extreme methods to reach these kinds of results. Living in a land with a hostile climate, under very difficult conditions, their initiations resemble the land on which they live.

By etymological definition, a shaman is a person who has died and returned to life. *Shaman* means "one who was twice born." It's the original meaning of the term, which comes to us from the Native culture of

Siberia. A shaman knows how to pass into other worlds to communicate with the spirits and return. Many shamanic initiations thus contain a ritual death as a symbol of this ability to travel between worlds. This has been documented by a non-Native anthropologist, one of the first to travel to the high north and study the Inuit. This anthropologist documented seeing an Inuit shaman initiating a young person into his craft. When his apprentice was ready, they both went onto an ice floe and dug a hole in the ice. They were accompanied by the anthropologist, who observed all. The shaman then tied his apprentice to a long pole and lowered him through the hole into the ice-cold water. He fixed the pole to the ice floe and left the place. Three days later he came back, pulled his apprentice from under the water, called his spirit back into his body, had him change clothing, and then requested a report on his journey to the other world.

The west teaches us the dissolution of desires. Its winds are dry and strong. The animals of the west are the brown bear and the black bear, and its period of the day is the setting sun. Sunset is the time when the sky is often afire with brilliant colors, an effect highlighted at the time of the autumn equinox. The west also holds the medicine of transformation, herbal medicine, and introspection. The one who best teaches introspection is the bear, who, when winter comes, enters his *ouache* (a bear cave or shelter) and sleeps until spring. We do the same thing, in a sense, when we have moments of solitude, when we reintegrate our cave, which is the center of our head and heart. There we have perception of a completely different reality and can renew our being in this contact with Spirit. The bear also knows all the plants that heal. In First Nations legends it is often the bear who comes to reveal to the people the use of plant medicines.

In autumn, all of nature experiences profound transformation. The leaves on the trees go from green to all the fiery colors of red, orange, and yellow. The fruit and vegetables ripen and are ready to harvest.

It's contraindicated to sleep with your head toward the west. In that direction sleep might be uneasy, and the body may tend to be feverish. It's better to go to bed with the head facing northward, where the energies are quiet and where the telluric currents cleanse our etheric field while they pour over the length of our body during the night like a river.

The color of the west is red (black in the Algonquin culture). The crystal associated with the west is amethyst. The west teaches us maturity and represents adulthood and the experiences acquired during a good life.

Center

And now, we come to the center. Here lies the wisdom of balance and equanimity. We are the center of the four directions. It's in the middle of the circle where we learn balance and equanimity. This ability to be of equal humor under all circumstances is the trademark of great men and women of wisdom. Little import is given to individual events by these wise ones; through it all they remain serene. They understand what consciousness is and that only the essence, the spirit and the soul, is eternal. Everything physical passes and transforms into something else in the eternal dance of the elements. And this dance is created and transformed by the consciousness of Great Spirit and humans. As one Native elder said: "Am I breathing? Yes, thus, everything is fine! I have stopped breathing? Ah well, life continues in the spirit world. Why, then, get excited?" Obviously, it is much easier to speak of equanimity than to master this steadiness of heart and mind on an everyday basis. Yet it's the stuff of true wisdom. The center of the four directions, which is also a direction, is the essence of the Medicine Wheel teachings: balance and wisdom.

Living in balance is an important aspect that the teachings of the four directions convey. For example, from the east we see forms arising, the first idea of a project, how inspiration comes. But to realize this project we need the experience and vision that comes from the west. In the south we perceive all the details, all the different aspects that are important for the realization of the project. From the north we see the archetype, the unmanifest potential in all its perfection, which is necessary in order to integrate all the details into a complete vision. In the south we find the courage to act and to manifest our vision, yet the north might indicate when to do this and when it's best to wait until circumstances are right. All these attributes are important for manifesting what we want to accomplish.

The wisdom of center helps us to include others, to find a balance within our universe as co-creators of our reality. We can illuminate the world with our enlightened understanding. Our ultimate offering, as human beings, is to acquire this ability to shine wisdom and light to the world. When we are at one with our soul and the world, our mere presence is sufficient to promote peace and healing around us.

I trained for twenty-five years in the First Nations Bear Clan lineage school of sacred studies. Their priestcraft tradition is ancient, pure, and powerful. For those who train in this priestcraft, there are sixteen tests that are taken in the course of a lifetime. The first consists of illuminating a dark place with the light emanating from one's own body. One must emit light for all to see, and that why this test is held at night or in a dark place. The priests of the Cherokee tradition in precolonial times had meetings in temples that were underneath large earth mounds. This is why they were sometimes referred to as mound builders. These underground temples had no lighting, yet they could all see clearly in these dark subterranean rooms, as their beings emitted enough light for all they needed to see.

Communicating with the Four Grandfathers of the Cardinal Directions

The Dance of the Four Directions is one way to spiral with creation. Everything in the universe breathes, grows, flows, and expands in spirals. This is why the dance and martial arts of these nations were sometimes called the Dance of Four Directions. As its name indicates, this dance is done in each direction. It's a way of contacting our internal spirals. This dance, common to many nations, begins with a simple imitation of the existing spirals in the trees, the wind, the water, the earth, and the movements of animals. There is a spiral in the steps of a bear, a dance in the comings and goings of the partridge. By imitating these spiral movements and by repeating them in four directions, we activate the stream of energy coming into us from the emptiness to fill us with light. This is why sunrise is an excellent time to practice movements to the directions. This spiral movement allows us to free the energy knots that form in us as a result of trauma and other disturbing circumstances, erroneous thoughts, or simply due to a lack of movement. It is said that when this dance is practiced every day during a period of at least three months, certain changes occur inside the body. As you dance in nature, be attentive to the sensations felt in your hands when you feel the vibrations coming from the various directions. After dancing several times around the circle, you will notice that one direction seems to be stronger than the others. This is an indication that it's your primary direction.

Each of us has a fundamental or primary direction. When we know what direction we are most attuned to, we can use this knowledge in several ways. One understanding is that oftentimes the opposite direction is our weakest aspect. This might encourage us to meditate more often on the attributes and wisdom of the direction opposite our primary direction. Other ways to use this knowledge are for protection and inspiration. For protection, stand or sit with your back to your fundamental direction. For inspiration, sit or stand facing your primary direction.

Another way of finding your primary direction is to look in every direction, once with open eyes, then blindfolded, and then again with eyes open, for about ten minutes each time. After looking in one direction, write down your feelings, impressions, and observations. Repeat this in each direction. When finished, let it rest. You should already have an impression as to what your primary direction is. Read your notes the next day. This should confirm what you felt the day before. Having a personal relationship with your cardinal direction will help in allowing a clearer perception of yourself and the world around you.

First Nations people don't have and don't need sacred books, bibles, scrolls, or the like. We read from the book Great Spirit wrote and continues to add to every day. That book is nature. All that is written in that huge volume is true. In it there are no mistakes, no errors, and no misinterpretations. The books written by human beings are always subject to interpretation; there is room for error or unclear or unhealthy intentions. Not so in the book of the world. It takes much contemplation and time spent alone in nature to begin to decipher the alphabet and meanings written on the world by Great Spirit.

In the center of the four directions, we are within nature. These teachings are vast. I have given but a small part of the teachings on the four directions; there remains a lot for you to discover, and you do not need a book to make these discoveries. They are there, just there, in the natural world that surrounds us. It is simple enough to just spend many hours and days in contact with the source of all life, Mother Nature.

SMOKE OFFERINGS AND PURIFICATION: SMUDGING

In Native America, smoke offerings are also a means of purification. This is called *smudging* by indigenous peoples. All First Nations peoples on Great Turtle Island* smudge the people and the place at the beginning of healings and important events. In this way we prepare the space and the people by purifying any unclear energy that may have a useless or harmful influence. We chase away evil spirits, hungry ghosts, and any energy that could be a nuisance to our activities.

One of my teachers, OhShinnàh Fastwolf, studied the effects of smudging by means of scientific experimentation. She was trying to understand why all First Nations peoples in Canada and in the United States, representing many different and diverse environments and nations, use the same sacred herbs for smudging. As she has multiple

---

*Great Turtle Island is the name used by Native American and First Nations peoples for North America. In the Haudenosaunee (more commonly known as the Iroquois Confederacy) the myths of the creation of humankind on planet Earth describe the coming of Sky Woman onto a planet covered with water. She calls a giant turtle to rise up from the depths to land upon and spreads two handfuls of dirt onto the turtle, which expands to create North America. You can still see the form of the turtle on a map: the North Pole is the head, Quebec and Alaska are the upper legs, Florida and California are the lower legs, and Mexico is the tail. For all First Nations the turtle symbolizes the earth.

advanced university degrees and was a tenured professor, she teamed up with researchers to try to elucidate this practice. They discovered that the smoke of these plants capture positive ions in the air and carry them away. Positive and negative ions are an energy charge in air molecules. Positive ions are a vehicle for pollution, as they bond dust particles to air molecules. Negative ions are beneficial and have the opposite effect. We find negative ions in high concentration by the sea, as saltwater creates negative ions. Thunderstorms also produce a high number of negative ions, as do pine forests and granite mountains. This is why the air is so vivifying in these environments. They are saturated with negative ions.

There are on the market today air purifiers that generate negative ions. When these devices have been used near a wall for a few months and are moved, we see the outline, the silhouette, of the machine on the wall. This is due to the fact that the negative ions produced by these kinds of devices cancel the positive ions in the air molecules. The particles of dust carried by the positive ions will then agglutinate on the closest surface, in this case, on the wall nearest the device.

OhShinnàh discovered that smudging works the same way. It carries away the positive ions, leaving the space open to more beneficial energies. We could surmise that the smoke of these herbs, by eliminating the vehicle of pollution, also prevents positive ions from carrying evil and harmful energies. All the immaterial subtle beings of the universe still need a vehicle to move around in the physical world. Our theory at this time is that the ill-intentioned spirits and all forms of heavy and evil energies and emotions, as particles of dust, use the positive ions to move. By chasing away these ions, we eliminate adverse energy charges.

Many therapists and health practitioners all over the world appreciate the effects of smudging because it eliminates all the heaviness in the electromagnetic field (the aura) of the person being treated. It's also used before the arrival of clients to clear the healing space and create a neutral environment. As well, it's used to clear the stagnant energies eliminated by the person during treatment.

One very important aspect of smudging is to always open a window every time you do smudging inside. This will allow the evacuation of smoke and the positive ions. Thus the first thing to do before smudging is to open a door or a window. Without an opening, purification with smudge is ineffective, as the positive ions cannot be evacuated and the smoke will increase the pollution in the air.

Teaching Story

Mad Bear was a very powerful medicine man of the Tuscarora nation, who lived in the northeastern part of the United States. A family asked him to purify a three-story house that was haunted. You might not believe this, but having worked with these predicaments I can tell you they are very real to the families who have these problems. Nobody's perfect: Mad Bear forgot to open a window before beginning to smudge. He had not yet ended clearing the first floor when a dreadful noise was heard coming from the third floor. Quickly, everybody rushed upstairs to see what had happened. One of the windows of the third floor, as well as its frame, had fallen down into the yard as if something had to leave in a rush, tearing away all that hampered its flight!

So, when purifying a house, always open a window. When purifying a dwelling, I open the doors and a window in every room. I begin smudging on one side of the main door and follow the wall, taking good care of going in all the corners. This is important as the heavy energies tend to accumulate in corners. We smudge everything, even the closets and the cupboards. When we finally come to the other side of the door, the whole house has been cleared. It is recommended that you purify your house at least once every three months. It's important to clear any new places where we live or work: new house, new apartment, new workplace, etc. We also smudge after any disturbing or traumatic events. Chiiyaam, a specially formulated liquid smudge, described in the box on page 61, can be used when there are no windows or when smoke is a hindrance or is disturbing to people in the place we wish to purify.

All the herbs used for smudging have specific qualities.

- **Wild sage** is very masculine and the one that purifies best. It has a powerful fragrance, burns easily, and produces lots of smoke. It's not a coincidence that sage also means wise old man. Sage contains testosterone, a male hormone, so we consider it a male plant. Sometimes women will take sage as a tea to balance their hormonal system. There are several wild sages or artemisias that we use; those most frequently used are white sage (*Salvia apiana*), desert herb (*Artemisia tridentata*), and prairie sage (*Artemisia ludoviciana*). They grow wild in different areas of the continent. In all regions there is one or more of these sages available. They are strong plants that contain lots of essential oils that insure excellent combustion.

- **Sweetgrass** (*Hierochloe odorata*) is the most feminine smudge herb. We also call it Hair of Mother Earth. This type of grass is always braided before use. Oftentimes we burn sage to clear away all negative influences, and then sweetgrass to attract beneficial energies and favorable circumstances. Sweetgrass does not burn all that well. To solve this problem, we break it up in small fragments and mix it in with the other smudge herbs, or we light the end of the braid and sway it to encourage combustion.

- **Canadian cedar** (*Thuya occidentalis*) presents the perfect balance of feminine and masculine polarities. It is also called Tree of Peace after Deganawidah, known as the Great Peacemaker, a very important messianic figure in North America, especially for the Iroquoian Six Nations. Some First Nations think this tree is the white pine. We associate Canadian cedar with healing, peace, and serenity.

- **Juniper** (*Juniperus communis*) is used to cleanse the place where we sleep, to have beautiful dreams, and to protect the dreamtime. Juniper is often used by those who are doing dreamwork. It has an influence on the brain that fosters sleep, and it favors lucid dreaming, which means being conscious that we are dreaming while in a dream.

We always burn smudge in a seashell to obtain the complementarities of the four elements. In America, the herbs and the resulting ash symbolize the earth; the match and flame represent fire; smoke represents air; and the shell, water. We often use an abalone shell because of its great resistance to heat, the ventilation offered by the small holes on the side of the shell, and its shining beauty. All the colors of the rainbow meet in the mother-of-pearl of the abalone shell. We say that the abalone comes from the great Mother Goddess of the Pacific Ocean. We find this shell on the West Coast of the United States and in Mexico. First Nations exchange them for smudging purposes and to make ornamentation from its mother-of-pearl. You can find jewelry made with abalone on the market as well.

▣ Smoke Offering

Here is one way of making a smoke offering:

1. After lighting the smudge, begin by slowly waving the shell at your feet, then moving up in a wave so the smoke goes throughout your energy field. This purifies your intention.
2. Offer the smoke to the sky, to the earth, and to the four directions. We start in the north because the spirits and the grandfathers live there. Then comes the east, the south, and the west. Present your offerings to our Heavenly Father and Earth Mother. Once these offerings are completed, you are ready to begin whatever it is you're preparing for.
3. To cleanse a home or a building, wave the smoke everywhere, in every corner and cranny. We often use a feather to do this.

The four cardinal directions and the grandfathers invariably answer our prayers. Their energy is everywhere. Each time you make a smoke offering, you will get a response from the directions. This is a common belief shared by indigenous peoples all over the world, as well as by many ancient traditions. You may not feel each direction in the beginning, but bit by bit you will begin to notice them if you are attentive.

Sharing this practice of smoke offering with others strengthens community spirit. Smoke offerings are common to all religions. As the spirits can sense fragrant incense, it serves to establish a link, a connection. We say that the smoke that rises and disappears in the air brings our prayers to the spirit world, Ungawi, the world of ideal form.

Chiiyaam, the First Liquid Smudge

Many years ago, in 1995 and 1996, I was regularly invited to offer healing to Natives from the north who had been flown into Quebec City to be hospitalized. Oftentimes these patients were placed in intensive-care units after major operations. In this environment it was impossible to perform the ritual purification by smudging with cedar, sage, and sweetgrass. The presence of medical oxygen, closed windows, and many hospital employees made the use of incense and smoke impossible. The very dense energy fields found in such environments and the fact that oftentimes the patient was plugged into various medical devices made it much harder to do the healing energy work that was requested of me without purification.

I then had an opportunity to meet some people who had an essential-oil distillery. As I was talking with them I suddenly had the idea: why not use essential oils rather than smoke? We spoke of extracting the essential oil of the sage that we use. It is the very special, very strong variety that grows in the American Southwest, which, as it turns out, contains a lot of oil. Sweetgrass, on the other hand, does not contain enough essential oil for it to be distilled by this method, but once back home I came up with a simple method to extract its essence. Cedar essential oil was already available on the market. The mixture of these three sacred herbs with corn spirits (alcohol) gave an auspicious result, but didn't smell so good! In fact, it smelled like cat piss!

Then one of my students in France put me in contact with a French perfumer, Michel Roudnitska, who invited me to visit. He graciously taught me the traditional high French perfumery techniques and methodology. I also worked with Mikael Zayat, a specialist in essential oils from Bromont, Quebec. With the knowledge gained from these two experts, I worked for three years on improving a product that became known as Invocation's Liquid Smudge. When I finished my research, I was astounded to realize that this liquid smudge was actually a lot more efficient than our traditional smudging with smoke.

It took me some time before I really understood why this product, which is now called Chiiyaam, an Algonquin word meaning "peace," was more efficient than traditional smudge. My discussions with a scientist gave me part of the answer. When we burn our sacred herbs, the fragrant molecules that are doing this work have been freed into the air by combustion. However, they have also been altered and partly destroyed by that intense heat. With essential oils, the fragrant molecules remain intact. Also, being a liquid, Chiiyaam allows me to do a shamanic ritual to encode the liquid with specific intentions. As we know, liquids are capable of holding specific vibrations.* That is why I hardly ever use smoke to purify anymore, even for offerings, except for certain ceremonies or when making offerings outdoors. I now favor Chiiyaam for purification purposes, and Miwah[υ],[†] our second Native essence, created with sweetgrass extract and twenty-one other essences, for offerings. Any person who has heightened subtle vision will immediately perceive the clearing and luminosity in rooms where Chiiyaam has been used. Miwah[υ] will create an ambiance that attracts beneficial energies and favorable circumstances. They act in accordance with the intention of the one who is using them, as the molecules of these liquids have been organized in a crystalline structure that conveys the user's intention. It's a healthy alternative to smoke in enclosed spaces.

Both the perfumes and traditional smudge can be found on our website boutiqueaiglebleu.com/en.

---

*For example, see the work done by Matsuro Emoto on the memory of water, as described in his book *The Hidden Messages in Water*.
†The meaning of this Algonquin word is "something natural that gives good energy and makes one feel good."

RESTORING THE BALANCE OF
MASCULINE AND FEMININE

It is said that our communities now need to be governed by women. I think this is true, as women today have more maturity than men, yet the general tendency is that women are getting more and more masculine and men more and more feminine. This is happening because the wisdom that leads to knowing who we are as true human beings is being steadily denied us by all forms of civilization. Oppression and discrimination against women are commonplace in all societies, and those women who do make it up society's ladder do so by being very much like men. There is now a tendency for the feminist culture, which is having more and more influence in the world, to return this oppression toward macho men. The swing from a culture where most all men were misogynistic and women very submissive to a feminist culture where men are encouraged to be more feminine and women more masculine and domineering is not a balanced change. True harmony comes from having community structures and roles that are clear, harmonious, and respectful of both polarities. For this to happen there needs to be the deep and profound education and inner psychological training that come from experiencing traditional rites of passage.

We need to reevaluate how we define ourselves as women and men, as this leads to a better understanding of how to enter into right relationship. We are beings of relationship, despite modern tendencies, and only with right relationship and communication can we work toward healing our world of unnecessary suffering.

In all Native cultures there are coming-of-age ceremonies for girls that happen when a girl becomes a woman, which is on or in the days following her first moon time. The whole community will assemble and honor that new possibility for giving life and celebrate the person who has undergone this transformation from a girl to a woman. For any female who experiences this type of honoring ceremony it anchors in her the understanding of her deep and holy importance as one who can carry life for the community. This is why women and men must never allow others to display a lack of respect toward any woman.

As men have no comparable natural cycle that initiates them into adulthood, they celebrate the transition into manhood in powerful, often extreme initiation rituals that enable them to acquire the attitudes and positive behavior expected of real men. An example of such an extreme initiation would be the vision quest. After a year of preparation, the boy is asked to climb a mountain or a platform built high up on a very tall tree and stay there for several days, sometimes as many as nine, without eating, drinking, or sleeping. In this way they learn to develop control over themselves, one of the qualities men are expected to demonstrate. They are also attuning to the spiritual world, where there is no need for food, water, or sleep. They cry for a vision, to learn from Spirit their role and mission on earth and their power as men. In this atmosphere of solitude and the darkness of night they face their internal devils and fears and are initiated into the virtues of courage, mastery, and control that leads to maturity. From boys they are thus transformed into men.

As our civilization has eradicated these rites of passage, men no longer receive the initiations that teach them how to be men. That's why there's a general consensus among many wives that their husbands often act as another one of their children. There is a general lack of maturity and control over their emotions by men in our world. Proof of this is easy to find. Just listen to our elected politicians discussing politics!

Women too no longer have a highly respected and honored initiation into womanhood. Rather than having time off to go to the moon lodge for a few quiet and very spiritual days, as they would in a traditional setting, women now have to hide their blood shedding. They now have menstrual pain, premenstrual syndrome, uneven cycles, huge mood swings, difficulty in commanding respect from men, and other similar difficulties.

Another of the great differences between indigenous cultures and modern, civilized society involves sex. Sex today has been influenced by religions, which portray sex as something shameful, bad, or evil. This is the cause of many problems today. The laws imposed by governments reflect the many taboos around sex, whereas in Native culture sex is a completely natural and wholesome experience. The reality is that sex can be seen everywhere in nature, in both the minute and gigantic manifestations of nature, in the attraction of atomic particles and in the gravitational force fields of the planets and stars.

Love and the will to procreate are the most powerful inner motivations that can arise in a human being. Putting this in a box as the Church has tried to do is impossible. The best example is the vow of celibacy that Catholic priests have to take and the huge number of scandals stemming from inappropriate conduct on the part of these clergymen, which lately has been coming to light.

Many other problems arise from the attempt to control people's sexuality. Unable to control these primordial impulses, they explode out of socially imposed strictures, and because of conditioning around shame and blame they manifest as sexual violence, disrespect, and other negative behavior. The end result is sexually transmitted disease, sexual deviation, sexual violence, rape, sexual abuse, pornography, prostitution, the sex trade, and so on. All this emanates from the misconception that sex is bad or evil. These deviations did not exist in Native nations before the coming of European colonizers. There is nothing more natural or more normal than making children in a sacred way, or loving another person and sharing that love in a sensual manner. And how that happens cannot be put in a box. That liberty only belongs to the intimacy of the two people involved, and no one should be the judge of their sharing. Making laws or rules that dictate how people should love one another leads to many horrible problems.

We must rediscover the traditional rites of passage that have been created for men and women and perform them again. There is great wisdom in understanding and honoring the differences between men and women and learning to develop the qualities that go with our sexual polarization.

4

The Fundamental Laws of Healing

There are three fundamental laws that will help the practitioner of the healing arts in his or her work. These principles are the philosophical base from which the practitioner can evaluate their inner preparedness to help and to heal others. These three laws apply to all forms of therapeutic and healing intervention. Music therapy, crystal therapy, psychotherapy, physical therapy, herbal therapy, massage therapy, even modern medicine can benefit from understanding these laws. They govern the appropriate application of therapeutic techniques and protect the therapist or healer. The laws that govern matter, spirit, the emotional body, and the mental body are all the same and have the same source. These principles are essential for giving our healing practice a solid base and appropriate protection. These three laws are: unconditional love; non-attachment; right intention.

THE FIRST FUNDAMENTAL LAW OF HEALING: LOVE

When we speak of love we are referring to unconditional, universal love, which is quite different from romantic love. There is no wanting to own, to keep, to restrain in universal love as there is in a romantic relationship such as in a formal, exclusive marriage-type relationship.

Universal, unconditional love gives itself freely to all, in the same way that the sun shines on all beings equally.

The battery, or basic energy source, that allows for life and any manifestation in matter to be stable and coherent is love. This energy keeps the planets circulating around the sun and the electrons circulating in the atom. In all things it's the same basic energy—that of attraction—that keeps things in coherence, thus maintaining the forms of all things. To understand this, picture a planet as a living being. It has its own motives and aspirations. So it's going in a specific direction and then it encounters this great source of light and heat, the very source of love, the sun, and thus starts orbiting around it. If it didn't have its own character, direction, and aspiration it would run into the sun and disappear. The same with a man and a woman as they orbit around each other, melding together, creating children, and then moving on in their own direction, as love keeps them orbiting around each other and their children in the great dance of life. They remain individuals, but their coming together creates life, just as the sun shining on the earth creates all living things. That is the nature of love.

The wisdom of love is compassion. Compassion is at the heart of any healing relationship. You must want to help others. There needs to be that deep impulse when confronted with suffering, that sense of empathy that makes you to want to help and to heal. Being in a therapeutic profession is not a job, it's a vocation. If you are doing this as a means of providing for your needs only, you're going to encounter problems. Being confronted by people's suffering on a daily basis, if there's no compassion or empathy, will soon have a negative impact on your emotions and morale. If you have a desire to help that comes from the spirit of compassion and love, offering healing to others will in fact energize you.

We must not confuse compassion with pity. When you pity someone you are uncomfortable around their suffering. So you immediately offer advice and try to find solutions, barging in with suggestions before the other person has finished speaking. When you come from a place of compassion, you listen to all the person has to say. You do not get emotionally involved in their suffering. From the heart comes a profound desire to help. It's this impulse that comes from the heart, a sentiment, not an emotion, that is the basis of all healing. This is why it is said that compassion stems from unconditional, universal love.

Compassion arises in meditation, when we sit in silence and sense the mystery that lives within us. Others will then appear as a reflection of that same mystery. From that feeling of unity with others arises the desire to help and to heal in a spontaneous, free-giving way.

Compassion is giving to another person what we ourselves wish to receive. Through feeling this sense of togetherness—that we are as one—we can learn to share those resources of love that are within us.

This love and compassion must be extended to ourselves, as clearly this kind of love cannot be experienced unless we love ourselves first, because it is only when we love ourselves that we can love others. We must feel compassion for ourselves before we can have compassion for others. As the saying goes, "Charity begins at home."

So to help others, we must start with ourselves. OhShinnàh Fastwolf suggests that students who wish to be caregivers should set aside one day a week just for themselves. Their day off should be used to do only what they like doing. That way, for the rest of the week, they will have joy in their hearts when taking care of their clients or patients.

All beings seek happiness. A person coming to you for healing is seeking happiness above all. Thus the first thing a person coming to you for help will look for is to see if you are happy. That person, upon seeing you the first time, will be looking for this, and this can happen deep within, on an unconscious level, as our spirit being knows and senses these things instinctively. If you are happy, the deep, unconscious message this person receives is, *Ah, here I will find what I'm looking for!* The healing has already been put in motion and you haven't even done anything yet. The opposite is also true: if they don't feel on a deep level that you're a happy, balanced person, the profound, even unconscious message they will get is, *I'm not finding here what I'm looking for.* If they see you in joy, they will immediately feel at ease, they will trust you and your care. Inner joy can be seen; it has a certain power of attraction. Then, consciously or unconsciously, each person who consults you may think, *This is exactly what I'm looking for, happiness and joy.* Their healing has already begun.

Thus we begin by helping ourselves first. Enough rest, pure water, a healthy diet, a balanced lifestyle, and not too much work, even if we love what we do. You have to learn how to say no, always a difficult thing for a caregiver. Know your limits and accept yourself as you are. The Heart Meditation described in chapter 8 supports the vigilance that we must have for ourselves. It is an inexhaustible source of healing energy, and ultimately it is the energy of love that truly heals.

The technique we use when healing is in fact secondary; it is indeed the love you have for the person you are helping that will ensure cohesion, therefore true healing energy. The therapeutic technique serves as a tool or vehicle to convey that love and compassion to the person. Embodying love is the essential thing you must do if you want to take care of others, but you must work on it to achieve it.

The universal love of which we speak here does not come from us. Love is one of the three great energies that gives rise to all physical manifestations.* All life arises in our world through the meeting of the energies of Father Sky and Mother Earth. In our spiritual practice it is good to visualize this meeting of polarities in the heart to better feel and manifest love and compassion. Love is the energy that insures the coherence of molecules and solar systems. When love is deficient, the result is dissolution, degeneracy, decrepitude, and death. We know that love is continually created in abundance by heaven and earth. If there is a lack of love it is because there are obstacles or impurities blocking its influence and manifestation in our bodies, hearts, and minds. Our work then would be to use prayer, spiritual practice, and the four elements to purify ourselves of the toxins, conditioning, traumas, illusions, and ignorance that present obstacles to the expression of love and compassion.

*The will to be, love, and active intelligence are the three manifestations of the Divine within all human beings.

We must make it very clear that we can never run out of love! As you help and heal, love and compassion are all-pervasive and abundant, as they are continually created through the meeting of sky and earth in the heart. Love does not come from us; it flows through us. Thus, never fear that its healing energy might not be enough or could ever stop flowing. Also, do not buy into the perception that you are using your own energies to heal. Those who work with that thought are often tired after helping others. A sign that you are doing it right is when you feel energized after healing another person. As love flows through your channels to help and heal, there is always a bit left behind. This is the sure sign that you are in harmony with the first law of healing: love.

THE SECOND FUNDAMENTAL LAW OF HEALING: NONATTACHMENT

Nonattachment is a healer's psychic insurance policy. It provides you with a protection that prevents you from feeling guilty or inadequate if an illness persists or from puffing up with pride if the person recovers. This is a trap that every therapist can fall into. However, nonattachment to results allows the healer to accomplish his or her work with confidence. You should not be attached to the results of what you do, as it's the person, ultimately, who makes the decision to heal or not to heal. All humans have free will. In healing, you are only a vector of healing. A healer offers his or her presence; the client welcomes, or not, what is offered; it's the person's own decision. Some ask to be healed, but in reality they really wish to keep their illness, because they are attached to it; the illness gives meaning to their life, it defines them. These people will not get better no matter how hard you try or which techniques you use. In this understanding of your work, if the person who comes to you does not heal, you don't have to hit yourself on the head with a hammer blaming yourself. Likewise, if they do heal, you should not think of yourself as better than God the Father! Your responsibility as a healer will always be to do your best—that's it.

I'm well aware this is easier said than done. That's why we need to meditate on and integrate this second law. This is the therapist's emotional health insurance. If you understand this principle it will ensure that if you have success you will not become arrogant and boastful, but remain humble and human. If you're not successful, if the person's condition doesn't improve, you will not blame yourself, feel guilty, or run yourself down.

As always, a holistic therapist should never work on the illness, but rather on the whole person. You should strengthen and help them with their sense of evolution and development so they may understand that their spirit is immortal and can still learn and evolve. This is the mark of a talented healer.

In all cases what must be understood here is that we remain unattached to the results of our interventions. Our responsibility is to do the best we can. The result is not of our doing.

THE THIRD FUNDAMENTAL LAW OF HEALING: RIGHT INTENTION

We can compare healing to an electric motor. Love is the energy source, or battery, but what carries or channels the current to the motor, which is the healing, is the electrical wire. That energy conductor is your intention.

Visualizing a clear image of what needs to happen with our therapeutic intervention will help channel the healing energy to where it needs to go. This is true for all forms of therapy, medicine, and healing.

Here is an example to help you understand the accuracy required to formulate right intention. Let's say a man has just injured his knee and consults you. The intention that might then come to your mind would be: *I want to remove his knee pain so that his injury can heal.* However, this intention is not useful. The words *pain* and *injury* indicate that your attention is focused on the problem. Your intent must express healing. You must visualize the knee as whole, functioning adequately, the man running effortlessly over a grassy field. The energy of love will follow your intention, and the knee will tune into your creative thought.

How you formulate an intention is the vehicle for what will happen as a result of your healing. The tool you use—in this case, crystal therapy—is the way your intention will be projected onto the person. So it is essential to properly formulate your intention; you should see the healing established and the person well, surrounded by all that is good and beautiful for them.

So the real power of your healing modality lies not in the specific technique, but in the strength and clarity of your focused intention. Performing therapeutic techniques with or without intention is the mark of either a good or an ordinary therapist.

It's helpful to understand that in fact illness is an illusion. It's an indication that the person needs to find their way back into balance and harmony, an alarm signal that something needs to change. It amounts to a transitory state, one the person either sinks into or escapes from, by changing the habitual patterns, frequencies, and intentions in his life path. Disease is one of the most powerful teachers there is, and to bear fruit as a teaching it needs to be accepted and then transformed.

From the void comes our spiritual essence that is all-knowing and all-powerful, that can accomplish everything and anything for us. Never underestimate the power of Spirit and know that channeling that power is done through the power of intention.

Thus we have love as the ultimate energy force to power our healing modality; the right intention to channel that energy in the most efficient way; and nonattachment to outcomes to insure the right attitude in your life as a health practitioner. These are the universal principles to meditate on and integrate into your practice.

Now that we have these excellent tools for our spiritual practice, let's delve into the crystals themselves.

Part 2

Crystal Attributes and Correspondences

5

Crystal Form and Structure

What makes certain stones crystals? A mineral substance in which the molecular composition is geometrically fixed in space, that is to say, where molecules are structured in a stable, geometrical way, all well-aligned with one another and reflecting that structure in a way that is visible to the naked eye, is what makes a stone a crystal. When you look at a crystal, you can see faces, angles, geometric planes, and sometimes a point. It is a reflection of the geometric order that exists on the molecular level. When the mineral substance reveals its crystalline structure through visible geometric forms, reflecting the shape it has at a molecular level, we call it a crystal. It is this arranged structure of molecules that gives the crystal its properties as an amplifier and transformer of energy. All types of energy that travel through a crystal will be influenced by its geometrical alignment. All precious and semiprecious gemstones are crystals in their molecular structure. This beauty in the shape and color is what makes them the flowers of the mineral kingdom. They are the most evolved beings of the mineral world. And as such they are doing a lot of work on many different levels and in many different dimensions.

There are some minerals that have a geometrically organized molecular structure, yet the geometrical shape of the molecular structure is not apparent to the naked eye. If we look at them under a microscope, however, we can see the thousands of little crystals of which they are made. We call these stones *microcrystalline*. Agate and jasper are examples of this.

There are other substances that we use that are neither crystalline nor microcrystalline, such as coral, obsidian, malachite, pearls, turquoise, ivory, and similar substances in which the molecular structure is not geometrically aligned as in crystals and microcrystalline stones. These amorphous stones are not used in quite the same way. They do not retain intention or programming to the same extent that crystals do. They are often more symbolic in this capacity than crystals, which have a well-defined energy pattern because of their molecular structure. The advanced practitioner will also be aware that these stones don't have the same fixed personality that a crystal tends to reveal. We will speak of them nevertheless, as they are also a part of the healing work of the mineral kingdom.

THE HARDNESS OF STONES AND CRYSTALS

Another important aspect of the language that relates to crystals refers to the hardness of the stones. A stone needs to be hard enough to resist daily impact if it is to be worn as jewelry. Since 1822, the science of mineralogy uses a scale of mineral hardness that ranges from 1 to 10. This was established by German mineralogist Friedrich Mohs and is called the Mohs scale. In this system, every stone is classified according to its hardness. A stone can scratch any stone that is of less or equal hardness. Glass, for example, which has a 5.5 hardness, will be scratched by quartz, which is a hardness of 7. Diamond, a 10, being the hardest, can scratch all other minerals.

Here is a short list of stones or substances to give you a general idea of this system:

Steatite (soapstone) 1	Opal 6
Amber 2	Quartz family 7
Coral 3	Topaz 8
Fluorite 4	Sapphire 9
Turquoise 5	Diamond 10

CRYSTAL STRUCTURE

An important quality of crystals relates to their structure. Science describes the smallest unit that demonstrates the basic geometrical structure of a crystal. These are groupings of crystal structures according to the axial system of their lattices. Each lattice system has three axes in a geometric arrangement. They describe three geometrical lines or six lattices that form a parallelepiped (a three-dimensional figure formed by six parallelograms) and the lengths and angles of these three geometrical lines. All crystals form into one of the seven lattice systems.

Here are the seven crystal families and some of the stones that organize into these structures:

Triclinic: All three axes are of different lengths and inclined toward one another. Based on a triclinic structure, i.e., three-inclined angles. *Labradorite*

Monoclinic: Three axes, each of different lengths. Two are at right angles to each other and the third is inclined. Based on a parallelogram inner structure. *Azurite*

Orthorhombic: Three axes, all of different lengths, at right angles to one another. Based on a rhombic (diamond-shaped) inner structure. *Topaz*

Tetragonal: Three axes, all of different lengths, are at right angles to each other. Based on a rhombic (diamond-shaped) inner structure. *Zircon, rutile appearing in other forms of crystal*

Hexagonal: Three out of the four axes are in one plane, of the same length, and intersect one another at angles of 60 degrees. The fourth axis is of a different length and intersects the others at right angles. Based on a hexagonal (six-sided) inner structure. *Aquamarine, emerald, quartz*

Rhombohedral: Axes and angles in this system are similar to the hexagonal system, and the two systems are often combined as hexagonal. In the cross-section of a hexagonal crystal there will be six sides. In the cross-section of a trigonal crystal there will be three sides. Based on a triangular inner structure. *Sapphire, ruby*

Cubic: All three axes are of equal length and intersect at right angles. Based on a square inner structure. *Diamond, pyrite*

STRUCTURE AND MEMORY

When I was in training to become a spiritual healer one of the exercises that I found very compelling was when our teacher went around the circle with a tetrahedron (one of the platonic solids) with just the outline, the lines of that bare form and their angles shaped with pieces of wood and copper wire. She projected a thought into this shape, and we were then to use our telepathic abilities to read this thought in that model of a tetrahedron. We found that she could encode a thought into this simple three-dimensional form and most of us could read it.

What she was trying to demonstrate was that as forms emanate from emptiness they take on geometrical forms, and these geometrical forms hold information. This is why we can encode intention into a crystal. The geometrical form of crystal molecules will hold your intention or a specific program and can also hold a lot of other information. This principle was demonstrated by Dr. Masara Emoto, a Japanese scientist who made many experiments to prove that water also has a memory. By crystallizing water into ice he could demonstrate that the different intentions that were put into the container holding the water before freezing would manifest in the shape of the resulting ice crystals. The water held the memory of what was written on the container, or rather, the thought form of the one who wrote it.

Water is not as organized as crystals. It is much more fluid and moving than crystals are. Crystals can therefore hold a lot more information and hold it in such a way that it can be amplified. Crystals are very powerful in this way.

This brings us to the five platonic solids. Named after Plato, who was one of the first to write about them, these are three-dimensional polyhedrons. A polyhedron is a solid formed by plane faces that have one shape (square, triangle, or pentagon), are identical in size, with all angles equal and all sides equal, with the same number of faces meeting at each vertex. There are only five solids or geometrical forms that meet these criteria (see color insert, plate 1): the tetrahedron, which has four sides (flat surfaces); the cube, which has six sides; the octahedron, which has eight sides; the dodecahedron, which has twelve sides; and the icosahedron, which has twenty sides.

I have found it a very worthwhile practice for the healing practitioner to meditate on these platonic solids. We use platonic solids that have been carved out of quartz crystal. Once we have a firm feeling and understanding of these forms, we can then visualize them and project specific intentions into them. By regularly visualizing these different polyhedrons with the same intentions within them, egregores (thought forms) are created that will quicken the manifestation of the intention. This is an excellent illustration of how crystals work.

The platonic solids are also noteworthy in that many spiritual teachings associate them with the five elements. Here are those correspondences: earth is a cube; water is an icosahedron; wind is an octahedron; fire is a tetrahedron; and sacred sound is a dodecahedron.

6

Working with the Five Elements

Many different healing traditions around the world have a five-elements theory. One that is well known is found in Chinese medicine, with the elements of wood, metal, earth, water, and fire. The ancient European alchemists spoke of air, water, fire, earth, and ether. Tibetan and Ayurvedic healing traditions have similar theories. The Native American Bear Clan Society where I studied speaks of earth, water, wind, fire, and sacred sound.

Forms emerge from emptiness as geometrical patterns that coalesce into the different elements that in turn create all that exists. This is the basic theory on which the different five-elements healing modalities of the different traditions in medicine are based. Everything is a combination of these elements as they dance with one another. Let's take a simple example: All that grows as plants and trees comes from the darkness and elements of the earth, quickened by the fire that comes from the sun. They need water to sprout and grow and oxygen and other gases brought in by the wind. And they need the space, the room, the sacred sound in which to manifest. The same process works in reverse. For example, when a tree burns, it first reveals the elements water and air through the vapor and smoke it gives off. Then the element fire, as the accumulated sunshine that is released in flames. Finally, there is the element earth with the ashes that remain after combustion. In fact, the elements are contained within one another. The easiest example of this is water: the earth element in water is ice; it is water when it is liquid;

it is air when it is steam; it is fire when the hydrogen and oxygen that it contains explode.

There is fire, water, earth, and different forms of wind (all that is gas, like oxygen) in every cell of your body. And you live on the earth, which is flying around the sun through space, that sacred sound in which all things manifest. You can hear that sound all the time. It's always there . . . Sometimes when I awaken from a deep sleep and come back into my body in the bedroom, it's very loud and is often the first thing I hear. Very difficult to describe, yet it's what creates and maintains everything.

Thus, working with the elements is a very powerful healing discipline. There are specific tools used in working with them. One that I was trained to use is called *matrix stone*. These are only given, in my experience, through a direct relationship with and transmission from an experienced shaman. Yet, as we have seen, many traditions work with the elements, and there are many ways of doing so.

The first step is getting to really feel them. Direct experience of the spirit within the elements is done through different meditations in which we are put in direct contact with the element. When that inner feeling and understanding is acquired—and in a traditional context there is testing to verify this—the practitioner can then transmit these elements and/or reharmonize them within a person for healing purposes. This kind of work exceeds the scope of this book, as it's through shamanic transmission that these exercises are given. Yet I firmly believe that we all hold that wisdom within us. As Socrates said, "Know yourself and you will know the universe and the gods."

Let's have a look at the elements and their associated stones.

SACRED SOUND/ETHER

Sacred sound (which in some traditions corresponds with ether) is the vibration that connects all things in the same interstellar, intergalactic, and infinite dance that is in constant evolution and interconnection. All things are connected with all the rest. Every plant is connected to a particular star, as are all human beings. All life is influenced by the planets and the rotation of the earth. When the earth is disrupted, which happens frequently these days, the animals, plants, and winds change frequency and sing differently. On a scientific level our assertions will someday be verified—if they have not already been confirmed. I've heard scientists explain that every time the earth has a global electrification, as with the use of radio waves, and then radar, and then microwaves, and now 5G waves, there is a great pandemic that sweeps over the world.

I remember an elderly woman from the Penobscot people, a lovable woman of wisdom who in her final years was quite exhilarated to see that this interrelationship that we speak of continually in all our traditions could now be explained scientifically by theoretical physics' superstring theory; I am convinced that this explanation is only the beginning. I believe that scientists will one day discover—if they have not already—that space is not as empty as it seems, and that it is animated by a form of measurable intelligence that contains a fluid capable of transmitting information over incredible distances faster than the speed of light. In fact, everything is information. The information available to us determines our capacity for self-fulfillment. That is why the almost entirely *intellectual* education that is offered in the institutions of the modern world has such a limiting effect on our potential for acquiring knowledge. An educational model that also includes emotional and spiritual knowledge and training would be far more holistic. I was fortunate enough to access information from other sources while I was still very young. I was thus able to go through all stages of the western educational system, from primary through university, without losing my natural ability to access spontaneous knowledge, which is an innate potential in all human beings.

The liver is the organ that is related to the element of sacred sound. It represents the ability to synthesize, from many nutrients and substances, what the body needs in order to function. It represents the intuitive capacity of the intellect and the world without form, the void from which form emerges, or the nonvoid, the emptiness from which all manifestations emerge. It cleanses and reconstructs.

To enhance liver function it is important to carry out an annual or biannual purification of the liver and gallbladder. The liver, or sacred sound, is in harmonious resonance with our whole being. For the emotional, mental, and spiritual levels it is essential to practice contemplation. Contemplation is a form of meditation that involves viewing things with an attitude of openness and compassion. When someone looks at others in this way we speak of it as empathy: full of compassion and devoid of attachment. By looking at the world this way, innate knowledge will appear spontaneously from the deeper recesses of our being, without our needing abstract, conceptual constructs. Definition through concepts or intellectual knowledge is slow, laborious, and incomplete compared to information received in contemplation. Knowledge received through contemplation is wisdom; it is knowledge that is spontaneous and immediate, complete and holistic. The intellect or mental body intervenes only when this knowledge needs to be communicated to others with whom telepathic communication is not possible.

"Aha!" I can hear you saying, "he's crazy!" Well, despite the fact that these words may seem to go against your entire education, they nevertheless reflect reality. Telepathy has been demonstrated so many times, in numerous studies and in the everyday lives of so many beings, that to question the existence of telepathy is merely to confirm the fact that modern-day education is remarkably shortsighted.

For example, birds practice flying together in the fall to prepare for migration; they fly in perfect formation, and all of them change direction at the same time, synchronized to the nearest millisecond. The same thing can be observed in schools of fish and in many other natural situations. So even animals know how to use telepathy.

Telepathy is easiest with people we love. Remember how you and a loved one sometimes say the same thing at the same time? This is telepathy. Remember how you knew who was calling when the phone rang? Of all the shamanic abilities, telepathy is the easiest. It opens doors to many different modes of communication—and not only with other people!

An acute problem today is that people are no longer capable of thinking for themselves and reaching their own conclusions without the approval of some external authority. This deficiency causes weakness in the liver and the many resulting liver-related diseases that are manifesting in the modern world. This leads to a situation in which a small number of people govern and manipulate the masses while making decisions that destroy nature, on which the lives of all beings depend. This mindset creates interference between humans and the universe; it deprives people of their access to the sacred sound that resonates in harmony with the whole and that provides all beings with the information they require at all times.

Taking time to observe nature, especially the nature that surrounds us, such as our gardens, helps us access the information we need to live as true human beings. Our beings do not feed only on food and water. We also need to find the cosmic food that connects us directly to Source. The connection that we have with the source of all intelligence and information in the universe—as there is order in this vast world—is right here, inside us, at every moment. The reflection of this informational field is found in nature, in the land, the skies, the stars, and the natural elements of this world. So taking time to contemplate nature is a vital, essential, irreplaceable activity. It is as fundamental as our need to breathe and eat.

Once you have succeeded in feeling this communion with nature— and this is something you feel rather than think—you can extend this contemplative vision to all other areas of your life. This will give you greater peace, creativity, joy, and efficiency in all your activities—and a healthier liver!

A healthy liver facilitates the synthesis and integration of all information, be it physiological, intuitive, or spiritual. A diseased liver amplifies anger and often gives people a loud voice and a tendency to shout. Too much anger damages the liver, while unexpressed anger can also be harmful to the liver. But it is possible to find constructive, positive, nonviolent ways of expressing legitimate anger by using a little creativity.

The crystals that work with sacred sound and the liver are: clear quartz, green tourmaline, heliotrope (bloodstone), green jasper, and labradorite.

FIRE

Fire is the element of transformation and energy. Inner fire is the capacity of the body to make its own heat. People who master inner fire are never cold. They can adapt to the coldest temperatures without any discomfort. Another characteristic of people who master inner fire is that they can procreate up to a very advanced age. This is particularly true for men. Inner fire is also the energy that transforms food in the bowels so that the blood can carry nutriments to the cells. The cells transform part of this food into heat, and transform the rest for specific activities of the cells or for cellular reproduction. In Native American spirituality, fire is associated with Spirit. It is alive, in the same way as the wind, the water, and the earth. At the beginning of all First Nations' major gatherings, a sacred fire is lit and is kept alight night and day until the end of the gathering. The fire is considered and treated like an honored guest. It is the connection between this world and the world of the Great Spirit, or Ungawi, the world of ideal form.

We can use fire to help manage our energy. For example, if our metabolism is slow and our humor gloomy, or if we are irritated and agitated, we could say that our fire is making too much smoke or is burning too fast. There is a risk of losing energy if we are either too depressed or too enthusiastic. Therefore it is important to learn to control our heart and our inner fire. For example, let's look at the fire of pleasure. Too much intense pleasure can be exhausting, and if there is not enough joy in your life, your heart and your digestion will lack energy. Your digestion could slow down and even everyday life may feel tiring. The heart suffers whenever there is too much or too little energy. In the long term, the heart may develop life-threatening pathologies if the energy is not balanced.

The best way to tame our inner fire is to remain vigilant and observe how our energy fluctuates. What irritates or saddens us? When do we feel heat or cold? Then try to either stimulate or calm your inner fire as needed. This can be done by simply visualizing the desired effect, or by practicing various other techniques.

Many people need to stimulate their inner fire. Various techniques can be used to do this. The simplest consists of exposing yourself to cold twice a day. For example, turning off the hot water and turning up the cold water at the end of your shower is an excellent way to stimulate inner fire. You can also remain naked for a few moments in a cold environment. When doing this, it is very important to inhale and exhale through the nose (not through the mouth). Breathe vigorously and do not block your breathing. The purpose of this is to stimulate the body via the skin so that it "ignites," so to speak—in other words, until it starts to produce heat. You shouldn't do this for too long, just a few minutes will be enough to start out. If you feel cold afterward, it means you have stayed in the cold too long. If you feel warm, it means you have ignited your inner fire. With practice you will notice that you no longer feel the cold as much, and your energy will be more constant. One of the great advantages of this practice is that seasonal colds and flu will be a thing of the past. The inner fire is in direct connection with your immune response.

It can also be helpful to gaze at a flame, such as a candle or a fire, and try to feel the internal correspondence, your inner fire. Notice how a candle transforms the atmosphere, making it warmer, more poetic, more comfortable, more comforting. Become aware that the fire of transformation of energy ultimately exists in every cell and in your heart, and it is possible to bond with this energy.

To calm your inner fire it is necessary to master the breath. Learning to breathe is an art and is too vast a subject to be covered here. But briefly, to calm your inner fire all you have to do is observe your breathing for a few moments. Once you are conscious of your rate of breathing, try to relax into the breath so that it can find its natural rhythm. Then introduce a brief pause between inhalation and exhalation, and between exhalation and inhalation. During this suspension of the breath, feel peace and bliss, calm and ecstasy in your heart. Continue this four-step centering exercise (see chapter 3) for a few minutes until your heart and breath become calm and serene.

Difficult emotions that indicate a troubled or diseased heart are hatred and cruelty. Positive emotions that are strengthened by fire that are experienced when the heart is healthy are faith, love, compassion, honor, and respect.

Stones that stimulate the fire element are fire opal, garnet, and ruby.

EARTH

The earth is the soft womb that welcomes us. She blossoms into an explosion of life during the day, especially in summertime, and covers herself with a beautiful, sparkling blanket of snow in wintertime. She carries us not for nine months, but all our lives. All our food, clothing, and dwellings come from the earth. How can we express the infinite love the earth unfailingly gives us? Through prayer and offerings! Expressing one's gratitude to the earth establishes within us a harmonious connection with all of creation, which fills us with the extraordinary joy of one who knows that we are safe, that we are fully accepted, and that we are where we belong: at home. Mother Earth is the human being's home. With her, and within her, we find health, joy, and fulfillment.

In the cycle of elements, the earth represents the abdomen because this element feeds the stomach, the spleen, and the pancreas. That is why feelings of insecurity, stress, and anxiety cause stomach ulcers. Compensating by eating too much sugar harms the pancreas and can cause diabetes. These emotions can also weaken the immune system, which in turn can harm the spleen. The antidote to these feelings is to connect with solid values. The greatest wealth a person can possess is one's family and one's home and garden, the place where we and our loved ones can cultivate biodiversity. After gardening, the next most regenerative activity for these organs is singing, especially singing with others or in a choir.

Our relationship with nature is only complete when we understand our mission on earth. We are the guardians of this earthly paradise. We were not driven out of the wonderful Garden of Eden; we exiled ourselves. We can recreate that paradise by cultivating our gardens. You can begin today, wherever you are. Growing edible sprouts from seeds in your kitchen is an excellent first step and will provide you with delicious, living food. Put some flowers on your windowsills to cheer the place up—and why not create a roof garden with flowerpots? Knowing the earth and understanding the role of every species of plant and fauna is the very basis of humanity's mission. We can then co-create paradise. In that paradise we become kings and queens of our domain, living happily with our loved ones.

Recent research shows that people who live on the upper floors of tall buildings die younger than people who live in a family home at ground level. My elders have been saying this for years. It is logical, rational, and obvious to those who understand human beings' relationship with the earth. You must have a personal, intimate relationship with Mother Earth, otherwise you will be lacking the essential connection that makes you a real human being.

The digestion, transformation, and distribution of food throughout the body requires calm and stability. A unique study, although somewhat grotesque (typical of a certain scientific attitude) has proven this. A scientist gave a dog a large meal, then sent it on a hunt for several hours. He then killed the dog and dissected it, only to discover that the food had not been digested. Another dog, fed the same meal at the same time, but that had been allowed to rest in its kennel, had completely digested its meal. Peace and quiet is essential for proper digestion. We don't really need this kind of cruel "research" to prove this; popular wisdom has always known it. So how can we create calm and stability within ourselves? Well, nature does it for us naturally.

We would be omitting a crucial aspect of healing with earth if we didn't mention clay. Clay poultices and clay taken internally to heal and detoxify is a master healer. We can help almost any physical condition with clay. When we allow water to infuse clay in powder form, it undergoes a radioactive process that makes it a living, intelligent material. A simple example: if we treat a flesh wound with a clay poultice, it will heal so well it won't leave a scar. Clay is the first mineral building block of life on this planet. All those interested in healing should consult the many books that explain how to use this simple healing agent. Our family has always used it for many different health problems. Clay is probably the foremost household tool in a healthy lifestyle. Takes work and regularity, but clay is not expensive and has a wide range of uses.

An imbalanced earth element gives insecurity, stress, angst, and anxiety. A balanced earth element gives composure, security, sympathy, and empathy.

Stones that work with the earth element are agates, all black stones, citrines, and carnelian. But all crystals and stones contain some earth element.

Tread softly on Mother Earth. Sing, commune with nature, and may your prayers be beautiful and free. Know that you are loved and safe, protected by Mother Earth, who now needs you to protect her too.

WIND

The wind, or the breath of life, is an invisible yet ever-present element, and as such is indispensable. It is the movement of life, the ever-changing spirit of creation. It is invisible, yet so very present and powerful. We can stop drinking for days, stop eating for weeks, yet it's impossible to stop breathing for more than a few minutes. They say that the wind is the voice of the spirits. When we perform rituals, we honor and pay attention to the winds. They speak to us and express the approval or disapproval of the spirits.

Good-quality air is essential if we wish to remain healthy. Breathing fresh air is increasingly difficult in cities and in the workplace because of pollution and contamination. Large buildings, for example, have ventilation ducts that collect mold, fungi, and dust that can be extremely harmful to one's health. Our homes contain all kinds of invisible dust, various pollutants, gases emanating from building materials or furniture, and so forth. Our air is polluted. But air needs to move and flow, to inhale and exhale. That is why we talk about the element wind rather than air; this living element is always in motion.

Wind corresponds to thought. Even though it is invisible, the wind can either refresh and delight us with a beautiful breeze that makes the leaves dance and sing in the trees, or it can destroy everything in its path with the power of a tornado or a hurricane. Similarly, our thoughts, even though they are also invisible, can create or destroy. We must learn to be the guardians of our thoughts, to become aware and conscious of the creative power of our mental projections. As real human beings we are responsible for what we create, and we must take time to reflect, particularly on the way we express our thoughts. As an example of what this entails, we would be wise to avoid categorizing people by judging them or by focusing only on their negative aspects.

Our voice expresses our innermost being. We must learn to express ourself sincerely and also to listen. Expressing our feelings and emotions allows us to dissociate from them. This gives us perspective, a step back that helps us understand them better. For this to happen, it is essential to share them with someone who knows how to listen. Someone who is quick to offer advice and suggestions does not know how to listen. Active listening is about being attentive and accepting that what is being expressed is that person's reality. Sometimes we can ask questions to help the other person express what they need to share. Advice should only be offered if it is asked for. To offer suggestions and unsought advice is to negate the innate wisdom of that person. A good confidant knows how to limit one's interventions, keep secret what has been expressed, and listen with all one's heart.

The sounds of the voice and song itself comes from the breath. Breath is the expression of Spirit. There is nothing more pleasant and therapeutic than to sing for our loved ones. There is no prayer more powerful than one that is sung. We should be attentive to the sound of our voice. We must learn how to soften a loud, intimidating voice, and avoid being violent if we speak words of anger, because they can break the peace like a gunshot. There are voices that harm, and there are voices that heal. The most therapeutic voice remains neutral, without influencing the atmosphere of the person listening.

The sound of sorrow, as when someone cries, and the flowing of tears frees the lungs of unhealthy energy. It is very important to accept when someone is crying without inhibiting what that person needs to express through their tears. The admonition to stop crying, all too often said to young children, conditions people to refrain from crying. In time, unhealthy energy can accumulate in the lungs, which may then develop various pathologies. Too much grief over a long period of time also harms the lungs. In situations where there is too much sorrow and bereavement, it is good to alternate with periods of joy, or at least rest, before again expressing bereavement and sorrow.

Sadness, grief, and depression are the negative emotions of unhealthy lungs that do not integrate the wind element appropriately. Healthy wind within gives courage, determination, affirmation of self, and honesty.

The only stones that can work with the wind element are the white stones and crystals, such as opal, moonstone, and pearl. It's far better to work with essential oils when working with the wind element. As such, I have created five wonderful shamanic perfumes for the elements, including Yuutin, which addresses the wind element.*

WATER

Ah, water! How can we describe the joy we feel at the shores of a great lake or the feeling of immense reverence when we look at the ocean? How can we put into words the sweetness of the rain and the bliss of a brook bubbling with energy? The greatest rivers of the world inspire holiness and smaller rivers and streams life!

We have our own internal waterways: our arteries, veins, lymphatic system, kidneys, and bladder. Water corresponds to the emotions. That

---

*See the 5-elements perfumes at www.boutiqueaiglebleu.com/en.

is why we associate the fall, autumn, with water, because it is a tempestuous season of major changes, maturation, and often lots of rain. Maturity and transformation are the qualities of autumn. These qualities are at the heart of what water has to teach us.

Water adapts to all the forms it meets. Whatever the shape of the vase or glass into which you pour water, it will immediately adopt that shape. But it never ceases to be water, always remaining faithful to itself. When it evaporates it cleanses itself and rises up to form clouds, as pure as it was at the beginning of time. Then it falls again to nourish the earth and all her beings. It cleanses everything, sweeping away everything in its path. Give it enough time and it will wash away the highest mountain.

This gives us a very clear picture of how the emotions work. Our emotions adapt to every situation in life. However, despite its apparent diversity, the energy that underlies all emotions, water, is always the same. That is why a wise person knows how to express his feelings when it's appropriate, but will always remain faithful to himself, never allowing himself to be trapped into believing that the emotions exist in their own right. An emotion is merely energy in perpetual transformation. If we wait a little, it will change. Take the moon, for example: it changes its appearance every day, but never ceases to be the moon.

There is an important distinction to be made between feelings or sentiments, which are of a more permanent nature, and emotions, which fluctuate. Love (unconditional, not passionate) is a sentiment that always remains; it is at the heart of every atom, molecule, cell, solar system, and galaxy. Joy and peace are also sentiments. Pleasure, envy, enthusiasm, fear, anger, grief, sorrow, anxiety, desire, mirth, and so forth are emotions. We must recognize their changing nature and see the underlying primordial energy they convey—essentially, joy, love, and peace. Think of waves breaking on the surface of the sea during a storm, while in the depths of the sea all is tranquility, peace, and silence. The true, unchanging foundation of the emotional body is peace, joy, and love.

The wisdom of water tells us that it is pointless to try to block the flow of our emotions, to dam the river, to calm the waves. They must be expressed; they must flow and spill over, because such is their nature. On the other hand, you should never lose yourself in this perpetual movement or get caught up in the emotion as if it were something permanent, because that is simply not the nature of emotions. We should rather admire the many ways our emotions reflect life's diverse situations while understanding that they are all just temporary. There is no need to panic, to overreact, to be carried away by the waves of emotion. Notice how a branch floating on the water of a lake follows the movement of the water but stays pretty much in the same place. So it is that the surface of our being can move and dance on the waves of emotion, but the true nature of our being always remains the same: joy, love, and peace. Being conscious of this gives us flexibility, malleability, and adaptability, without losing a sense of who we are. We must remain real human beings: co-creators of the world with the Divine. We can learn from our emotions, but we must never be a victim of them. That is a sure sign of maturity, of someone who understands their essential nature.

The kidneys, which are the very foundation of life, are the physiological link with generations of our ancestors. The current system would have us forget the history and spiritual heritage of our ancestors in order to better control and manipulate us. By submerging people in a stressful lifestyle, with tiring workloads, excessive formalities, bureaucracy, and constant control, this system distances children from their families and parents from their communities. The nonsensical garbage that people see on television and in electronic and media entertainment has replaced stories, folklore, songs, dances, music, traditions, community, wisdom, and knowledge of nature. That is why there are so many diseases of the kidney, bladder, and prostate, as well as a general loss of meaning in life. Having no direction in life has created a new plague affecting the younger generations: suicide! A society whose young people commit suicide is a very sick society indeed. Many families today have no land or garden to pass on to their children. Therefore, these young people have no roots and no understanding of the essential values that sustain life. There are young people today who have never seen the stars, who think that eggs come from the supermarket, and that the ultimate purpose of life is what they see on computer and television screens.

We have allowed this situation to happen, so it's up to us to change it. Recognizing the legacy of our ancestors is not as easy as it used to be, but on the other hand, wisdom lives on in the hearts of all people. We must learn, just like water, to adapt to the world as it is, but at the same time we must build our lives on solid values—on our relationships, nature, and life. In nature you will always find joy, love, and peace. The most precious gift you can pass on to your children is a piece of land or a garden, a little spot of paradise that you have preserved for them. That way they can come to understand the true meaning of life: to be a co-creator of a paradise on earth and to blissfully contemplate a world filled with beauty and love. They will understand that it is water, earth, fire, wind, the plants, the animals, and the clouds that nourish the earth, and that make it possible for life to exist. This will make them want to dance and sing and build a healthy and harmonious life for their children. They will become real human beings.

That is the message of water. Water has memory, as proven by homeopathy and by the work of Japanese scientist Masaru Emoto.* Thus what flows in our veins, as well as what flows in the rivers and streams of the earth, carries the memory of the world and the hope for future generations.

An imbalance in the water element will manifest as fear. A balanced water element within gives ease of emotional expression and a strong connection with one's ancestors and, with that, primordial knowledge and wisdom.

The stones and crystals that work with the water element are celestites, aquamarine, and opal.

---

*See Masaru Emoto's *The Hidden Messages in Water.* New York: Atria Books, 2005.

7

The Colors, or Rays, and Their Properties

Divine energy orients light in specific rays that create and influence the many different aspects of creation. Everything in the universe is mainly composed of energy. Energy is essentially frequency. The lower the frequency, the denser the manifestation. As you go higher in frequency you go to sound, then to light, and then to cosmic rays. Light will manifest different frequencies, which manifest as different colors.

All of creation is actually made of vibrations, frequencies, and those stem from the one light. Scientists thought they had found the smallest unit of matter when they discovered the atom. Yet as they progressed in the study of the atom they found that it is actually 99.99 percent empty. The atom is composed of tiny particles that vibrate within that space, creating the illusion of physical matter. Thus vibration can be described as a specific frequency that responds to what created that frequency: the power of intention—specifically, Creator's intention to manifest the multiverse. This is responsible for everything that exists in our known universe.

The color of a crystal is one of the main attributes that determines the effect it will have on our health and energy. Thus it's important to have a good understanding of the colors, or rays as they are sometimes called, as described below.

The three primary colors, blue, red and yellow, symbolize the three laws of manifestation. Blue is the will to be, to live, and to exist in a physical body; red represents love, compassion, devotion, or the soul and emotional being holding the whole being in coherence with the intention; and yellow relates to Spirit, creative intelligence, and mind.

Sunlight reveals seven colors when it passes through a crystal prism or a cloud of raindrops, creating a rainbow. Each color orients light energy in a specific way.

We look to the rainbow to find the range of colors and their attributes. They display in the following order: red, orange, yellow, green, blue, indigo, and violet. Red, orange, and yellow are warm colors, red being the hottest and yellow the coolest. Green is a neutral color and represents that health is a state of balance and equilibrium. Blue, indigo, and violet are cool colors, blue being light and easy, indigo deep and profound, and violet a spiritual, very elevating color, not easy to live with, but very inspiring.

To give you a general guide in the choice of colors, and thus of the crystal that displays that color, we will orient ourselves by following the energies of cool, warm, and neutral colors.

When there is chronic illness, a problem that has been there for some time already, there is usually a depletion of energy. Thus you should generally use a warm color to provide energy to the person in need of healing. When there is acute pain or illness, usually meaning it has come on suddenly or recently and immediate help is needed, there is usually inflammation involved, which means too much energy is concentrated in one place. This calls for a cool color, to refresh, dissipate, and reduce pain and inflammation.

If you want balance, stability, and energizing yet soothing, life-giving vitality and neutrality, then go to green. Green is always good. When in doubt, choose green. It's the color of healing.

Now, let's look at specifics.

RED

The color red, which is stimulating and energizing, corresponds to the first energy center at the base of the spine. It's associated with the musical note C and is the slowest of all color frequencies. Red is the color of passion, love, and vital life-force energy. Red is very strong, so strong in fact that we should always harmonize with green or blue after having a session with the color red. If we have applied red for a longer period of time and have had good results, then we will start reharmonizing with a green or blue ray stone for several days at the end of the cycle of red treatments.

The red ray stimulates and strengthens the constructive energies of the body. It can also give instantaneous energy. For example, on a long night drive, if you want to stay awake and remain vigilant you could use a ruby tincture or a ruby essence. The red ray is used for the immune system, for the blood, and in some instances for the heart when there is slow or low energy. A good example is anemia, where the blood is tired, lacking in energy, and iron-deficient (note that when iron rusts it turns red, its innate color). Thus the pathologies that benefit from the red ray include red blood-cell deficiency, eczema, depression, fatigue, despondency, and all the degenerative diseases. By degenerative disease we mean cancer, senility, Parkinson's disease, multiple sclerosis, and the like.

Crystals of the red ray are ruby, which is the strongest, red garnet, rhodochrosite, and red jasper. Rose quartz is in a class by itself and we'll describe it later. Of course there are many other red crystals, but as I mentioned earlier we only speak here of those that we have used over the centuries. As all crystals work in different ways, we like to be confident of our choice in stones when they are used to help and to heal.

ORANGE

The next color in the rainbow is orange, which is revitalizing and stimulating, a warm, harmonizing color. It's associated with the second energy center or chakra and the musical note D. This color will work with the digestive system and recharge the etheric web. It has an impact on the throat center because of that center's correspondences with the second center.

Carnelian is our favorite orange stone. Carnelian reactivates the power of true expression, and if you have blockages in the throat center it will help with different types of speech problems. Like red, orange is also a warm color. It's got a lot of energy and is stimulating, but it balances things out, whereas red is more brutal and omnidirectional. Orange is good for the digestive system and organs. In the elements symbolism it's the color of the stomach, spleen, and pancreas. It's also the color of choice for all psychosomatic pathologies. A very important orange stone that we'll talk more about in part 5 is Madeira citrine.

YELLOW

Now we go to the fastest vibration in the warm color spectrum, which is yellow, and an even higher vibrancy, the color gold. These colors correspond to the musical note E and the solar plexus. Yellow gives energy like the other warm colors, but on a higher, more subtle vibratory level. It works with the nervous system and the brain, for inspiration, for projects, for intellectual capacities, and for the nervous system. Yellow can also be used to help the eyes and nerves. It can remove calcium deposits in those suffering from arthritis and excess mucus in the lungs.

Some stones that have the yellow ray are golden citrine, golden beryl, and yellow topaz.

GREEN

In the middle of the spectrum we have green, the healthiest color. That is why you'll find it in all natural environments; where there's rain, the foliage is coated in green. Green corresponds with the musical note F and, of course, the heart center. Green is a neutral color. It's stimulating yet relaxing at the same time. If you don't know what color to use, go to green. Health is a state of balance, thus green has that vibration. When you need balance, equilibrium, equanimity, go to green. When you are working with the heart, go to green. You can start with strengthening the heart with red when that need is there, but always finish with green when there's a heart problem. Green is a much-needed color today on all levels. Green refreshes and tones the body. It's used for many afflictions. In the elements system green is associated with the liver and gallbladder.

The king or queen of all green stones is emerald. There is also green tourmaline, green jasper, and dioptase. Malachite is to be mentioned here as well, but note that this stone is not crystalline.

BLUE

The blue ray is electric, soothing, and relaxing. It corresponds to the throat center and the musical note G. This is the color we use to bring down fevers, to assuage migraines and headaches, and to calm inflammation. Anything that needs to cool down calls for blue. For example, if you have a small burn and you immediately think blue and send that color there, it often disappears instantaneously. Use blue for unwinding and relaxing. It's very useful for infections, as blue is antiseptic.

The blue ray crystals are aquamarine, celestite, blue garnet, azurite, and dioptase. Celestite is a favorite for migraines and headaches. Aquamarine is for the prostate and all problems related to the water element in the body. Azurite works miracles with tendinitis.

INDIGO

Indigo is the deep blue, very dark sapphire, deep sea, evening sky blue color. Indigo relates to self-knowledge, intuition, and wisdom. Whereas blue relaxes, indigo will put you to sleep. It's associated with the sixth energy center, the forehead/third eye, and the musical note A. Indigo brings us to very deep levels of relaxation. It's good for all the openings in your head, thus the sinuses, ears, nose, eyes, and anything related to the lungs. It's used to go into deep levels of meditation, contemplation, and divination.

The indigo crystal par excellence is sapphire, which is a deep blue stone. Also of note is labradorite, a very special stone that has indigo and other related colors. Other examples of indigo stones are lapis lazuli and sodalite.

VIOLET

With violet we have the stimulation of the upper faculties of the human mind and spirit and a calming effect on the lower energy centers. Some use violet as an appetite suppressor. The crown center and the musical note B, the note that drives upward to the next octave, are associated with violet. We use violet for that which needs transformation. A typical application would be for helping to transmute addictions arising from a compulsive character into a more useful mode of expression. Other uses are in helping and healing stress, nervousness, high blood pressure, epilepsy, neuralgia, and mental disorders that are not hallucinatory or schizophrenic.

People on a profound spiritual quest or with high religious standing will wear amethyst, a quartz family member of the violet ray. Amethyst is not recommended and actually contraindicated for schizophrenia, among a few other pathologies we will study later in this book.

COMBINATIONS OF COLORS

Then there are white and black and variations on these two colors, which are actually the same in that both contain all colors, yet in opposing dimensions. So combinations of black or white with other colors in stones give us a great variety of diverse effects. For example, pink is a combination of white and red. This gives us pure love, unconditional love, nonromantic love, and all-encompassing compassionate love.

White

The color white represents the presence of all the colors of the spectrum. The light that comes from Spirit is clear, and when it goes through a prism it reveals the seven colors of the rainbow. This is clear light. White light, while it has all the colors, is more opaque than clear. For example, white powder on glass windows in bathrooms—you can't see through these powder-coated windows, but light does come through. You need a clear window to see through. This distinction between white and clear will be further clarified a little later.

Black

The color black also contains all the colors of the spectrum, but it retains the colors rather than shining them out as white does. An example of this distinction from white would be how you dress for specific occasions. If you want to shine, to teach, to perform, to display, you wear white. If you want to be discreet, low-profile, and keep your energy to yourself in a more protective mode, you wear black.

These are simple descriptions of that aspect of the energy that crystals carry in the form of color. To be able to choose the right color you need to integrate not only the mental, intellectual aspect described here, but also the feeling the color imparts to you. Always remember that you are the one setting forth an intention, which the crystal will amplify for healing. Both need to do the work; a crystal by itself doesn't do much of anything. Also, what works for me might not work for you in all circumstances, so you should get a feeling for them by sitting with the colors. Go into your meditation space and use the colors one by one, giving yourself time to feel them. There are many ways to do this, just use your imagination. The easiest way is to visualize them as they shine through your whole being.

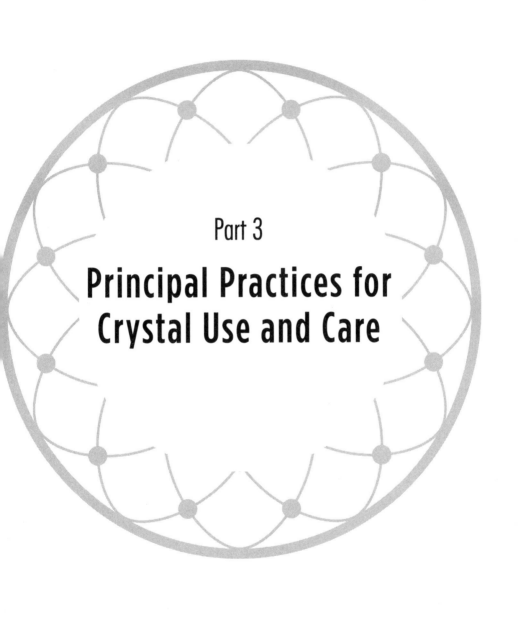

Part 3

Principal Practices for Crystal Use and Care

8

Creating Sacred Space

In this chapter on the practices that refine a crystal practitioner's ability to work with these jewels of the mineral kingdom we will show you how to create sacred space-time in your body and mind, your home, and outside in nature. The first practice is creating a turtle altar in your home.

THE TURTLE ALTAR

A wise Cherokee priestess once taught that every race of humanity has its specific responsibility on earth. The white race is responsible for inventions; the black race is the guardian of the rhythms of the world; the yellow race deepens our understanding of community structures; and the red race is the guardian of the Earth Mother and nature. The turtle altar or shrine carries this name because it is the altar or shrine of the Earth Mother. Indeed, all First Nations of North America called this continent Great Turtle Island. The turtle has always been for us a symbol for the Earth Mother, and as crystals are her bones we are going to learn how to create this altar.

Formerly, people always had a shrine in their homes, a place dedicated to their spiritual practice. When we leave this world and pass through the doors of death, the only thing we take with us are our memories, our meaningful relationships, and our highest thoughts. All the rest is short-lived. It is thus wise to give time to daily spiritual practice. The creation of a sacred space in one's home—namely, a turtle altar—will make your meditations and reflections more inspired and raise them to a higher frequency. Seeing that inspiring space of beauty in your home will make it easier to find the time to sit in prayer and meditation on a regular basis.

We find on the turtle altar seven essential elements: a candle, some water, a crystal, some salt, some corn flour, a *machikoué* (a maracas or rattle), and a shell containing some sage.

- The **fire** of the candle represents Spirit, the omniscient light, the essence of the earth. In former times this fire was in fact the central fire of the tipi, the wigwam, the kiva, the longhouse, or the hogan, representing the essential fire of life. All Native homes had a fire in the center of the dwelling. It was for more than just utility; it was a place for connecting with the spirit world. As you light a candle on your altar, you pray that the spirit of the earth will bless your abode.

- **Water** symbolizes the blood of the earth. It is also an offering so that all the lost spirits and hungry ghosts who seek solace may quench their thirst. It is the fresh, cool water that heals, nourishes, cools, and calms. It represents mirror wisdom, the enlightened mind that sees things as they are. As you place the water bowl on your altar, you pray with these words: *May all beings who are thirsty find water to drink, and may we see the nature of our spirit, who we truly are.*

- The **crystal or stone** represents the bones of the Earth Mother, her skeleton. Only if you live alone should you use a one-pointed crystal. Best to use a multipointed cluster of clear quartz crystals (see plate 2). The crystal symbolizes perfection in form and pure intention. It is the symbol of our unmanifest potential and an amplifier of the beneficial energies created by the shrine. Its largest termination or point is directed northward, aligning the altar with the electromagnetic energies of the earth. As you place the crystal in the right direction, press it firmly with your fingers, applying pressure to activate it and align it with the north. Thank it for its help.

- **Corn flour** feeds the lost souls and hungry ghosts. We offer the sacred corn so that all beings have enough to eat. This yellow, luminous flour symbolizes the uncountable blessings of Mother Earth. If the disembodied spirits, lost between worlds, come into your house, they will find on the altar a spiritual food that will lead them toward the light. As you place the small bowl of corn flour on the altar, say these words: *May all those who are hungry find food to eat.*

- **Sea salt** represents the flesh of Mother Earth. Salt is a mineral synthesis of the elements that are indispensable to life. In the Bible, man is called the "salt of the earth" because his role is to promote the well-being of all life on earth. Salt on the shrine acts as a magnet to attract all negative vibrations and anchor them in the salt structure (which is in fact a kind of crystal), thus neutralizing dissonant subtle energies. Place the salt on the altar holding this thought in mind, and say a few words to confirm your intention.

- The **rattle,** or maracas, called "life-force shaker" in our tradition, represents our spiritual practice, our will to remember what is important, which is to have a daily time to think and meditate in unity with the essence of our being. As you place it on the altar, shake it, make music, and remind yourself that if you don't shake a rattle it won't make any sound. In the same way, even if you have the best teachings, if you don't practice them, they won't give you any results.

- The **shell** with sage is used for purification. It represents the purity of our intentions and the will to continue to cleanse and purify ourselves. Burn a little sage to purify the space that you have just created.

Now that all these elements are on the altar, sing a heart chant or any spiritual chant you know to activate the altar. Test the energy coming from the altar before doing the chant and afterward. Look to the light that has been created. You have created sacred space!

These elements are the skeleton of the altar, its simplest expression. Once these essential elements are laid on the altar, you can add your own personal medicine, those objects that have a particular importance or a symbolic value to you. It can be a picture of a spiritual elder, a rosary or a mala, a feather, or any other object that is a part of your medicine. For example, a healer will keep her healing crystals on the altar so that they become infused with spiritual energies, thus more powerful when used in her healing practice.

Once the altar is installed and blessed, we give offerings, part of the shrine ceremonial. The water should be changed every day, the bowl rinsed three times and filled on the fourth. This new, fresh, cool water represents the light of our being. In the same way that water reflects the sky, we can, by cleansing ourself every day, become crystal-clear and acquire mirror wisdom, the ability to see things as they are. Periodically we also renew the salt and the corn on the altar. Sometimes the altar receives offerings of food. But the most important offering is our prayers and meditation.

This altar becomes a symbol of divine light, blessing our house and protecting it. It enhances communion with Source, that atom within our hearts that is connected to the whole universe. The energy that is generated by the shrine increases in time as we do daily spiritual practice in front of it. It will thus help to harmonize our environment. The presence of the altar also serves as a reminder of the importance of spiritual practice. It is very easy to get caught up in the hustle and bustle of everyday chores and work and forget what is essential. The presence of the shrine reminds us that it is good to take time every day to pray, meditate, and meet with our inner self. In time, remembering to practice becomes easier. We have a special moment with ourself in front of the altar, this place of beauty that we have created. The shrine is the reflection of our inner beauty. It is easy to soak in this light because it's the visible demonstration of our own light. I've often pointed out to my students how there is the presence of heightened luminosity when an altar is created. All have noticed the reality of this phenomenon. We can easily perceive more luminosity in a room where a turtle altar has just been activated.

The rites practiced in front of this shrine will remind us of our purpose in life. We can also use the altar to create what is called *harmonic resonance magic.* This magic is done by reproducing on a smaller scale things that we would like to see manifest on a larger scale. If, for example, we wish to pray for rain, we can water a plant on our shrine while visualizing the same thing happening as rain falls on the surrounding gardens and fields. In harmonic resonance, echoing our thoughts, nature will tend to respond to the vibrant energy field this creates. The altar represents the earth. It is the planet that is there, right in front of us, shining in beauty with all its elements. And we are an integral part of Mother Earth.

Our thoughts, words, and actions are the wood with which we build our tomorrow. All that happens we have in some way created. Our thoughts are alive, our words resonate in the world, and all our acts create waves that one day will return to us. We are responsible for the seeds we sow.

This is a safe and strong place to implement your daily practice as a crystal healer. It's also the best place to keep your crystals when they are not being used.

WORKING WITH THE ENERGY CENTERS

Sacred space by itself is useless unless we honor it. If we acknowledge sacred space then it becomes imbued with higher frequencies. These higher frequencies will then aid us in our healing practice through harmonic resonance as they refine and augment our capacity to channel healing energy to others. The best way to honor sacred space is by doing spiritual practice there. Here is a simple and efficient practice to align, purify, and enhance your energy centers.

A clear quartz crystal can help calm the kundalini. This is the special energy contained in the first energy center at the base of the spine, also called the *serpent fire.* When it is stimulated or awakened it will seek a path up the central channel into the other energy centers, or chakras. If the other energy centers are not open, this can cause problems. An awakened and enlightened human being will have the kundalini rise all the way up to the forehead, to the third eye. Illustrations that show Egyptian pharaohs with a cobra on the forehead depict this. When a prematurely awakened kundalini gets stuck in the second energy center because it can't flow upward through the central channel there will be a lot of disharmony in sexual expression. That goes for each of the energy centers as well: if kundalini cannot flow all the way up, there may be problems associated with the particular energy center that is blocked. The clear quartz crystal can cool this energy down.

There are seven or eight chakras, depending on the tradition. Here is a brief summary of each center, or wheel, and its function:

- The first center is at the sacrum, at the perineum. Here we find the coiled serpent known as *kundalini,* which contains the fundamental energies and the original instructions we received when we came into this world.
- The second center is behind the umbilicus. This center accumulates and coordinates all energies of a physical nature, giving a healthy body when all is flowing the right way. This center has many neurons and synapses, so it is often called our *third brain*. It also carries the intelligence necessary to coordinate all the activities of the physical body. We accumulate energy of a physical nature in this center.
- The third energy center is called the solar plexus. It coordinates our emotional energies.
- The fourth energy center is the heart. This is our second and by far our most important brain! It coordinates everything that has to do with understanding, love, compassion, and essential communication with other life forms. It holds the divine atom of communion with our essential spirit.
- The fifth energy center is at the throat. It coordinates mental capacity and the ability to communicate through speech. Skillful means to accomplish and realize our potential are nourished by the energy that comes from this center.

• The sixth energy center is at the forehead and also includes a secondary center at the back of the head (the occiput) and the center of the head (the pituitary and pineal glands). All that is spiritual and our higher guiding principle comes from these centers. It condenses energies from the sky to nourish the body's glands.

• The seventh energy center, or wheel, is at the top of the head and is like an opening through which we receive heavenly energies and commune with other subtle centers above the head.

• The eighth energy center is between the heart and the solar plexus, the point of vulnerability at the end of the breast bone. It is our main connection with the universal mind of creation and the entry and exit point of the light body when traveling out of body or shamanic journeying. For many people beginning on a spiritual path, this very sensitive center needs protection. There are many ways to protect this center, the easiest is by wearing a clear quartz pendant (see pages 191–93).

🔅 Purifying the Energy Centers with a Clear Quartz Crystal

This is an exercise for purifying the energy centers that follow the spine in the center of the body, along what is called the *central channel*. These centers are known as chakras in the Hindu tradition. They are wheels of subtle energy that coordinate the innumerable energy exchanges and spiritual potential we carry.

Note: It is not a good idea to work on any specific energy centers individually. When we work with the energy centers, we must work with all of them.

Before beginning, the crystal used in this exercise must be purified with the technique taught in chapter 9 (see pages 126–27).

1. Choose a clear quartz crystal that is not too big, as you will be putting it on your forehead. Take a few moments to relax, creating a quiet ambiance, and then center. Take your crystal and gaze into it for approximately ten minutes. Then lie on your back in a comfortable

position, laying the crystal on your forehead. If it's a one-pointed quartz crystal, the direction of the point is not important, but if it rests well on your forehead the end pointed down, toward your body, is the best angle.

2. Find yourself in the crystal, and as you merge with it you both become clear, transparent light. This light emanates, entering into your body first at the base of your spine, into the first energy center. As you are in this light, you can also see this light. And so look at this first energy center, and as you look at it check for any blockages or hindrances in the energy flow there. If you see anything that needs correction, use this light that you are, which has merged with the light of the crystal, which is in a pure form and thus attuned to the laws of the universe, and correct what needs correcting.

3. After seeing what you can do in this first center and doing it, move up into the second energy center just below the navel in the center of the belly. Look at this second energy center from within the clear, transparent light, and correct anything that needs adjustment, removing any blockages and harmonizing any hindrances with the clear light to make this energy center as efficient as possible.

4. Continue in this way through all the remaining energy centers: the solar plexus, the heart center, the throat center, and the head center. There are three centers in the head. One is on the forehead, one is at the occiput at the back of the head, and one is in the center of the head where the pineal and pituitary glands are. Begin at the back of the head, then the center, then the forehead. End by bringing the light up to the very top center of the head.

5. You have now completed this exercise. Thank your crystal and purify it for a few minutes in saltwater.

OFFERINGS

As mentioned in chapter 2, there are three aspects to spiritual practice: offerings and prayer; physical exercises that have an energy aspect to them, also called breathing and stretching; and meditation. We describe here some of the ways of making offerings.

One of the simplest ways to offer prayers of gratitude is through offerings. These become a physical, concrete way of manifesting our thankfulness for the gift of life. The more we express gratitude, the more we receive. The more we feel thankfulness, the more we are in harmony with the universe and our life purpose. Gratitude is a beauteous form of pure joy. If we give thanks upon awakening, expressing gratitude to Creator for being alive, it will be difficult to be sad or bad-tempered the rest of the day. To have a human body and to be alive is such a blessing. In fact, all the suffering and obstacles we face are opportunities for growth. The most difficult experiences in life often have us learning important lessons really fast. The more things are difficult, the more reason we have for saying thank-you.

When we give thanks every day, we awaken a very special magic: we offer something to the universe. And when we give, the universe gives back to us in return. It's a universal law, exemplified by the simple act of breathing out, then breathing in.

Teaching Story

An old Huichol medicine man, Matsuma, went to teach in Southern California.* At the time of his stay there had been a drought that had been raging for three months. During that time, the earth had not received a single drop of rain. The ground was so dry that it was cracked. During a break in the teachings, certain students asked the elder if he could do something about the drought. He had been waiting for that request, as he had seen the dire state of the land that had great need for rain. He immediately went outside, under a blue sky, for two or three minutes, giving a simple offering of corn flour. He then returned and continued his teachings. Fifteen minutes later, the land was blessed with torrential rain. To the bewildered students, the old man simply

---

*As told by one of his students, Brant Secunda.

declared, "The thankfulness of men is food for the gods." By "gods," he meant the spirits of nature. Let us feel grateful for what we have, honor the universe, and it will give us back in return. In fact, the old man had not needed to ask for rain. His only thought was to give an offering of thankfulness to the spirits of nature. This was sufficient for nature to immediately send what was required by the environment.

We emphasize how important it is to physically demonstrate our thanks to the world. It's not sufficient to simply think *thank you*. Offerings are a more physical, overt way to demonstrate our thoughts and feelings of gratitude. The simple exercise mentioned in chapter 2 and practiced by many Native peoples will make it easier for you to feel what I'm trying to convey. At your next meal, before beginning to eat, take a small piece of each food from your plate and put them on a piece of bread or in a small bowl. At the end of the meal, take your offerings outside and give them to nature. When you have given this offering, just stand silently and be attentive for a few moments; notice what is happening around and within you.

Offerings are a testimony to our thankfulness for the beauty of the universe all around us. All Native nations have traditional offerings that are appropriate for different circumstances. As a general rule, North American First Nations will offer tobacco, sweetgrass, corn flour, cedar, sage, or juniper. These plants are sacred in the memory of all First Nations of North America.

It's the same with all that we consider sacred. Think of wine. This substance is very important for Christians, who consider it symbolically as the blood of Christ. Far from being considered harmful, it's on the contrary supposed to bring them toward even higher levels of consciousness. This shows that everything lies in the intention with which we do things. The spirits of nature recognize sacred substances because they are encoded in the memory of the world and in the traditions of the people. When sacred substances are offered, the spirits of nature answer our requests more readily because they are in harmonic resonance with ritual conventions established for millennia between humans and the nature spirits. If you work with a sacred substance, you are in the presence of an energy that revives ancestral memories and community with the spirits of nature.

The cycle of reciprocity and its magic will begin to bless your life when you take time to share and express your thankfulness to nature. Nature, the world we live in, is the foundation of our consciousness. It is through nature that we can start to understand our relationship with Great Spirit. Through nature the Great Mystery (the Divine, or Wakan Tanka in Lakota spirituality; Gitche Manito in Algonquin spirituality) is always talking to us, showing us the truth and the laws of the universe and the path to be followed to reach an even greater unity, a deeper relationship with our essence.

The greatest offering of all is the way we live our lives. One of my friends who has since passed on, whom we all called Chief Thundercloud, was a very tall, slender Cherokee man who gave magnificent teachings on water. Everywhere he went, he purified the waters. I've seen people give him a glass of murky polluted water; as soon as he placed his hand above it, the water became crystal-clear. This man began his work as a medicine man in a hospital, where his son was dying of a very serious disease. The doctors had abandoned any hope of saving him, saying he only had a few hours to live. Having promised his wife that their son would live, Chief Thundercloud asked to be left alone with his son. He placed his hands over the boy and offered a prayer to Great Spirit, offering his life in exchange for his son's life. To offer one's own life is the greatest offering. He felt a great energy moving through his body, then through his hands. In the moments that followed, the young man awakened from his coma. He was well again. His parents were elated. The next day, Chief Thundercloud realized that he had to honor his commitment. He thus left his job and dedicated the rest of his life to helping others by healing, teaching, and doing what he thought Creator expected of him. He became a well-known and respected medicine man. Even if he has now passed on to the spirit world, his teachings on water remain and are still very important, especially today, in a world where pure drinking water is becoming scarce because of man's ignorance of the laws of nature.

Offerings are an excellent way of entering into right relationship with the natural world around us. Choosing the most appropriate offering often depends on our lineage. To all Native peoples, the ways of their ancestors are of great importance. The parents through whom we are embodied are not chosen at random. The choice of our parents is established according to criteria determined by karma, our love for people in previous lives, and the life mission that we came to accomplish. We are related to all our grandparents and great-grandparents and beyond, as from them we inherit both positive and negative aspects of the family that we build on or transform. They are a part of the earth we live on.

We say of our ancestors that they are the guardians of tradition and the guardians of the earth. They are there to help us and protect us. The ancestors are our main source of inspiration and represent the spiritual foundation of our being and our relationship with the places where we live. This is known to Native peoples all over the earth.

For example, the Africans who were captured and sent to Brazil to work as slaves in the plantations brought their cultural heritage with them. In their country of origin, they performed yearly ceremonies to honor their ancestors. When they arrived in Brazil they quickly realized that the land there did not belong to the white colonizers who had brought them there. They realized that the white people had stolen that land, which in reality belonged to the Native peoples who were the original inhabitants. They therefore adapted their African ancestor rituals to honor the ancestors of the Native peoples of that land, Brazil. The symbolism of those ceremonies share many of the characteristics of First Nations celebrations, notably, the ceremonial clothing, rituals, and offerings. These Afro-Brazilians choose to honor the ancestors of the Native peoples who were before them, even though they were almost completely exterminated by the European colonizers; they did this because the bones, bodies, and ceremonies of those ancestors are inherent to the land where they were living. These celebrations are very different from their original African ceremonies.

We see in this example the fundamental unity that exists among

Native peoples everywhere on the planet. The laws of nature are unchanging; they are the same everywhere. By living in accordance with nature, aboriginal peoples everywhere came to respect the same basic values and the same understanding about the world. There is between Native peoples of all lands (those who live in harmony with the land, with minimal technology) a real ecumenism that transcends all the differences that could separate them. We have important lessons to learn from this unity. Our world would glean great wisdom and understanding about the nature of the world and our fundamental unity as human beings if we truly understood the importance of honoring our ancestors and the ancestors of the land where we live. The following story illustrates this aspect of our world heritage.

Teaching Story

Many years ago I visited an intentional community* near Berlin, where I had been invited to teach and share on community values and techniques. This very special community was experimenting on new communal ways of life that were very different from those of typical German society. In the evening when I arrived, a large tent had been erected where meals were offered to participants. I was invited to eat, and we settled down to have supper. Out of the corner of my eye I perceived a white shape coming toward me. It was the spirit of an ancestor, dressed in long white robes, with a long beard who resembled Panoramix, a Galois Druid in a well-known French comic series. Very surprised, I saw him coming straight at me, looking very agitated. He wished to speak to me and was very adamant about it. I explained to him telepathically that I was with friends who did not see him, that it would be impolite to leave so soon, and that I needed to eat after a long day of traveling but that I would be out in a bit to hear what he had to say. He disappeared. Straight after the meal I went out of the tent and came nose-to-nose with my famous "Panoramix," who was still

---

*ZEGG is an ecovillage community located on the outskirts of Bad Belzig, Germany, about 80 km southwest of Berlin.

very impatient to speak with me. I asked him to wait a few moments so I could center myself to better understand him, as he was a spirit and not speaking with words, but through telepathy. I needed to be well-concentrated to understand properly. So I meditated a moment, then I turned to him and asked him what he wanted.

This ancestor told me that he was the guardian of the earth on which we stood. He had been holding important teachings for many hundreds of years, waiting for the opportunity to pass them on. Now there was a community living on the land, and he desperately wanted to pass on his wisdom to them. For the first time in a very long time there was a community, an assembly of people of like mind who were ready to live and share life on his territory. I could understand that: Native peoples everywhere live in communities. Modern-day society based on a relationship to money is the negation of right human relationship. Yet this ancestor was distraught, as nobody could see him and no one was listening. So I asked him, "What can I do about it?" He taught me a specific offering that would help them communicate with him. The offering of this lineage was a little honey on a birch leaf. What was interesting was that he also told me that the symbolism of his people was based on flowers. Our Native American symbolism is based on animal totems, hence the feather bonnets and other ceremonial clothing with animal parts. That honey was the traditional offering of the Natives of this part of the world made a lot of sense. It took me three days to convince this community they should do what the ancestor was asking!

This ancestor showed me a ceremony of former times and asserted that if people agreed to this traditional offering, he would speak to each of them. I knew that this community was not spiritual. They were more centered on social and sexual experimentation. They had spent five years in the Black Forest experimenting with sexuality—many rules, no rules, exclusive relationships, multiple relationships, etc. Finally, they had come to the conclusion that their only rule would be to have no rules except honesty. This was a very special community. Its members were open to spirituality, but it was not a major concern for them. I was thinking that

Panoramix had given me a real hefty mandate by expecting that I get them to do this. I had been invited to teach and share our First Nations ways on community, the theme of this gathering, but didn't have any status in the community other than having been invited to be a guest there.

I spent a whole day in my room trying to think of a way to do this. My new friends, noticing my absence, came to knock on my door, wondering what was happening. I explained to them that upon my arrival I had received a request from an ancestor, with ceremony and teachings for them, and that I wished to pass this on to them. I asked them to organize a meeting with a small group of influential members of the community, to whom I would explain what had come to pass. They did this and then told me that they would think about it and discuss it that evening. The next day, they agreed to try what was proposed. We settled on a time and place.

We formed a large circle in a field. I cleansed them with sage smoke and then offered some sweetgrass to invoke my ancestor's help. I lit a sacred fire to open a vortex to the spirit world. I spoke to them about the ancestor and asked them to carry an offering into nature and then to sit there quietly where the offerings had been made. We sang together, and then off they went individually, each one in a different direction with their offerings of honey on a birch leaf. Of the forty people who attended, thirty-nine were able to witness, in one way or another, the presence of this ancestor. Some of them heard steps but when turning around saw nobody. Others heard him in various other ways, and some even saw him and had conversations with him. They were very surprised by the experience and so was I. It had taken me ten years of spiritual practice to be able to communicate with my ancestors, and some of these people had succeeded straightaway. All that was required was to remember the spiritual traditions of the land where they now lived.

The preceding story is a good example of the strength traditional offerings have. This leads us to understand how important it is to research the traditions that are part of our domestic and territorial lineages. Every great geographic region has particular places and symbols that are important to those who have lived there. When we know them, it becomes possible to access the energy beneath the symbols and to know how and when to benefit from pilgrimage to these sacred places. Making offerings allows us to put into motion the wheel of reciprocity, that universal law that unites us with nature. As explained by Sun Bear, spiritual agreements were established between nature and human beings since times untold. If we respect and honor these agreements, we usually enter into harmonic resonance with nature, making it possible to harmonize the environment with our needs. As crystals are an intimate and important part of the earth's energy field and manifestation, we need to make offerings to them too. When we wrap our crystals in their red cloth "homes," a ritual described in chapter 9, we often include sage, sweetgrass, or sacred tobacco as an offering to them.

THE MEDICINE WHEEL

The ceremony that best facilitates the creation of sacred space outdoors consists of building a Medicine Wheel. This practice is common to many cultures around the world and is practiced by all Native American peoples. There are many different kinds of Medicine Wheels. They essentially consist of stones arranged in a circle on the ground in various configurations. The Medicine Wheel that I practice comes from Sun Bear's teachings. Sun Bear, from the Chippewa nation, was one of the best-known First Nations teachers of the twentieth century. He was one of the first to teach to all people, of all colors, as was predicted by the prophecies. He was also a friend, a mentor, and a precious support to me on the path in times of need. We traveled and taught together. There was a specific prophecy among his people that spoke of him. It said that one day a bear would poke a hole through the veil of the new world with his tongue. That's exactly what he did. Traveling all around the world, Sun Bear taught people in a very unique way about the reality of our situation, this global state of emergency in which we find ourselves, and how we can mend the sacred hoop by coming back into right relationship with Mother Earth.

One day, on the top of a mountain, this Chippewa elder, a Native of White Earth, Minnesota, had a defining vision. He saw all kinds of different animals coming up to him in procession, but when they got closer he realized that they were men and women in animal costumes. They then got in a circle, and there he saw that each one of them was carrying a stone, and after putting the stones on the ground they did ceremony and danced. A voice addressed him in his vision: *It is now time to bring back the Medicine Wheels.*

Inspired by his vision, the very next day Sun Bear shared his vision with his community and put in place a Medicine Wheel that matched his vision. Thereafter there were gatherings across North America centered around the creation of a Medicine Wheel for many years until his death at the age of sixty-three.

In recent years the Medicine Wheel has reappeared in many Native American nations. This means the return of a blessed place of power, the creation of a sacred space-time, and the presence of a vortex of energy that can serve as a place for prayer, meditation, ceremony, and healing. Moreover, the strength of such a vortex increases with time if the rocks stay in place. At my own Medicine Wheel, I'm always having to put the stones back in place after the bears move them to enjoy the ants that take refuge underneath.

Sun Bear created and published an earth astrology that is not based on the stars but on the earth, the plants, and the animals. It might be interesting to read if you wish to delve deeper into the subject.*

❧ Creating a Medicine Wheel

The following instructions are for building a traditional Medicine Wheel outdoors. You can also create a small Medicine Wheel in your house with crystals by following the principles outlined here. You will feel the energy that will be released if it has been built properly.

---

*Sun Bear and Wabun, *The Medicine Wheel, Earth Astrology.* New York: Atria Books, 1980.

1. The first step in creating a Medicine Wheel is the same as for any important ceremony: each person involved purifies him- and herself, then the place and the stones are purified with sage smoke. It is recommended to place the ashes of the incense on the stones that will be used. Sufficient stones must have been gathered near the place where the wheel will be created. The location must be prepared to accommodate the wheel (stump removal, weeding, etc.). Throughout the making of the wheel, one remains in silence to allow oneself to become inhabited by the sacred form that one is configuring on the ground.

2. Then comes the important task of choosing the stones. The size of the stone is in relation to the overall size of the wheel—*the larger the wheel, the larger the stones.* Thus the stones will all be of approximately the same size depending on the width of the wheel. Once you have established the general size of the stones you want, go out in nature, find a place that feels right and that has stones lying around, and *feel* them. This may seem strange to the western mind, but in fact stones are alive. Try to establish a psychic connection with the stones. And remember, it is with the heart brain or the gut brain that we communicate with nature, not with the head brain! In these relationships with nature we are dealing with the world of feeling, not intellect. When you become aware of a stone that would like to come with you to be a part of the Medicine Wheel, leave an offering in the place of the stone you take.

   To be able to feel, that is, to apprehend reality through other than the ordinary five senses, is an ability First Nations have brought to a very high level. Some teachers call this the sixth sense, or holistic perception. If you are familiar with traditional elders you know they don't speak a lot and won't give any credence to what you have to say unless they feel it. You can talk your head off and they'll hardly look at you. But if your heart is sincere and you have an honest quest, if you're silent and just wait, at some point they'll look at you and say just a few words, and yet that will feel as if they have given you a tremendous gift. That's the power of feeling. When Sun Bear was young he would train with his brother to develop this ability. They would stand about fifty feet from each other, one of them holding a large piece of wood up in the air at arm's length above his head, while the other would aim at the piece of wood with a .22 rifle, blindfolded! This is a very clear demonstration that feeling can be a *very* precise method of ascertaining knowledge!

3. Purify yourself and the space where you wish to build the wheel using sage or liquid smudge. Identify the center of the wheel and place the first stone there, the one for Creator. And since the geometry of the circle is crucial for the energy vortex, you can use a rope to measure the radius between the center and the stones that will be deposited in each direction, fixing the one in the north first, then in the east, the south, and the west. If need be use a compass. The distance must be the same between the stone in the center and those in the four directions.

   The stones in the circle between the north and the east will be those of the wild white goose, the otter, and the cougar (the puma); between the east and the south, those of the red-tailed hawk, the beaver, and the deer; between the south and the west, those of the woodpecker, the sturgeon, and the bear; and between the west and the north, those of the raven, the snake, and the elk.

4. Stones that correspond to the attributes of each direction are then placed in a line, starting from the north stone to the center. The three stones making a pathway from the north stone to the center hold the intentions of purification, renewal, and purity. The attributes of the east pathway are clarity, wisdom, and enlightenment. Those of the south are growth, trust, and love. The attributes of the west are experience, introspection, and strength. In each direction leading to the center, a line is drawn with three stones spaced apart.

   In a circle close to the Creator's stone and around it, seven other stones are placed in a circle. These seven stones are for the most holy Mother Earth, the Heavenly Father (Sun), Grandmother Moon, and the four clans of the elements: Thunderbird (fire), Frog (water), Butterfly (wind), and Turtle (earth).

▶▶ Clear Light ◀◀

Plate 1. Clear quartz platonic solids

Plate 2. Quartz crystal cluster

Plate 3. Blue Eagle's healing quartz crystal

Plate 4. Clear quartz crystal protection pendant

Plate 5. Diamond

Plate 6. Herkimer diamond

►► Crystals of the Red Ray ◄◄

Plate 7. Red garnet: uncut and unpolished (left), cut and polished (right)

Plate 8. Red coral (left) and carved red coral bead (right)

Plate 9. Rose quartz shaped into a heart

Plate 10. Ruby

▶▶ Crystals of the Orange Ray ◀◀

Plate 11. Carnelian

Plate 12. Madeira citrine (left) and golden citrine (right)

▶▶ Crystal of the Yellow Ray ◀◀

Plate 13. Golden topaz

►► Crystals of the Green Ray ◄◄

Plate 14. Amazonite

Plate 15. Bloodstone

Plate 16. Chrysocolla

Plate 17. Malachite

Plate 18. Turquoise

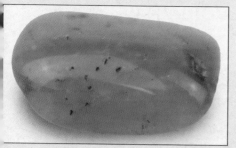

Plate 19. Chrysoprase

Plate 20. Emerald

Plate 21. Green jasper

Plate 22. Green tourmaline

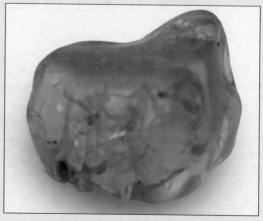

Plate 23. Jadeite

Plate 24. Peridot

►► Crystals of the Blue Ray ◄◄

Plate 25. Aquamarine

Plate 26. Azurite

Plate 27. Celestite

Plate 28. Dioptase

►► Crystal of the Indigo Ray ◄◄

Plate 29. Sapphire in the author's eagle bolo

▶▶ Crystal of the Violet Ray ◀◀

Plate 30. Tumbled amethyst

Plate 31. Amethyst protection pendant

▶▶ White Crystals ◀◀

Plate 32. Moonstone

Plate 33. Opal

Plate 34. Pearl

▶▶ Black Crystals ◀◀

Plate 35. Black tourmaline

Plate 36. Obsidian mirror

Plate 37. Smoky quartz

▶▶ Multicolored Crystals ◀◀

Plate 38. Agate

Plate 39. Labradorite

Plate 40. Watermelon tourmaline pendant

▶▶ Other Stones ◀◀

Plate 41. Amber

Plate 42. Pyrite

5. Now that that the wheel is completed, you are ready to activate it. Everyone takes a seat outside the circle it forms to feel the energy it releases before it's activated. Then the Medicine Wheel is activated in the same way as you activate a turtle altar: you simply welcome the Medicine Wheel, palms open toward it. The heart chant is launched, inviting the wheel to manifest itself in these times, in this place, and in these stones. After chanting you will find that the energy is generally much stronger. Take the time to feel it. It is by moving around the wheel that we can detect it. When you get close to the activated wheel make a full clockwise circle before you go inside. It's like a greeting of respect for the sacredness it expresses. When you want to get inside the wheel, take one of the pathways that lead to the center from any direction; you can go out of the center in any other direction along the corresponding pathway. What is respectful is to always follow one of the four stone paths. When you get out of the wheel, go clockwise around in a full circle again. Then take a few steps backward looking at the wheel, then bow to greet it and thank it. You can then walk away from the wheel as normal.

6. Once all stones are in their specific places and the wheel has been activated, you can move around the wheel until you feel the urge to sit or rest in a specific place. And then, just do that . . . Meditate on that spot. The Medicine Wheel is a place for contemplation, meditation, ceremony, and healing. In time its energy will radiate out and bless all the land around you. In time you will find other ways of deepening your connection with creation through the Medicine Wheel. You have created sacred space. Now give it some time!

⌃ Heart Meditation ⌃

This three-part meditation is very important. It's the first practice I teach in my classes, and I regularly come back to it. It's also frequently integrated into other meditations, as it is a foundational practice.

Always begin any meditation with purification. We prefer to use liquid smudge unless we are meditating outdoors. Sage smoke is an effective purifier, but being smoke it carries particulates that can be harmful to the lungs. Thus Chiiyaam offers very efficient purification thanks to the shamanic encoding that is used to make it (see chapter 3). It contains sixteen essential oils, all of them used in purification practices around the world. When you have sprayed this perfume on your hands and brought your hands around you, clearing your energy field, then either offer the scent on your hands to the four directions and to the earth and the sky, or spray once in each direction.

⌂ Uniting with Spirit

We begin this meditation with an offering to the four directions* and then by offering a prayer. Here is one I often use, although it varies every time. You must pray with your heart, thus your words will arise spontaneously. This is a transcription of one of my prayers, offered at a crystal seminar meditation.

> *Creator, Great Spirit, O Great Mystery,*
> *O Most Holy Divine Mother,*
> *Heavenly Father,*
> *Mother Earth,*
> *Wise protectors of the four directions,*
> *Guardian spirits who watch over us,*
> *Grandfathers and grandmothers, ancestors who walked*
>   *the earth before us,*
> *I humbly pray to thank you for all that has been given to us.*
> *Thank you for the gift of life.*
> *Thank you for our food and clothing and the shelter in*
>   *which we live.*
> *Thank you for the spiritual practice and teachings and for*
>   *the spiritual lineages that have enabled us to receive*
>   *these teachings.*

---

*Available at ancestralwisdomtoday.com in the Member Area under Tools/Chants.

Thank you for all those who help us and love us.

Thank you for our families.

Thank you for the trials that are sent to us, for all the
lessons that life gives us.

Thank you for all those who have made it possible for us
to live and communicate together.

Thank you for these days in which we live together, and
for the medicine that we can share, and for all those
who have made it possible.

And we pray that you bless the Most Holy Mother Earth.
That you bless her valleys, mountains, and plains; her
streams, rivers, lakes, oceans, clouds, and rain; her fires,
volcanoes, lightning, and winds from the four directions.

Bless the bones of Mother Earth, her crystals, stones, rocks,
and metals.

Bless Mother Earth's hair, her vegetables, fruits, trees,
plants, herbs, seaweeds, and forests.

Bless the children of Mother Earth, those who fly in
the air, swim in the waters, crawl on the earth, the
quadrupeds and the insects.

Bless the young and the children, the old and the elderly,
all those who have left this life and all those who have
not yet been born.

Bless all those who guide and teach us, all the teachings
they carry and all those who walk with them on the
sacred path.

We pray that these crystal teachings be honored, carried
with respect, and produce much healing for all our
relations.

We pray for ourselves, who are in need of healing,

For the earth, which needs healing.

This is my prayer.

Aho!

⌂ *Uniting Heaven and Earth*

Sitting straight, the spinal column like a tree, a link between heaven and earth, we now visualize coming up from the crystal heart of the earth a spiral of light, spiraling in us and around us, going up into the sky, purifying and clarifying our whole being . . .

We now visualize another spiral turning in the opposite direction, coming down from the sky and turning in us and around us, and then going deep into the earth, purifying and clarifying our whole being.

We then visualize both spirals together at the same time, rising and descending simultaneously, uniting us with heaven and earth.

These two spirals coming from the Earth Mother and Father Sky meet in the heart and the child that we are in our heart. This meeting creates great spirals of rose-colored light emanating from the heart. The energy of love, compassion, and understanding flows out in a spiral of rose-colored light, spreading out in horizontal spirals, filling us with beauteous energy, and from there, flowing out into our homes and out onto the land . . . across regions and countries . . . spreading across the whole earth . . . carrying the energy of love, compassion, and understanding to all beings. We are entering into right relationship with everything that exists through the light of the heart nourished by Mother Earth and Father Sky. We understand our deep connection with everything that is, that what is without is also within, that everything that's happening within is also happening without, and we want to nourish this energy of the heart.

Then we sing the heart chant.*

⌂ *Uniting with Source*

Sit in silence for a few moments, seeing and feeling the unity and interrelatedness of all things. After a few moments, allow the rose-colored light of love and compassion that was sent from the heart out into the world to come back to us. We gather it all up and pull it

---

*Available at ancestralwisdomtoday.com in the Member Area under Tools/Chants.

back into our heart, retaining the connection with all things and feeling in the center of our heart the presence of Great Spirit. This is the part of us that knows so much better than we do what's good for us, that part of us that can do everything and anything for us if we give it power over our life. We murmur to our heart, *May thy will be done.*

We now see our soul, that speck of divine will and light, our true being that resides in our heart, that of Creator, Spirit, our spirit that is linked with Creator, our eternal soul. We see it as a golden sun in the center of our chest. As we breathe in, the golden sun grows in size . . . At the end of the inhalation there's a moment of suspending the breath, where we commune with this light . . . Then we breathe out, and that energy radiates throughout our body. At the end of the exhalation there's a moment of suspending our breath, where we commune with this energy. This moment of communion brings us to ecstasy and bliss.

Again we breathe in, as the golden sun grows in our heart. At the end of the inhalation there's a moment of suspending the breath, where we commune with the golden sun. It is beauteous joy, and as we breathe out it radiates throughout our body, healing us. At the end of the exhalation we again suspend our breath, and in so doing we unite with Source.

Continue for a few moments longer with this four-step breath.

Now, crossing our hands over our chest, we offer thanks for giving our souls this moment of sacred space-time. Then we put our palms together in a prayer mudra and in thankfulness we salute the lineage and students who have made it possible for us to receive this meditation.

9

Caring for Crystals

We need to approach crystals with care and a specific methodology. Before beginning any work with your crystals, it's a good idea to purify the room where you'll be working. It's also a good practice to purify yourself and purify the person on whom you'll be working before doing a therapeutic intervention. We described how Native Americans do smudging and how a Native liquid smudge, Chiiyaam (see chapter 3), can be useful in doing this. But we also need to purify our crystals. How do we do this?

PURIFYING YOUR CRYSTAL FRIENDS

There is a technique for purifying crystals that has been verified by countless crystal healing practitioners. This was taught by OhShinnàh Fastwolf, who received these teachings from a Cherokee elder, Keetowah.

✦ Basic Purification Technique

1. You will need a bowl made of a natural material (glass, ceramic, stoneware, wood). Do not use plastic or metal.
2. Pour either natural spring water or distilled water into the bowl and add a pinch of sea salt, the exact proportion being a quarter of a teaspoon per liter of water.
3. Immerse your stones, crystals, and jewelry in this water for seven days and nights the first time. The molecular structure of a crystalline stone

gives it its ability to remember, to register the energies in its environment. Immersing your crystals in water for this period of time if you are cleansing them for the first time will ensure that their memory, former programming, and positive ions, which have been able to accumulate around the electromagnetic field of the crystals, are completely purified. Subsequently, after using or whenever needed, twenty minutes is sufficient to cleanse. This step is very important. As your crystal is going to be used in therapy, you must know what information it is holding. The crystal does not discriminate among the information it records in its structure. It holds everything, the good and the bad. If you're working with a crystal to help and to heal, you need to know exactly what the crystal is holding. This is why you must imperatively erase the crystal's memory before using it to help and to heal. How this works is due to the electrical charge in the crystal's molecular structure that holds information. Salt is also a crystal that has a tendency to be cubic (as can be seen if you look at unrefined coarse sea salt). When salt dissolves in water, the salt crystals create an electrical charge in the water molecules that is stronger than the charge that's holding the information stored in a crystal's molecules. This does two things. First, it erases the information being held by the crystal. Second, it replaces the positive ions around the crystal with negative ions, which are beneficial.

I remember a friend who often complained of discomfort and pain in his throat. I noticed he often wore an amethyst around his neck. When asked if he had purified the crystal he said no, he didn't even know that this needed to be done. We purified it and he never once complained about pain in his throat again. This is a good example of why we need to purify the stones we wear.

It's a good idea to keep the bowl you use to purify your crystals near your bed, because then you will remember to purify your crystals every day. You will be able, for example, to put your jewelry into the bowl before you go to bed and take out the crystal with which you sleep. The following morning you can remove your jewelry and put your night crystal back in the bowl. They only need twenty minutes to purify once the weeklong initial purification has been done.

A crystal that is worn for protection or therapeutic reasons needs to be purified daily. A crystal that remains on a table, desk, or other piece of furniture only needs to be cleared maybe every few months. When you get a better sense of a crystal's energy, you will feel when this needs to be done. Of course, when you use a crystal directly in a client's energy field you will need to purify it immediately after use and as many times in a day as you have clients.

As I had been with crystals for many years before learning this technique, I tested it in several ways and found it to be very useful. One test that's easy to do and you could try yourself if you have several crystals and precious stones, is the following: Clear for a whole week half of them. Then put them beside those that have not been cleared, in a place where you can look at them frequently. You'll notice that those that have been purified are more luminous; they shine in a different, more intense manner.

Be careful that all jewelry put in saltwater is made of noble metals: silver, gold, or platinum. Cheap materials may rust or be damaged by saltwater. It is not necessary to purify red coral or pearls for a week, just a few moments in saltwater, preferably by moving them softly through the water, is sufficient to clear them. The same is true of malachite. This is because coral and pearls come from the sea and malachite is not really crystal; its internal structure is not organized in a specific molecular pattern.

CARE AND MAINTENANCE OF CRYSTALS

Now that your crystals have been purified, it's time to energize them.

❖ Basic Energizing Technique

1. The proper method is to put them in running water. The ideal situation is a small stream. Embed them among some rocks to be able to find them

easily and leave them there for a few hours. They love this. You can do this by the side of a lake where there the waves come and go over them, that also works nicely.

2. When I don't have time and absolutely need to energize crystals that are working a lot, as I have pure water running through my faucets at home connected to a well that delivers water from the earth, I put them on a piece of wood and let the water from the faucet flow over them for an hour or two.

Be very careful if you're energizing your crystals by the side of the Pacific Ocean, as it is said that the Great Mother Goddess loves to eat crystals! Many a student of OhShinnàh in California has lost a few crystals this way. If you are by the Pacific Ocean and letting the waves come and go over your crystals, stay there and check the waves. If you see a very big wave coming in, grab your crystals and move them. We don't experience this problem with the Atlantic Ocean. And, of course, it is saltwater, thus it should also purify your crystals at the same time. In Native lore the Pacific Ocean is called the Mother Ocean, and the Atlantic Ocean is called the Father Ocean.

Crystals need time-out the same way you do. We all like to go on vacation, to have a day off from work to renew, rest, recharge. Well, so does the crystal. You can test this by putting crystals that have been under running water among crystals that have not. Do this in a place where you see them frequently, as the light phenomena through which the crystals express themselves are often perceived from the corner of your eye. It is not in the visible light spectrum, but we can still see it, it's just that it's another type of seeing. As you're working with crystals I'm sure you will be able to perceive this, but the first time it will happen by chance. Another way of working with your subtle vision is by locating your vision between your two eyes on your forehead. This is the energy center that sees things with clarity on other invisible spectrums of light. For this reason it's often called the third eye. This is an important center to cultivate and practice, as seeing the energy around people and emanating from people can be useful when we are healing with energy as work with crystals entails.

The second thing that's important in caring for crystals is to protect them from breaks and scratches and stray energies. First, you must know that although crystals are very hard, being stones, they also have cleavage angles through which they can break like glass. If they are struck at the right place, they can shatter. Also, a harder crystal can scratch a softer one. For example, diamond will scratch all other crystals, as it's the hardest.

This is why we wrap all of our crystals separately, and we do this using red cloth. Red is the slowest of all vibrations and it puts up an energetic wall that prevents stray energies from permeating the crystal, thus protecting it. When your crystals have been properly purified and energized, wrap them, and when you take them out, even months later, they will be ready to work.

Not only do we wrap crystals in a bit of red cloth, we also put them in a special bag, which we call the *crystal home*. I like to have a different bag for every crystal so I know which one is inside. Crystals can exchange energies when touching one another, so this is another reason why they are wrapped separately. Of course, always use natural fabric, 100 percent cotton or silk or linen or bamboo or hemp—any natural fabric will do. I also recommend that as an energy practitioner you yourself should always wear natural fabric. There is plenty of information on the harm that is done to one's health with synthetic fibers.* As an energy practitioner you should also know that artificial, synthetic fibers influence natural energies and prevent a lot of the healing energies from coming to you and through you to the other person. Always wear natural fabric.

As we always need to test the techniques with which we work, there are a few simple ways to do this. I find that when I have a programmed

---

*Brian Clement's book *Killer Clothes: How Seemingly Innocent Clothing Choices Endanger Your Health* (Hippocrates, 2011) reveals the harmful effects of clothing not made from natural fibers.

crystal that is used for a certain kind of work, I can feel this program is active when I take the crystal out of its cloth home. However, I discovered another way of testing at the very beginning of my crystal career. At that time I was going to gem and mineral shows, where many different vendors and specialists in the field of gemology, crystallography, and lapidary were selling their wares. I would go to these shows to buy crystals for my students and clients. You can imagine these big, gymnasium-size rooms filled with tens of thousands of unpurified stones and crystals, and a sensitive energy healer walking in the midst of all these confused energies! I had a very hard time. I would rush through and make some very bad purchases. I did not take the time necessary to compare prices and quality. After two of these experiences, I felt I needed to find a solution to this problem. So the next time I dressed from head to toe in red clothing. The only thing that wasn't covered in red was my head. I was relieved to find that I could walk slowly through the whole show and take my time, compare prices, compare quality, and make much better purchases.

Of course, if you are carrying a crystal and you want its programming active in your energy field, don't put it in red cloth. This is a given.

Things to Avoid

Some of the information you'll encounter out there includes some bad practices when it comes to crystals. Some tell you to put crystals in pure salt, not saltwater, to purify them. This is actually detrimental to the energy field around crystals. It pits them, which produces holes in the energy field around the crystals. To remedy this situation you need to bury them in the earth for twenty-eight days. This will allow them to restructure themselves and reform their etheric web, calling on the earth's energy field to do this. As we consider crystals to be living beings, I would also suggest apologizing to the crystal before doing this. Always set right relationships with the crystals. And then, of course, purify and energize and find it a proper home in red cloth.

Other erroneous information that's out there suggests putting crystals in sunlight or in moonlight to energize them. What really happens is they will take on solar energy or lunar energy. This is okay if you're working with these energies. But your crystal is no longer neutral. It will be working either with solar or lunar energies. If, for example, you have a crystal that you have put in the sun and you are going to work with a woman's menstrual problems, where you absolutely need to draw more lunar energy, you might have difficulties in getting a favorable result. We want neutral energy conveyed to the crystal, and this is done with running water.

BLESSING A STONE

Bless a crystal whenever you want to give it to someone so that it holds a specific intention and the power of the directions. If you do not have a spare crystal on hand, you can also do this to a piece of natural fiber, some piece of cloth that you want to send to a person, although the crystalline structure of a stone will hold the energy of your blessing in a stronger way than cloth will. The following is a simple ceremony that will help you convey blessing energy to a stone or any object. We do this with all of our medicine.

⏃ Blessing Ceremony

1. Take two stones with crystalline structure, one that you will bless in this ceremony and another that will be left by itself. (This is to test the technique so you'll see the difference between the blessed stone and the one that wasn't blessed. Always test the techniques you learn.) Energize your hands by rubbing them together vigorously in an up-and-down movement, palm against palm, and then evaluate the energy in each stone. Now select the stone you want to energize. Center yourself (centering exercise, chapter 3) and energize your hands a second time as before. Place your palms toward the crystal that you have chosen with the tips of the thumbs and index fingers touching, thus the hands

will form a triangle. Orient the palms of your hands toward the east, calling in the energy of the east into your hands. Bring that energy over the stone. When you feel that the stone has taken this energy, the energy of the east, you will feel this by a slight pressure coming up under the hands (or whatever your specific code is). Now do the same thing with the south. The palms of your hands holding the shape of the triangle made by the index and thumb tips touching are now facing south. Call on the energy of the south to come into your hands, and then bring them down over the crystal until you feel the energy has been absorbed by the stone. Repeat this to the west and then the north.

2. Now bring your two hands—in the same position as before, thumbs and index fingers forming a triangle—up along your central channel until they are overhead, and then bring them down as if gathering all the energy in your energy field. Bring this energy down over the stone, with the specific intentions you have for this blessing. Allow that energy to enter the stone until you feel an answer from the stone under your hands. Then, with your hands still forming a triangle, turn your hands slowly in a clockwise motion, as the sun turns in the sky, and on the third turn separate your hands rapidly, away from the stone. This is so that the energy stays on the stone. As your hands are magnetic and they work with energy, when you separate them rapidly the energy will not follow your hands, but will remain on the stone.

3. Now take the two stones and evaluate the difference in energy between them. You will note that the energy around the stone that has been consecrated by this ceremony is a lot larger and more focused.

Crystals are very special beings that have a lot to offer. We have just reviewed the practices around basic care for them, and also the right attitude that will allow the proper foundation for crystal healing work. The next step is to enter into right relationship with your crystal friends.

10

Establishing Right Relationship

When there is a feeling toward a crystal, when there is more in your perception of the stone than it being just an inanimate object, but if instead you see it as a living, conscious being, then you have the basis for creating a relationship that will amplify both your and the crystal's ability to help and to heal. This kind of connection with your mineral ally happens on an emotional and spiritual level once you have understood the principles of healing and the attributes of crystals, as recounted in parts 1 and 2. The next step is to shift your relationship into an even more subtle and intimate connection.

GETTING INTIMATE WITH A CRYSTAL

Once it has been purified and energized, take your crystal into your meditation space. Allow the smoke from cedar or sage incense to pass over it and commune with it, with your heart, in that special space where you open to listen to the heart of things. One of the easiest and simplest ways of establishing a healthy relationship with a crystal is to sleep with it.

❖❖ Sleeping with a Crystal

1. To begin this practice, hold a clear quartz crystal in your hand when you go to bed. Left or right hand, doesn't matter.

2. Don't worry where it will go when you fall asleep, yet take note of this upon awakening, and also note the following:
   • How do you feel?
   • What do you feel toward the crystal upon awakening compared to the way you felt toward it before going to bed?
   • Did you sleep well?
   • Do you feel tired?
   • Did you have any dreams?
3. Thank the crystal upon awakening and put it in saltwater for a few minutes so that it can purify itself, and in running water if possible so that it can renew and be ready for another night's work.

I have received countless accounts of how this has been experienced. We have found that the crystal seems to move around on its own. As people notice when they wake up, it often naturally goes to the place where they are suffering from a health problem. In the beginning you feel as if you didn't sleep as well, and yet you feel completely replenished and renewed. A few people have found that simple problems that have been around for a while disappear during the night. We feel the crystal very differently, almost as if it's a person. Why this is so is easy to explain.

Crystals vibrate to the frequency of perfection in the natural world, the same world your body lives in. As you have established right relationship with the crystal and the underlying intention is health and healing, the body can draw on that frequency to heal itself. This works even better during the night as your conscious mental body is not drawing energy away from the physical body. That part of you that may resist the subtle energies is not in control during the night. The body and soul will automatically adjust to the frequency offered by the crystal, that of neutral perfection. You may feel a heightened awareness while sleeping and perhaps have the impression that you haven't slept. This feeling will disappear after a few days of sleeping with the crystal, as the conscious mind lets go of its interpretation of the state of heightened awareness. At that point you will start to feel completely rested.

Meanwhile, the crystal is active during the night. It's attracting positive ions, thus purifying your body. It is rebalancing the energy field of your etheric web. It will mend tears and holes in your energy field. It will guide your soul and spirit toward beings of light who can guide you in the subtle realms toward a greater spiritual evolution. It will ignite the fire of clear consciousness in your soul, enabling a pure path of right relationship and rapid evolution. Thank the crystal upon awakening and put it a few minutes in saltwater so that it can purify itself and in running water if possible so that it can renew and be ready for another night's work.

The Law of Harmony

One of the reasons why quartz crystals are so beneficial for our health and overall beneficial manifestation in this physical world is because of their near-perfect molecular structure, which is organized in a geometrical array. This perfection, which makes ordinary stones take on geometrical shapes of great beauty, thus inspiring their epithet "flowers of the mineral world," will interact with your own innate perfection and call it forth. Our spirit comes directly from Great Spirit, from the world of ideal form, the spiritual world. We have great, nearly unlimited potential. To call forth this perfection we can use what is called *the law of harmony*. The law of harmony is what allows us to resonate with our innate perfection. The law of harmony is demonstrated in many things. For example, if you press on the pedal of a piano that releases the strings so they can vibrate, and hit one of the lower C notes, all the C notes above it will also start to vibrate. This harmonic resonance illustrates the law of harmony. Thus, when you enter into right relationship with a crystal friend, its innate perfection will enter into harmonic resonance with your innate perfection. The very ordered and harmonious geometrical molecular array of the crystal will entice your own perfection to shine forth. One of the best ways to initiate this process is to sleep with your crystal.

SHAMANIC JOURNEY TO MEET
A CRYSTAL FRIEND

To better understand how crystals feel, hear, and experience their lives as living mineral beings, we use a special technique, shamanic journeying. There are many different ways to experience out-of-body phenomena. We can experiment with these methods in order to really understand a crystal. This kind of journeying can also lead to the discovery of your crystal totem.

In all realms, the plant kingdom, the mineral kingdom, and the animal kingdom, we have what we call *totems*. These are life forms that are specifically attuned to your unique life path and soul incarnation. We can enter into relationship with these totems to help us in many different ways. Although a lot of this information has been lost as people have grown further and further away from the natural world, that does not mean that you do not have these totems. It's just that the method of discovering them has not been taught. Not all people absolutely need this information, yet for a crystal practitioner it's very important to better understand how the beings of the mineral world, these beauteous flowers of the mineral kingdom, experience life, as that is essential in understanding how we can best work with them.

The first thing we need to understand when it comes to shamanic journeying is that we experience life in many different dimensions. We are multidimensional beings. We can describe this more easily by giving a name to the energetic aspect of who we are: the light body. We call the physical body, which is a temporary vehicle for our soul and spirit, the shadow body. The physical body is very important as it carries our ability to evolve from one lifetime to the next, progressing toward greater and greater manifestations of peace, love, joy, and light. We are creators learning to create paradise and eventually whole other worlds. As of now, we are attempting to create better circumstances in our own life and that of others. It is in our soul and spirit that the memories of all the lifetimes we have ever experienced are stored, and it's in these spirit bodies that we can travel outside the physical body.

We have a great deal of attachment to the shadow body. When we incarnate on earth we temporarily forget all our prior experiences. This is important, as we come here with a fresh outlook on life. It is possible to remember past lifetimes, but that is not necessarily useful. When we go back to the spirit worlds we have an opportunity to review all that with our guides and spirit teachers, and that is the appropriate time to remember all of it. Yet we have great attachment, as we feel we are this body and identify with it. This is one of the meanings of ego. This attachment to the physical form can prevent us from flying free on a shamanic journey or from identifying with other life forms. Thus to be empty is a basic principle of the shamanic experience.

There are three keys to shamanic power:

1. The first is to be centered, to be all that we are—mind and body synchronized with our mission in life, our potential standing at the ready. Practice the centering exercise (chapter 3) frequently.

2. The second key to shamanic power is to be empty. This is difficult to describe, as it defies language. It's the ability to be available, unfettered by thoughts or feelings, completely and entirely in the present moment, yet beyond time and space. As I said, difficult to describe . . . One way to practice emptiness is through the suspension of the breath between breaths in the Heart Meditation (see "Uniting with Source" on pages 124–25). In that suspended moment we can experience communion with the divine aspect of our soul. That communion results in bliss and ecstasy. If we're not empty, then we won't be able to establish that level of communion.*

3. The third key to shamanic power is allowing things to happen through us. When the energy of universal consciousness feels it can flow through us to respond to the needs of the people, then extraordinary things can happen. Frank Fools Crow, one of the most powerful

---

*There are extensive references to this emptiness in *Dancing the Dream: The Seven Sacred Paths of Human Transformation* by Jamie Sams (New York: HarperOne, 1998).

medicine men in recent history, a holy man, describes this as being a hollow bone through which Great Spirit can blow into the world. As with everything in life, this takes training—and it also defies description. Yet, practice, practice, practice makes (near) perfect!

As we journey to meet crystals we have to let go of all identification with our shadow body to be able to become one with the crystal, to better feel how a crystal experiences its existence. These three keys of shamanic power will unlock the door to that experience. So, in the shamanic journey described here, you need to remember these two terms: the *light body* and the *shadow body*.

Usually, whenever possible, I have my students doing spiritual practice for a whole year before going on a shamanic journey. This is because of the problems that can arise if the energy body is weak or unabalanced. The light body needs to be strong and balanced before doing out-of-body traveling. A book can never substitute for hands-on training. Yet because we need many Rainbow Warriors today to protect Mother Earth, we give the opportunity to all to walk the narrow path. If you can journey with someone who is a trained shamanic practitioner, that would be best. If not, there are certain precautions you should implement before and after journeying.

⚡ Journeying to a Crystal Cave

Do not attempt to do the full journey described here before practicing the relaxation part, the first step of the exercise below, at different times of day, to attain a profound state of relaxation. This is an ability that's always good to master. To do this relaxation, I recommend recording the meditation in a slow, even, neutral voice, following its instructions as you listen to some drumming while relaxing in a reclining position on your back, your arms alongside your body, palms facing the sky. You can use my *Earth Drums* recording* or have another person drum an unwavering,

---

*At https://aiglebleu.bandcamp.com/album/tambours-de-la-terre-m-re-earth-drums

steady beat during the journey. Stop the drumming or the recording immediately upon returning to your physical body.

You must be well-grounded before and after this exercise. Thus, find a special tree with which you will establish a relationship. Go to it a few days prior to the shamanic journey and give it offerings and ask it to be your grounding anchor. You will embrace this tree before and after the journey. After the journey, upon embracing the tree, you will call back all of yourself. You want all of your light body back in your shadow body. Ask the tree to ground you and make sure all of your light body is back in the physical. Having a Herkimer diamond close to you during the journey and holding and carrying a smoky quartz afterward will help, but this is not essential, though I highly recommend the smoky quartz.

Start by purifying the room with liquid smudge or sage. Then begin the following meditation:

1. Take several minutes to relax every part of your body as you travel within, going from your feet to your head, feeling heavier and heavier as all your muscles, organs, and bones relax completely. If any part of your body does not seem to relax, tense it and then let it go. You can do this several times to that specific area until it relaxes.

2. Lie down and center (centering exercise, chapter 3). Now breathe in blue light through the nostrils and exhale through the nostrils all that is no longer needed. Again, breathe in and out, slowly, naturally. Then, upon inhaling the blue light a fourth time, send it into your feet as you exhale. Relax your toes, the soles of your feet, your heels, and your ankles using the blue light. Moving up the body, relax your calves, your knees, your thighs, inhaling the blue light and exhaling it into areas of your body. Relax your bones and muscles that attach your legs to your hips. Your legs feel very heavy, completely relaxed. Relax your hips, your sexual organs, your bowels, and your stomach. Relax your diaphragm, your lungs, and your ribs. Relax your spine starting at the bottom, moving up, relaxing vertebrae after vertebrae up to the neck. Relax your shoulders, your arms, your forearms, your wrists, your palms, your fingers. Your

arms are completely relaxed and feel very heavy. Relax your throat, your neck, your mouth, your tongue, and your lips. Relax your cheeks, your eyes, and your forehead. Relax your scalp, your brain, and your ears. Your whole body is now completely, entirely relaxed. You feel very heavy, as if you're melting into the surface on which you are lying, so heavy that you become light, so very light, floating like a small white cloud in a great blue sky.

3. Now visualize your body of light resplendent in its beauty and perfection. Take several moments to really feel and become that light body. Then visualize the shadow body that you are. Take several moments to really feel and become that shadow body. Now infuse the shadow body with the light body. Merge both bodies, filling the shadow body with the perfect light of your spirit. Your shadow body and light body become one. The light body and the shadow body now form a single being. They open the doors of spirit.

4. You now find yourself on a prairie at the foot of a great mountain. As you walk toward this mountain, you see sparkles, the reflection of sunlight, as sudden bursts of color in your eyes. As you go to the mountain you find that these lights come from many hundreds of different kinds of crystals that grow on the mountain, reflecting the sunlight at certain angles. You are attentive to the crystals as you walk up the mountain. You hear a sound, a high-pitched, single sound. You understand that there is a crystal calling you, singing to you so that you may find it. Walk toward the sound. You see caves and grottos on the mountain. Maybe that sound comes from a crystal in one of those caves . . . Continue walking toward the sound . . . And now you see it, you see that crystal shining its light toward you. Stop and admire it, feeling its vibration, its frequency, the energy coming to you from that crystal. Ask the crystal's permission to enter into its lifestream. Feel its response. Now your light body merges with the crystal. Enter into the crystal and become one with it. You are the crystal! You see as it sees, feel as it feels, hear as it hears. You are a crystal, and you exist in just this way . . . Let the drumming continue to play awhile, for as long as comfortable, but give

yourself a time limit. It can be until the end of the recording or some other predetermined stopping point.

5. It is now time to come back to yourself. Thank the crystal for sharing its life with you before leaving it. You sense how your relationship with this crystal has evolved, having shared its lifestream.

6. Now walk down the mountain . . . onto the prairie . . . back into your shadow body. Have the drumming stop upon coming back into your body. Move slowly, beginning with your fingers and toes, moving up your body, turning your head from side to side, feeling every part of your body as you stretch . . .

7. Be sure to record this experience and all your journeys in your journal.

One of the comments I've heard over the years when students come out of this journey is that it is difficult to do so. Ending the drumming seemed to help, and yet many say they would have liked to stay in this deep meditative state—a good indication that they succeeded in penetrating into the life of a crystal, which can span millennia.

Experiencing a crystal's life in this way can help you to better understand them. Shamanic journeying can allow you to integrate the second pillar of crystal work, which is knowing that crystals are living beings. Now it will be easier to work *with* the crystal to help, to heal, and to gather and store information.

A variation on this journey is to go into the earth rather than on top of a mountain. To do this, we usually follow a stream until it falls deep within the earth, and there we listen for the crystal friend to call to us. In using this variation, be sure to follow all the steps of this meditation in the order given.

We now have several techniques that have the same intention: to create and affirm your relationship with a special member of the mineral kingdom in order to help and to heal. Practice these methods and you will gain a friend who will work wholeheartedly to help you and all those who come to you for help and healing.

11

Using Crystals to Help and Heal

There are many ways crystals and stones can be used for healing and making life more rewarding. They are the most organized beings in the universe because of their molecular structure. They are near-permanent because they have maintained their incarnation as the beautiful flowers of the mineral world for millennia. As they maintain their organized structure, transforming and amplifying all types of energy for very long periods of time, they have fascinated humankind for ages. Thus by their sheer beauty and eternal presence they evoke great treasures of the mind and spirit. These are the attributes that make crystals so fascinating to work with. They will always remain firm and steady in their faithfulness to incarnate the life mission Creator has bestowed on them. Once you have a crystal friend, you have a friend forever.

Energy follows thought, which is the ultimate creator of all things. It is said that we are in a dream, Great Spirit's dream. It is through the thoughts of Great Spirit that the universe is created. The circumstances and accomplishments we manifest in life always begin as thoughts. It is this energy, the energy of thought, nourished by our empathy and compassion and then oriented according to a specific ray of the crystal prism, that can be amplified and channeled through a programmed crystal.

There is a consecration ceremony that will assist in establishing a bond with a crystal. Like a human being, each crystal has a specific frequency at which it vibrates. This makes it more apt to do certain work over other kinds of work. So consecration facilitates your understanding the crystal's purpose.

CONSECRATING A CRYSTAL

The consecration ceremony is a twenty-seven-day ritual that will help you commune with your crystal and perceive its specific gifts and then apply them to healing situations. We use this ceremony to consecrate the crystal to act in a specific way, and in specific circumstances, in a sacred manner. All healing has a sacred component to it, if you understand the notion of holistic healing. The best time to start a consecration ritual is on the new moon. If not possible on the new moon, any other time will do.

The Consecration Ceremony

1. Begin by purifying the crystal for seven days in saltwater.
2. Find an appropriate bag and a red cloth for the crystal's home.
3. Go to some running water on a sunny day.
4. Purify yourself and the crystal with sage smoke or liquid smudge. Then center yourself (centering exercise, chapter 3) and rub your hands together vigorously. Hold the crystal up to the sun and ask it why it has come to you, what specific gift it carries. Then listen.
5. Place the crystal in running water for two hours.
6. After the crystal's running water bath, center yourself and rub your hands together vigorously. Hold the crystal up to the sun and ask it why it has come to you, what specific gift it carries. Listen.
7. Place the crystal back in its bag after wrapping in its red cloth, with some offering of sweetgrass or sage enclosed in the bag with the crystal. Put the bag on your altar. Every evening for fourteen days during your meditation bring the bag to your heart and commune with the crystal.
8. For the next two weeks, repeat the previous step every day, removing the

crystal from its bag and cloth, communing with it, and then wrapping it and placing it back in its bag.

9. Then go back to the stream, purify yourself and the crystal with sage smoke or liquid smudge. Center yourself and rub your hands together vigorously. Hold the crystal up to the sun and ask it why it has come to you, what specific gift it carries. Listen.

10. Give the crystal another running water bath. Can be shorter than two hours.

11. Your crystal is now consecrated.

You will most likely feel how your relationship with your crystal has changed during this ritual, which takes place over a lunar month. It's a very powerful way to encode the crystal with its innate abilities. It confirms and consecrates a powerful collaboration and a respectful relationship that will enhance the crystal's power and your ability to work with it.

PROGRAMMING A CRYSTAL

You are now ready to prepare to program your crystal. The difference between programming and consecrating is that programming is most often for a temporary, one-time use, whereas a consecrated crystal will always be used for what it has been consecrated for. To program a crystal, you will begin by centering (centering exercise, chapter 3) until you feel focused and clear. In brief, the equation for programming a crystal is: inhale = intention / exhale = manifestation of intention.

⚏ Programming Technique

1. Do the centering exercise (chapter 3), while holding the crystal in the palms of your hands.

2. Formulate an intention as a firm thought form established in your mind. If you have any doubts on how to establish a good intention, review the third law of healing in chapter 4.

3. Inhale deeply, holding your intention firmly in your mind. Exhale from your mouth, sending your intention into the crystal as you hold the crystal between cupped hands in front of your mouth, not losing a single atom of your breath that holds this intention. Now your crystal is programmed with that intention.

Simple! Creation myths have great wisdom in them, and you will see in many of them the story that Creator created human beings by breathing his life-giving breath on clay statuettes representing man and woman. As Creator does this, they start to breathe and live.

This programming is active for about twenty-eight days.* After that it's a good idea to re-energize and reprogram the crystal. You can program a crystal with several intentions as long as they are compatible. Simple example: moon, water, sound intuition, harmonious moon cycle in a woman, etc.—all this is good. However, moon and sun together don't work, they cancel each other out. Fire and water same thing.

Test this. The way we tested this during our crystal seminars worked well. I would ask if anyone was experiencing pain anywhere. There always were a few people. I would then ask a few questions to find the best intention (color, crystal, etc.). If I had two people it would expand the reach of the experience. I then told the students to program their crystals with those specific intentions. If we had two people, I would have half the class doing one and the other half the other. We would wait a few minutes, and then ask the people being treated what they were experiencing. The range of impressions was impressive, but the results were consistent: pain always decreased and many times disappeared.

SIMPLE PRACTICES FOR CRYSTAL HEALING

As for the practical aspects of working with crystals in a healing mode, there are many ways they can be used therapeutically.

---

*There are ways to program a crystal permanently but this is beyond the scope of this book as it requires sacred knowledge and ritual training.

The easiest and probably one of the most pleasurable and fun ways to work with them is to wear them as jewelry. A cut stone has the same properties as a natural stone, but when they are cut, faceted, and polished, to be used as jewelry, they can be even more beautiful. The metal—gold, silver, or platinum—on which the stone is fixed will amplify its energy. This is one way to integrate the energies of a particular stone on a daily basis. You can wear crystal jewelry when you are seeking healing or in circumstances when you are looking to amplify a specific intention.

It's important that only noble metals be used in crystal jewelry— silver, gold, or platinum. Sometimes copper and bronze are used, but they have a tendency to oxidize and the color may change. Gold, silver, and platinum will not be affected when they are purified in saltwater. If you are working with a piece of jewelry that is only coated with a noble metal, the underlying metal alloy may react to the water and the salt. It might rust or lose its shine. Noble metals like silver, gold and platinum also lend specific energies: gold, a very solar energy, and silver, a lunar energy. Platinum is associated with Neptune, Venus, and Mercury. It is a recently discovered metal and does not have as many astrological associations as the other noble metals. Nevertheless, it's the most precious metal used in jewelry and is more neutral than gold or silver.

Of course, you need to purify a piece of jewelry for a whole week before using it, and following that it is recommended you program that crystal, as we need to encode it with a specific intention or orientation for it to do its work properly. This is one of the secrets of healing that we emphasize in this book. A clear intention will orient the energy of the crystal. We need to have the energy going in a specific direction to create balance. Balance, equilibrium, is the state of harmony that is synonymous with health. When there is imbalance, there is disease and discomfort. This is because we are not in harmony with the laws of the universe or because our soul needs that suffering to learn specific lessons, such as control over one's body and mind or humility.

All stones that are hard enough to be worn without the danger of breaking upon light impact can be used in jewelry. Depending on the type of work it is doing you will want to purify the stone more or less often. If the healing work to be done is important and urgent, it should be purified every time it is used. If it is only there to produce a specific energy related to your work, it can be purified once a week. To know when it needs purification you need to tune into the life of that piece of jewelry and that stone, as every stone has a distinct personality. The ability to tune in will come in time. The more you work with crystals, the more accurate you will be in perceiving what the crystal needs. The more you work with energy, the more you will become proficient in perceiving different types of energy.

The first energy field around the human body, as noted in chapter 3, is the etheric web. This energy field will call on the energy of the piece of jewelry to bring it into balance. It is not necessary to wear the piece of jewelry over the site of a specific problem. In other words, if you are using peridot to work with your pancreas, you can still wear the peridot on your finger or around your neck; you don't have to place it over your pancreas. Your etheric web will bring the energy of the peridot to where it is needed.

There are different colored stones that can work together to create a powerful synergy. The metal of that piece of jewelry will combine with the energy of the different stones. Thus, several stones can be used together on the same piece of jewelry if they are compatible. The principle is quite simple: you can wear any two colors that are adjacent on the spectrum. The order of the rainbow determines adjacent colors: red, yellow, orange, green, blue, indigo, violet, red, and so on. Thus, red can go with yellow or violet; yellow can go with red or orange; green can go with orange or blue; blue can go with green or indigo; and violet can go with red or indigo. You can amplify any colored stone with a transparent, clear crystal. This is the most common use we see. For example, you can have an emerald with tiny zircons or diamonds around it, as all these clear stones will amplify the effect of the green emerald.

Note that certain colors will cancel each other out. For example, red and green together do not work. And black or white stones should not be combined with colored gems.

Use your intuition and then verify your choice of stones with the person for whom you are preparing the combination. Kinesiology (muscle testing) or dowsing are both effective testing methods. You can wear different types of jewelry at the same time as long as they don't touch one another. So if you have rings on your fingers, skip a finger so that the different stones don't touch. It's the same principle that we use when we wrap our crystals individually in red cloth. Crystals can exchange energy if they are in contact with other crystals.

Another way of benefiting from the energy of a crystal or stone is to carry it in a small pouch or in a pocket. For this it's better to use a polished or tumbled stone, as a raw stone can be abrasive and poke holes in your clothing. Multifaceted, polished, or tumbled stones all have the same energy as the uncut stone. Only rarely does a stone lose its sheen when it is polished. Those who cut stones know this, in which case if this happens they say that the stone has "died" or has "lost its water." This is a rare occurrence, however. In general, a stone that is cut and polished will retain all of its energy and sheen. You can benefit from the specific vibration of a particular crystal by carrying it on you—in your pocket, for example. But if you do this avoid any contact between the crystal and any coins, since they have been touched by many other people. A small pouch for your stone can come in handy; that way you can slip it inside a pocket or pin it on your clothing.

Another way of working with the power of a stone is to program a clear quartz crystal to the specific energy of another stone that is needed (see "Programming Technique," this chapter). Quartz crystal, being clear and very harmonious to the energies of the human body, can be programmed with the energy of any stone you wish. This is really practical. With a well-prepared clear quartz crystal you have the potential of having all the different semiprecious and precious stones that you wish to work with, simply by programming your quartz crystal, for example, as an emerald, or a ruby, or a sapphire. First you must purify the quartz crystal, and then program it with the vibration of another stone. Of course, before doing this you will want to have a clear sense and feeling for the energy of the specific stone you want to work with. So at some point you will need to meditate a bit with the real stone. You don't need to own it; you can borrow it or take time at a gem and mineral show to sit awhile with any crystal you borrow from a vendor or from a friend. Once you have really felt the energy of a specific stone and it has been integrated into your mind, then you will be able to program your purified quartz crystal with any mineral energy you wish to work with using the programming technique provided earlier in this chapter (pages 145–46).

Yet another way of working with a crystal is to simply visualize that stone and its energy. Your mind is what's doing the work. The crystal is only amplifying your energies and thoughts. The real battery that brings forth the energy for healing is the mind; the crystal is only there to orient, amplify, or transform the energies with which you want to work. Thus you can visualize in your mind's eye the aspects, beauty, and energy of a specific crystal, and then let that image infuse your being. This is especially useful when you don't have that specific crystal. When you have cultivated yourself through regular meditation practice, your thoughts will be well-focused for this task. You will be able to maintain concentration and thus send a specific crystal energy to another person with precision.

Teaching Story

I was once approached by a journalist who wanted to write an article on my work for a French magazine in Quebec. Our interview went well, and she wrote a nice article. When she presented the article to the editor of the magazine, however, he was not satisfied with it and he wanted to change so many things in her article that she could no longer support it and felt a lot of anger over it. As she was telling me this over the phone, I could clearly feel that there was a personality conflict between her and her editor. Aquamarine is the stone of choice to harmonize human relationships. I went into my meditation space and I visualized these two people enclosed in a huge aquamarine crystal conversing with each other and reaching an agreement. A week later, the journalist called me and said that she had met with her editor and they had arrived at a compromise that fitted her needs. The article was published.

CRYSTAL ESSENCES

A very powerful and efficient way of using crystals to help and to heal is in the form of essences. This is where we take pure water and infuse the energy and specific programming of a crystal into the water. As water has memory and can adopt and hold that information, it will retain the energy of the specific crystal friend that we put into it. When you take this water internally, it will affect your body and physiology very rapidly. Normally, within twenty minutes your body will have integrated the specific frequency and vibration of the crystal essence. It's a bit like the way homeopathic remedies work. There are only minute amounts of any material in a homeopathic remedy; similarly, in a crystal essence there is only the presence of vibration and frequency.

A stone essence takes about four hours to a day to make, with the time spent on doing the actual work being around thirty minutes. The dosage is as follows: use anywhere from half a cup to a few drops under the tongue, between two and four times a day or as needed. The essence will begin to work within twenty minutes. To obtain the maximum effect you should not take any other type of essence or medication for twenty minutes before ingestion of an essence, and you should not eat any food or drink anything immediately before and after using the essence. As essences only contain water, you cannot overdose on them, the exception being any stone of the red ray, which can call too much on a person's energy reserves. Always harmonize with green or blue after using ruby or garnet essences. Also, be careful with Herkimer.

If you don't have the specific crystal (emerald, ruby, sapphire, etc.) with which you want to make an essence, that is not a problem. If, for example, you want to make emerald essence but you don't have an emerald, take a clear quartz crystal and program it as an emerald first, and then program it with your specific intentions. In this way you are sending two programs into the clear quartz crystal.

Avoid making essences with azurite, soft chrysocolla, and dioptase as they may leach harmful substances into the water. Avoid making essences with coral, malachite, and turquoise as they do not have a crystalline structure thus will not hold the programming.

⚜ Making a Crystal Essence

1. Begin by filling a large clear glass bowl with pure spring water or distilled water.

2. Go outside into the sunlight and do the centering exercise from chapter 3. Energize your hands by vigorously rubbing the palms of your hands against each other and then blowing on your palms (as described in detail in chapter 12). Hold the specific crystal and program it as described. The more specific your intention, the more effective your essence will be.

3. Now put the crystal in the water.

4. Energize your hands a second time.

5. Place your hands over the water, tips of the thumbs and the indexes touching, palms facing toward the water. Send the same intention into the water, but now with your hands. This takes longer than when you energize your food. It can take anywhere from two to five minutes before you receive a response coming back from the water, felt with the palms of your hands. This response indicates that the water has taken as much charge as it can hold.

6. Now move your hands in a clockwise circular motion three times and separate them rapidly. As your hands are magnetic, they will draw the energy back into them as they move away slowly. This is why we remove our hands rapidly.

7. You can put some type of clear netting or cloth over the water so that dust and insects don't fall into it. Meanwhile, the sunlight will impregnate the water with your intention. Leave it in the sunlight for three hours or all

day if you wish, but three hours is sufficient. You can still do this on a cloudy day, but a sunny day is much better.

8. Remove the crystal from the water. Bottle the water you have obtained, storing it in a cool, dark place. The fridge is okay, but if you have a root cellar that's better.

The charge will remain in the water at full intensity for about a month. The second month the charge is still there, but it starts to weaken after three months so you would best redo your essence with fresh water.

With essences you can work with a lot of specifics that address certain issues of the person you are treating, or you can also work in a more general way. For example, say you have a green emerald essence, a blue aquamarine essence, and an orange carnelian essence in your fridge. Depending on the people who come to see you, you can offer them some of these essences. There is no need to take a full glass, a spoonful, or a few drops if using a dropper bottle, is sufficient, but as it's only water the quantity doesn't matter. You can even make tea with an essence and it will still have the desired effect. If you have a family member who's depressed, you'll be going with the orange carnelian water to perk them up. If you have an overexcited and overactive child, this calls for the blue aquamarine water. I expect you get the drift of how you can work with this.

These are some of the ways we can work with crystals. In the next part of the book we will learn how to do hands-on healing using crystals. The first step is learning how to work with our hands. The laying-on of hands is a universal method of healing found in traditions all over the world, and this practice can be amplified by using a clear quartz healing crystal. But first, we will close this part of the book with a meditation.

When you have memorized and practiced the Heart Meditation (pages 121–25) for a few weeks or months, then you can progress and learn this one. Once you have memorized it, feel free to practice the one that gives you greater energy, clarity, and serenity. Both meditations are fundamental in understanding and feeling the reality of your light body. We are beings of light, as are the crystals. There are more advanced meditation practices available at ancestralwisdomtoday.com, but these two should keep you busy for quite some time.

⌂ The Three Suns Meditation ⌂

Note: The chants referenced below in bold are available at ancestralwisdomtoday.com*

Between the inhalation and the exhalation in this meditation, we suspend the breath a few seconds, doing the same between the exhalation and the inhalation.

Begin with an offering and a chant to the four directions.

Sit upright, the spinal column a link between the sky and the earth. Start by following the breath without influencing the length of the breath, just following it, being within, conscious, and aware, feeling the inhalation bringing us vitality, energy, and light. The exhalation releases all that we no longer need. Allow the breath to find a relaxed, natural rhythm without influencing it. Pause . . .

Sense a spiral arising from the crystal heart of Mother Earth, rising through us up into the heavens, purifying and clarifying our whole being. Now another spiral comes down from the sky and spirals within us, moving down into the earth, purifying and clarifying our whole being. Pause . . .

These two spirals meet within the heart, and as they meet within the heart you see a great yellow sun. This is your soul, the divine, immortal, eternal essence of your being. Your soul knows better than you what's good for you and can do anything and everything for you. This yellow sun, as you breathe in, expands in your chest. At the suspension of the breath you come to a place of ecstasy, communing with your soul, this great yellow sun. As you exhale this light pervades

---

*With a free membership, readers can access the chants by going to the Member Area/ Tools/Chants.

your whole body. At the suspension of the breath, before completing your exhalation, you are for that moment in communion with the great yellow sun. Continue for a few moments with this four-step breath. Pause . . .

From the center of this yellow sun you see a tiny speck, which is a red sun. It flows down from the heart through the central channel to the second energy center situated in the stomach behind the umbilicus. As you breathe in, this red sun grows and expands, and at the suspension of breath it radiates throughout the body. As you continue to exhale, this red energy brings healing to your physical body, and at the conclusion of the exhalation you feel this healing happening. As you inhale again this red sun expands in your stomach; at the suspension it radiates throughout your body; and as you exhale this light, which is everywhere in your body, in every cell, promotes profound healing. At the end of the outbreath you feel the result of this healing. Pause . . .

The red sun remains in your stomach, glowing and warming you. Back to the yellow sun. This time you see a tiny blue star arising at the center of your head where the pineal and pituitary glands are. As you inhale, this blue speck becomes a blue sun that expands to fill your head. At the suspension it radiates throughout your whole body. At the continuation of the exhalation this blue light heals all that is of the mind, in all cells of your body. At the suspension, before the next inhalation, you feel the results of this healing. At the next inhalation, the blue sun expands. At the suspension, it radiates blue light throughout your body. At the conclusion of the exhalation this blue light now creates healing in every cell. At the suspension at the end of the exhalation you feel the results of this healing. Pause . . .

Now the red sun rises up and comes to float beside the yellow sun. The blue sun sinks down and floats up close to the yellow sun. They are like the three points of a horizontal triangle. This triangle of three suns starts turning, slowly at first and then spinning in a clockwise circle, faster and faster. Round and round and round and faster and faster and faster, and soon you cannot distinguish them from one another. They become one brilliant white light that shines in all directions, without limitation of time or space. You are this light. You are in this light. You are a breathing white light that beams throughout the whole universe. You travel on this light, to where you want to be. You are but white light breathing in space. You send this light to all those who need it. Compassion, understanding, love, and light are freely given to those who cry out in the night. You give freely out to the world the pristine energy of universal, unconditional love from the heart. Pause . . .

At this point, begin the heart chant.

Now, bring it all back—all this light comes back into your heart. It becomes once more this yellow sun, your soul. You still feel the world, the universe, as a part of yourself. Pause . . .

Now rest in the space of emptiness. No thoughts, no concepts, equanimity and balance in the awareness of the here and now. Pause . . .

Sing your rejoicing, your gratefulness for this unity and healing. Chant your thanksgiving, your gratitude for this meditation that has been given.

Conclude with the creation chant.

Part 4

Advanced Healing Practices

12

Preparing for Hands-On
Energy Healing

As we start to move into hands-on healing techniques, we first need to understand the function of the electromagnetic fields that surround all living things. These are the subtle, invisible, yet measurable energy fields around us. Some call this the *aura,* yet a more precise scientific term is *electromagnetic energy field.* It can be measured with scientific equipment—at least the first field can. Yes, there are actually five fields, and people with advanced subtle vision can see all five.

THE ELECTROMAGNETIC ENERGY FIELDS
OF THE HUMAN BODY

All disease begins in the electromagnetic field before eventually manifesting on the physical level. A strong electromagnetic field protects against disease and maleficent energies. For those who are well-trained there are ways to work with all five fields, however, this is too advanced a subject, in my humble opinion, to be given in a book. So here we will only consider the first field. It extends from 15 to 20 centimeters around the body and is called the *etheric web.* It is seen as rosy lines or a luminous halo around the body. It acts as an interface for the other fields and for all cosmic and telluric energies that reach us.

The etheric web is the physical body's energetic blueprint. This explains why an amputee can sometimes have pain in the missing foot or hand: the etheric web is still there. As far as our physical health and well-being are concerned, this is the most important field. I like to call it the etheric web as it has a web like a lattice or a grid that reflects the way it communicates energy. There are apparatuses today that can diagnose thousands of bits of different information from all parts of the body in a few seconds by reading this energy field. To my knowledge, these devices are widely used in Germany and Russia and in a few select places in North America.

The second field is known as the *astral field* or *emotional field*. It extends around the first energy field, about 30 to 45 centimeters from the body. It can be seen as electrical charges, points, clouds, or circles of color around the first energy field. This corresponds to our emotional body and that's why this field is always moving and displaying different colors.

The third energy field is called the *lower mental field*. This is the rational, objective, linear mind that thinks, using logic and acting as a memory bank. It's often seen as moving pale yellow lines around the astral field.

Then we have the *higher mental field* that represents our subjective, holistic, circular, abstract mind that's responsible for abstract thought, intuition, creativity, the arts, and fantasy. It surrounds the lower mental field and is often seen as small, pale green, circular cloud formations.

The fifth energy field, the *spiritual body,* is our spiritual connection with the world of ideal form. It connects your soul and spirit with your immortal spirit and soul, often called the *oversoul,* that part of you that remains in the world of ideal form. It's often seen as moving fingers of blue, indigo, and violet light penetrating from outside the fourth field and going all the way through all the fields into the physical body.

Of course, everyone is unique, and there can be many variations to the aspects these fields may display to one's subtle vision, provided you have attained that level of cognizance.

In addition to these five, there are some mystery schools that speak of a sixth and seventh energy field. We do not consider them as energy fields that manifest around a person, but rather as energy fields of cosmic reality that are there whether the person is there or not. The reason they have been documented is that they often visibly manifest around people of very high spiritual attainment. For example, the halo often painted above the heads of saints in Christian iconography portrays such a field. As I have no experience working with such fields and they are not used in therapeutic work with crystals, they will not be discussed here.

THE ENERGETIC HANDS

With this background, it's now time to get some basic training and practice under our belt. This is (literally) the hands-on part of our work, as you must first learn to work with your hands before you can use crystals. It's important that we realize that if we are not centered and have not trained our mind and feelings to focus on specific intentions, as described in chapter 2 on the three preliminaries, and if we do not take proper care of our crystals as described in chapter 9, then the use of crystals can actually be harmful. One of the many reasons we start by using our hands before using crystals is that it's nearly impossible to make mistakes when doing hands-on healing with only your hands.

In the palms of your hands you have a secondary energy center called *the eye of the hand*. It is called this because we can see, or rather *feel*, energy with our hands, and we can also send out healing energy through our hands. Your body knows this instinctively. For example, if you bump your knee on the sharp side of a table, the first thing you will do is put your hand on it and rub it. Your body knows that there is healing energy in your hand, and so you instinctively do the right thing. Another example is when you encounter a friend or family member who is in anguish and crying. What's the first thing you do? You put your hand on their shoulder or you embrace them. The hands will go exactly where they need to go to give reassuring healing energy. Thus your body knows instinctively what it needs to do. Now we need to take this further and make our hands a conscious healing tool. And as with all things, this needs practice.

The first step in doing energy healing is learning to feel and evaluate the energies and vibrations coming from the first energy field, the etheric web.

⚡ Sensing the Etheric Web and Energizing the Hands

1. Put your hands one in front of the other, palm facing palm, and bring them closer together and then farther away from each other several times until you feel a ball of energy between your hands. Look to where that sensation is the strongest. Everybody feels this differently, but when you find a resistance or a vibration or a repulsion between the palms of your hands you have found the width of the etheric web where they meet. That is the first energy field around your hands.

2. Continue by vigorously rubbing the palms of your hands against each other and then blow on your palms. Do this three times the first time you try this exercise. We call this *energizing the hands*. When you do this, the elbows should move; they must not be close to the body but out away from the body a little. This movement will also help with centering. Imagine that you're creating heat in the palms of your hands.

3. Now return to step 1, bringing your palms closer together and then farther away from each other until you find that ball of energy. You will notice that the energy field has doubled. What's happening when you energize the eye of the hand is that you stimulate the capacity of your hands to feel and receive energy, thus doubling the energy field. Your hands are more perceptive now, and they're sending out more energy.

Now we need to learn how to perceive the variations in energy in the first energy field. Everyone feels this differently. This is the first stage of learning hands-on healing, learning what your specific symbolic reading type is. As everyone has a different way of experiencing the energy fields and the variations when there are problems in this field, we must discover what our own hands-on code is.

▣ Learning to Perceive Variations in the Energy Field

When we work with the hands and feel resistance or vibration or frequency or a repulsion or whatever indicates that you have met the exterior limit of the etheric web, then follow this field. Use these next steps to learn how to perceive variations in the energy field.

1. Start by trying this with a plant. Just like we humans, all vegetation has its own electromagnetic field that varies according to the health and species of the plant. You will notice that depending on what part of the plant you scan there are going to be variations in its energy field. The field can be wider or smaller; it can have a different feeling when the plant has broken parts; you can sense differences around the flowers, the stem, or the leaves; and you can sense differences between a healthy plant and a sickly plant.

2. Now try this with animals, if you have a domesticated animal that will tolerate you doing this around them. This is very interesting to try, as animals have specific reactions to this that can be very revealing.

3. The most telling experience is when you try doing this with people. Bring your hands to about 15 to 20 cm (around 6 to 8 inches) from the body until you feel the etheric web. Follow this outer limit to the etheric web, being careful that the palms of your hands really stay at the outer limit of the first energy field. When there are variations on what you are perceiving, ask questions. When you feel these variations in the energy field, ask the person if there is anything happening in that specific location in their body. This is how you are going to begin to recognize and perfect your specific hands-on code of perception.

CULTIVATING VITAL ENERGY

The next step in preparing for hands-on healing involves increasing your vital energy. We can compare the vital energy that can be transmitted through hands-on healing to an electrical system. If you send a high voltage of electricity through a thin wire it will burn out, it will short. This doesn't happen with your hands, however, as your body automatically takes on the amount of energy that it can process through your system. *It's important to understand that we are not drawing on our own energy.* If you did so you would rapidly be depleted. In our Native practice we draw this energy from heaven and earth, as they meet in the heart. As such, there is an unlimited supply of energy available if the channels are open, as when energy is given it is immediately replenished, like water flowing through pools in a quiet stream.

Our spiritual practice is what slowly increases the amount of vital energy that we are able to channel. Regular spiritual practice, we insist, is the basic requirement for all crystal practitioners. Another way that we can augment our vital energy is by increasing the vital energy in the food that we eat. We do this by sending healing energy and a clear intention through our hands into our food before we eat.

⚟ Increasing the Vital Energy of Food

1. Begin by tasting every kind of food you have on your plate. You want to compare before and after, so remember what they taste like.

2. Then energize your hands. Rubbing them vigorously, one against the other, one time, is sufficient once you've mastered the prior exercises.

3. Put your palms toward the food at about 15 to 20 cm (around 6 to 8 inches) and send through your hands the intention *to help and to heal.* You will feel at some point, usually after a few seconds, the same energy you felt when at the edge of the etheric web of another human body or a plant. This indicates that the food has taken on as much energy as it can.

4. Now taste the food. You will find the food tastes better and has attuned itself to your specific needs. It will be easier to digest, and you will need less to feel full. In time your energy level will be heightened.

Over the years in my crystal seminars I have received a number of testimonials on what people experience when doing this with their food. But what always comes back consistently, in every single seminar, is that the food tastes better, that you don't need to eat as much to feel satisfied, that digestion is easier, and there is a sense of reverence that makes the experience of eating more fulfilling. By honoring the food we eat and thus nature, which has provided it to us, we integrate ourselves into the greater scheme of things. The odd instance of someone who doesn't taste or feel a difference is resolved by doing the same exercise first with a glass of water. As water is neutral to the taste, this helps. This is very simple, just trust your feelings. Everyone has what's needed to experience this.

It's important to practice tasting the difference in the food when we increase its vital energy and notice the digestive ease as a result of doing this practice. As always, testing is important, as it allows you to do this with conviction. The emotion, the feeling, the experience will lend its energy to the thought behind the theory to give maximum energy to the work you do. Theory and practice, knowledge and experience need to go hand-in-hand. It is said that this practice also pleases the nature spirits, since they see it as evidence of your gratitude and that you're honoring the food they have provided you.

Teaching Story

I once had an experience in which the Montreal organizer of my crystal courses had invited me to her favorite Japanese restaurant. I ordered chicken teriyaki and she ordered some sushi. As always, I energized my hands and sent my intention into the food. I didn't get a response from the food, so I energized my hands again and tried a second time to energize my food. Again I got no response from the food. I tried a third time with the same result. Then I tasted the food and it felt heavy on the stomach. This had never happened to me before. I was reluctant to eat this food. I felt I needed to trust what I was feeling. Good lesson here, always trust your feelings. My host, a bit disappointed in bringing me to her favorite restaurant, offered to change plates. I discovered sushi as a result and have been a real fan since then. She too did not get any response from the teriyaki, but she ate it all the same. The next day she told us she was sick all night.

I told this teaching story to another crystal class a few weeks later. That Saturday evening, a woman from the class went home and cooked supper for her family using leftovers and had a similar experience. Sunday morning during our opening circle she told the group that she had practiced energizing the food she had prepared. She didn't get any response. Remembering my story, she didn't eat the food she had prepared, but didn't trust herself to tell her family members, who ate the food and were sick throughout the night.

Always remember in your work with crystals, the work is happening on an invisible level of high frequency, so you must learn to trust your feelings.

Learning how to energize your food is very useful when traveling. When I go to a restaurant, I energize everything I eat. Sometimes a single item on the plate does not respond, and so I don't eat it. In all the years I've traveled I've never suffered from indigestion, food poisoning, or any similar problem, despite the fact that in my travels I have eaten in some rather dubious places.

Now you can go a step farther and use your hands to adjust the energy in medications, herbal remedies, and supplements. You can teach anyone who is sick how to do this, by holding the very simple, clear intention *to help and to heal* while energizing the substance. Their medication will have a greater effect and will be more helpful and easier to digest, with fewer side effects. Supplements will have more healing power and will have adapted to the person's specific needs. That's why it's the one who is going to take the medications and supplements who needs to do the energizing, as their own hands will communicate best the exact energies needed by that person's body.

13

Laying-On of Hands

We all need to train in healing with the hands alone before working with crystals in another person's energy field. We need to take baby steps. Even an advanced practitioner in other disciplines should move slowly and with precaution when using crystals. Doing hands-on healing with crystals is very powerful. It's possible you can aggravate a person's condition if while doing a treatment your concentration and focus slips. When working with your hands, however, it's nearly impossible to make any mistakes. This is a very simple, effective, and powerful treatment that can be used anytime, anywhere, because you always have your hands with you! It is thus very important to learn how to do laying-on of hands before working with crystals.

In Native tradition we have many laying-on-of-hands treatment modalities. These are quite elaborate and have many aspects that require specific spiritual training and exercises. It's impossible to teach these methods in a book. What we do have, though, is a method that was inspired by the work of Dolores Krieger, PhD, RN, and her Therapeutic Touch practice.* This is a technique enabling you to transmit healing energy in a beneficial way. It has its roots in ancient healing methods that exist the world over, in all traditional societies, where it's simply called *the laying-on of hands*.

OhShinnàh Fastwolf and Dolores Krieger were very close friends.

---

*See https://therapeutictouch.org.

During the final years of their lives they lived together in Montana. I visited them there and could appreciate how Dolores, who was well into her nineties, was active and could work away at her computer a good part of the day; she didn't display any signs of a diminished mental capacity. When younger, Dolores traveled the world to study with great healers who were renowned for their prowess in laying-on-of-hands healing. She then compiled the elements that most of them used in doing this type of treatment and simplified these methods to give us a powerful healing tool that anyone can easily learn.*

Throughout the world there are great healers who have demonstrated extraordinary results. Some of these practitioners have a lot of vital energy and a strong spiritual practice. Their energy meridians are wide open and therefore they can receive and emit powerful waves of healing energy. Yet even if we don't have the proficiency and ability of these great healers, we all have healing energy in our hands. If you have a pure and compassionate intention toward another person, your laying on of hands will be greatly appreciated and very helpful.

Laying-on of hands can be administered several times a day. For best results you'll want to repeat several days in a row. It can be done in a short amount of time, ten or fifteen minutes, or for a longer period of time if the person can relax in a reclining position. The energy exchange with the hands is instantaneous. The only negative effect is that it can cause some fatigue for you if you're doing it for longer periods of time. This all depends on your concentration and whether or not you're coming from the heart. If you understand what's been given here thus far, you will not give your energy away; you will be giving what is freely given by the sky and earth as they meet in your heart. As always, practice makes perfect. If you practice well, you will become an excellent healer. When done well you will actually feel energized after doing this healing. The energy that comes through always leaves a little behind.

So let's begin.

---

*As published in her book *The Therapeutic Touch: How to Use your Hands to Help and to Heal.* New York: Prentice-Hall, 1979.

❧ Laying-On of Hands Methodology

1. Center with the breath (see centering exercise, chapter 3). Then visualize roots of light going down from your feet into the earth. This will protect you from any stray energy, magnetic pollution, or malignant vibes that the person might release during her treatment. This dispersed energy will not stick to you if it comes into you; it will immediately ground into the earth, even if you're on the twentieth story of a high-rise building. Visualize a dome of clear (not white) light around you and the person you are going to work on. This is to protect the healing space. It's important that you be open to receiving sky and earth and the vibrations of those luminous beings who help you who are the guides of the person you are treating. Thus, to feel comfortable opening up, you are creating this dome of light that only allows luminous energies to penetrate your healing space. Visualize this great dome as large enough to envelop your client or patient and for you to move around in.

2. Firmly and vigorously rub your hands together, energizing the energy centers in your palms. Have the palms of your two hands facing the client and bring them closer to the person until you feel their etheric web (as described in the exercise "Sensing the Etheric Web and Energizing the Hands" in the previous chapter). Once you have felt the limits of this etheric web, stay at the surface and slowly bring your hands around the person's body at this level, experiencing the width, the vibration, and whatever indications you have discovered from doing the exercises in chapter 12 as being the code of perception your hands have that is uniquely yours. Be very attentive to the depth of the field. During this evaluation I find it useful to rebalance the etheric web if its depth has discrepancies. As noted in the last chapter, the etheric web should be the same depth all over. If you find places that are too deep or too shallow, readjust these by pulling or pushing with your hands. Put your two hands on both sides of the body and you can readjust with your breath and by visualizing the effect you want to achieve.

There can be a great many problems with the etheric web. Sometimes it's completely out of sync. I've seen a person sitting down and the only part of the etheric web that was attached to her body was her head; the rest was horizontal, as if she was lying in bed. I had to bring the whole thing down so it would integrate with her body. There can be a wide assortment of unbalanced fields. The worst I've seen was upside-down, the feet at the head and vice versa. Took me a while to understand what my hands were reading. Many things can be observed and are indications of what's happening with the person. I usually have one hand pulling while the other is pushing in the opposite direction on the other side of the body. It usually responds immediately, and the person will feel a difference immediately. But before you can read the person's field, the etheric web must be in place. Otherwise there's no precision in what you're reading. So this is the phase where you push and pull with your hands so that the etheric web is of uniform depth over the person's entire body.

3. While you're assessing the etheric web, be attentive to feeling if there are any tears or holes in the etheric web. I feel this as if there is suddenly nothing at that specific place. That indicates to me that there is either a hole or tear in the etheric web. Do this over the entire surface of the person's body. Ask questions. If you feel a difference in the vibration of the etheric web, ask the person if there is any problem at that specific location. Be aware that all health problems originate in the energy field before they manifest in the body. Thus the client may not yet be aware that there is a problem in that specific location. If the person says there seems to be no problem at that place, it doesn't necessarily negate what you have felt. Always trust yourself.

4. Now reflect on the color ray and specific intentions you think will be most beneficial for the person. The knowledge your hands have determined is the basis of what you will choose. The person might have described different ailments that are not corroborated by what you felt. Always go with what your hands tell you.

5. Once you have determined your intention for the healing, energize your hands a second time. Next, you perform the etheric sweep. Your hands are working as a broom as you bring them over the etheric web in slow,

sweeping, smooth, caressing motions all over, moving in the general direction of the floor to immediately ground any excess or undesirable energies. These sweeping movements will have the effect of soothing the person and will balance and soften her etheric web. Your hands will collect a lot of positive ions in the process as you release them from your client's energy field. To get rid of them is simple: just shake your hands toward the ground. I often do this periodically several times during a treatment as soon as I feel a buildup of stagnant energy around my hands. This sweeping has powerful effects. Your client will feel more relaxed, nurtured, and loved; her vital energy will increase and she will be energetically prepared to receive the rest of the treatment.

6. When you've rebalanced, caressed, and smoothed over the whole etheric web, begin the actual treatment. Concentrate in your hands the intention you have prepared, the color ray you have imagined will help your client, and the specific locations where you have discerned problems. I often use the visualization of a crystal of the appropriate color to add power to this part of the treatment. Symbols have power, and the image of the crystal in your mind will add power to your treatment. Palms facing toward the person, send healing energy to her with the specific intentions and appropriate color to those areas that need healing. Take all the time you need, but be attentive to your client's needs.

7. Once finished, you can now mend any tears or holes that you have found in her etheric web. Spread your fingers and weave them one over the other, imagining threads of light coming out of the ends of your fingers as if you were weaving the threads into a web of pure light that is covering and healing those tears and holes in the etheric web. Evaluate the results with your hands. When you feel the web is tight and all is covered, you have completed the mending of the etheric web.

8. Put your two hands on the two feet of the person you are treating. Imagine roots of light going through your hands and through the person's feet into the ground. This is to remove any stagnant energy that has been wanting to leave but has not yet found its way out of this person. You are

grounding and anchoring her into the earth's beneficial energy. Now put your two hands over her head or on her shoulders and call on the energy of Father Sky. You can also invoke any deity or god that is important to you. You are calling on divine energy to bless this person.

The treatment is now finished, yet it's important to share impressions and feelings with the person you've helped. This can be a very important part of the treatment. There is a need to do this at the beginning of treatment also. We all need to share and talk through the important experiences and challenges life continuously offers us. We don't need advice as much as a chance to get the stuff out there in the open so we can see it through the eyes of another person. When we've expressed our feelings and difficulties, they are shared by another, and that makes them easier to carry. We also see our problems differently, and our inner, innate wisdom has more room to offer the life lessons the experience of discomfort or disease is offering us. Thus the wise practitioner just listens and doesn't offer advice unless it is requested. But anything you've perceived during treatment can be shared afterward if you feel it is beneficial for the person to hear.

Be sure to put your hands under cold running water to wash away any residual energies.

You can do laying-on of hands with your client in any position, lying down, standing up, or seated. When the person is lying down it can be difficult to evaluate the energy in her back, so I prefer the seated position. But you can do this in any position as long as the person can relax in the position they're in.

You will want to practice healing with the hands for several months before you move on to the hands-on crystal treatment. This is important training. You need to develop a certain degree of mastery and some experience of the possible results you can obtain with hands-on healing. When you have developed confidence and reliability, you will be able to move on to the crystal treatment. You will then find that the crystal amplifies the work that you are doing with your hands. With a crystal you can be even more precise, as if you were working with a laser beam.

So to recapitulate, here, in brief, are the steps to help you remember the aforementioned sequence:

1. Center yourself. Visualize a dome of clear (not white) light around you and the person you are going to work on.
2. Energize your hands by rubbing them together vigorously. Evaluate the etheric field of the person by moving your palms across the surface of the etheric web. Adjust the depth if necessary. Consult with your client for feedback on possible problems related to what you are feeling with your hands.
3. Assess whether there are holes or tears in the etheric web and get feedback from your client.
4. Reflect on the color ray and specific intentions you think will be most beneficial for the person.
5. Energize your hands again and perform an etheric sweep over the whole surface of the etheric web, sweeping your hands like a broom.
6. Palms facing toward the person, send healing energy to her with the specific intentions and appropriate color to those areas that need healing.
7. Mend the holes or tears you have found in the field with threads of light coming from the ends of your fingers.
8. Ground the person by putting your hands on her feet and visualizing roots of light going down into the earth. Bless her with energy from the sky, using your hands over her head or shoulders.

Share with the person what she experienced. Remember to let cool running water flow over your hands.

This is a simple yet effective method of helping others. It can be used with anyone. It can be done rapidly if needed; it is always beneficial, and when done right it will even energize the one giving the treatment. As always with any discipline, you need to practice to master this technique. Start with your family and friends before integrating this into your healing work.

14

Healing Practices Using Quartz Crystal

Working with the crystals themselves will bring the skills you have obtained thus far, up to and including the laying-on of hands described in chapter 13, to a whole new level. A quartz crystal is a powerful tool with the precision of a laser beam that can refine one's healing work to a fine art. Do not attempt any of these treatments using a quartz crystal until you've gotten months of spiritual practice under your belt and have achieved positive results with the laying-on of hands.

You'll begin by finding the right crystal to do this type of work (see plate 3). This is a one-pointed clear quartz crystal. It should be smaller than your fist but big enough to clearly determine the crystal's C face. If it's too big, your hand will get tired and you'll lose concentration. If it's too small, you'll have problems getting the crystal's ray to work in the right position.

A one-pointed clear quartz crystal has six faces leading to a point, the extension of its six sides. Each side leads to a triangular face that leads to the point. The faces are all different. One is longer than the others, starts farther down from the point, and is often larger but not always. This longer triangular face leading to the point is called the *C face*. The crystal emits the ray of clear energy through that face. If you place that triangular face a few inches above and parallel to your palm and move a bit, you'll feel the energy that the crystal emits through that face, as if a small brush were moving over your palm. The choice of a crystal can often entail choosing one where the C face is obvious, making it easier to work with.

You will need to purify your crystal and enter into right relationship with it before using it for healing work. Review chapters 1 through 4 to make sure you've got this right. Please remember, these are powerful tools, and your aim is to help and heal. With insufficient practice or preparation you might not reach your goal of helping others. Patience and perseverance are always important virtues for a healer to cultivate.

Two exercises follow. The first is to help you evaluate the condition of a person to determine the best treatment; the second exercise guides you through the treatment itself.

❖❖❖ Pretreatment Evaluation Using a Quartz Crystal

1. Start by purifying the space in which you will be working, preferably before the person you're treating arrives. To do this use sage or liquid smudge.

2. Center yourself (centering exercise, chapter 3) and offer a short silent prayer, thanking Creator for the gift of being able to help others, and invoke your guides and the patient's guides to come assist the healing.

3. Visualize roots of light reaching from your feet down into the earth. This will enable all surplus energy to be grounded. If your client releases discordant energies, pain, or disease as a result of the treatment and your body channels them, they will pass through your body into the ground, thanks to the roots of light you have created. This way you will not retain anything that could remain with you. It is not necessary to be standing on firm ground to imagine these roots of light. They will be effective even if you're on the twentieth floor of a building.

4. Imagine a dome of clear light or amethyst light above and around you and the person you are working on. This is to protect your healing space. It's important that you be open to receiving sky and earth and the vibrations of those luminous beings who help you and who are guides for the person you are treating. Thus to feel comfortable opening up,

you create this dome of light that lets only luminous energies penetrate your healing space. Imagine this dome being large enough for you to be able to move around in it while your patient remains inside it. What I have found to be the best arrangement is for the patient to sit on a stool, allowing them to be restful while allowing you to bring your hands all around them.

5. Firmly and vigorously rub your hands together, energizing the energy centers in your palms. Move the palms of your hands toward the person receiving the treatment until you feel some resistance. This vibration, which is described in chapter 12 ("Learning to Perceive Variations in the Energy Field"), which you have practiced enough at this stage, enables you to access the depth of the etheric field and gives you an indication of the person's state of health. Be very attentive to the depth of the field. When evaluating I find it useful to rebalance the etheric web if the depth has discrepancies. The etheric web should be a uniform depth all over. If you find places that are either too deep or too shallow, readjust the web by pulling or pushing it with your hands, putting your two hands on both sides of the body and using your breath and visualizing the effect you want to obtain.

6. Assess the person's entire body, following the surface of the etheric field. Ask questions of the person if you come across any anomalies to find out what's happening at that location.

Once your evaluation is complete, you are ready to begin treatment.

▰ Healing Treatment Using a Quartz Crystal

1. Center a second time. Place the crystal on the person's spiritual plexus. This is at the point of the sternum between the cardiac plexus and the solar plexus. Put your other hand on the back of the person, palm toward them, away from the body, at the surface of the etheric web, to feel when the ray emitted by the crystal passes through their body. Then put the C face on the person's forehead. Same as before—place your other hand at the back of their head, palm toward the head, at

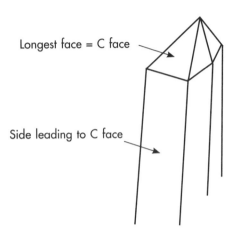

Longest face = C face

Side leading to C face

the surface of the etheric web, to feel when the ray passes through the person's head. Then place the C face of the crystal on the top of the person's head. Rather than putting your other hand underneath the person's perineum, trust the feeling that will come through your hand that holds the crystal. When you feel that the ray has passed all the way through the central channel of the person, slowly pull the crystal up toward the sky, the C face remaining parallel to the top of their head. Often we notice the person's head straightening on her shoulders at this point. This manipulation is done to open the energy centers of the person. This is why preliminary to the treatment it's important that you have already established a dome of light around the person and yourself, so that there is no vulnerability when the person's energy centers are open.

2. The next step is doing what we call a *crystal bath*. It's the equivalent of the etheric sweep described as part of the laying-on of hands (review chapter 13). Use the side of the crystal that leads to the C face (see diagram), parallel to the client's body, at the outer edge of the etheric web. The crystal has six sides each leading to one of the six triangular faces going to the point. You want the side leading to the C face, which is the longest of the triangular faces, parallel to the body on the edge of the etheric web. Try to be at the edge of the etheric web, not inside it. Throughout my years of teaching, this is where I've frequently

had to offer corrections to my students, who often do the crystal bath within the etheric web. It is much better to do it at the *edge of the web,* actually, right on the outer surface of the web. It's easy to determine this: bring your hands slowly toward the client's body and as soon as you feel resistance or whatever your personal code indicates to you that you have met the etheric web, remain at that distance. This is also what allows you to see any differences in the depth of the etheric web. With the side of the crystal that leads to the C face, move it parallel to the body at the edge of the etheric web all over the person's energy field. The movement is similar to the sweeping, caressing movement that you used in the laying-on of hands. This is very helpful. It will regulate the etheric web, giving indications to this energy field that it needs to harmonize and be consistent in its depth. It will also remove positive ions and generate negative ions, thus clearing, purifying, and energizing the etheric web. And it will smooth out those spots that were rough to the subtle touch.

3. Now, run your crystal through saltwater for a few seconds, moving it through the water with your hand to remove the positive ions that have been attracted to its energy field. This will regenerate its capacity to generate more negative ions. Wipe it dry and center yourself a third time.

4. If you wish you can train the person you're treating to do the centering exercise with the breath (described in chapter 3). You don't want the person to do this at the beginning of the treatment because some of the problems that can appear in her etheric web before evaluating it with your hands may temporarily disappear. So at this point it's better to receive the treatment and relax into the process and center at the same time. Assess the person's openness and the ambiance that has been created in order to tell whether she should do the centering exercise.

5. With a strong focus, program the crystal with your intention for the person, using a specific color and crystal—for instance, green/emerald, blue/azurite, orange/carnelian, etc. (see part 5 for more options)— which you have determined following your evaluation of the person's energy field. Program only a single color into the crystal. Include your

specific intentions to orient the energy in the right direction. Remember the focus on intention that we studied in chapter 4, on the three laws of healing; envision perfect health and a happy, vibrant person, and do not focus on the problem or pain the person is experiencing.

6. Holding the crystal about 12 inches above the person's head, the C face parallel to the crown of the person's head, send its programmed ray into the head. Ask your client to visualize from head to toe the color that you have programmed into the crystal. Here's an example of how to do this, using the blue ray: *Imagine a clear blue aquamarine light flowing down into your body through the top of your head, like a vivifying blue water that is washing away all that you no longer need. This blue light flows through your head and neck into your shoulders and down into your arms, to the tips of your fingers. It flows down into your breasts, your lungs, into your stomach and all your organs, into your hips, down your thighs, knees, and feet, down to the tips of your toes. You are now full of a vivifying aquamarine blue light.*

7. Now you're ready to work on all those areas where you have discerned problems. Orient the crystal's C face toward the body and beginning well outside the etheric web, move the crystal in a slow clockwise spiral, moving toward the problem and going up right close to the skin or clothing, all the while your spiral getting smaller and smaller, tighter and tighter. When you are very close to the body you should feel a small "hook." This indicates that you can now pull on that energy, removing from the client's body whatever has created disease or discomfort. Pull it right out beyond the etheric web and release it to the ground. It does so automatically, you don't need to do any specific gesture if you don't feel it, but you do need to visualize this happening to encourage that energy to anchor into the ground and dissipate. Continue the same movement, slowly spiraling from outside the etheric web right into the energy field close to the body, feeling that small hook and pulling it out. If we were to visualize the shape of this movement it would be like a cone with the larger end outside the energy field and the smaller end close to the body. After doing this a few times, use your other hand to evaluate

whether you have achieved results by evaluating the changes perceived on the etheric web. When you feel that you have completed the work at this point, tone the areas that you've just worked on by doing a small crystal bath on those spots. As before, this is with the side leading to the C face and not with the C face itself. Just bring it a few times over the spot that you have worked on to smooth out the etheric web there. Then move on to the next place until you've completed "washing" all the spots that required treatment.

8. With this crystal treatment there usually is no need to close up any holes. I've never had to do so, as when you do the crystal bath they automatically call on the crystal etheric web, so similar to ours, to mend them. Yet you might want to verify if all is okay at the places where you sensed holes in the etheric web, and then do a general toning like the crystal bath, but on those precise spots, to close any holes. If this is not sufficient then do the weaving of the etheric web that you learned in chapter 13.

9. It's important that you conclude the treatment by closing up the energy field as it's now completely open and the person is more vulnerable to outside energies. These could "eat up" those stray energies and that would not be helpful. So we need to close this up. There are two ways to do this. If you are a Native American practitioner and have sacred feathers, you can sweep with those feathers in a vigorous to-and-fro movement in front of the person, imagining that you are closing up the energy field. Otherwise, join the tips of your index fingers and thumbs, creating a triangle, and place this form in front of the spiritual plexus of your client, bringing it all the way up above the person's head to her crown, and then bringing it slowly back down to the spiritual center, with the intention to close the field. Then separate both hands in a rapid movement. The energy centers are now closed.

The treatment is now complete. Put your crystal in saltwater and put your hands under cool running water.

Now is the time to share with your client. Allow her to express everything she feels, as this is important in any treatment. A person needs to share what's happening to them so as to release any clinging or attachment to their suffering. It's important that you be a good listener and not comment unless your feedback is requested. After allowing your client to express herself you can share what you felt or noticed during the treatment. Always avoid doing this during the treatment as the relaxation that the person experiences is important and beneficial to a healthy exchange of energies.

Although this treatment is very powerful, when the person returns to her daily routine and lifestyle, where the patterns of discomfort or disease originated, she can easily fall back into the same energy patterns that created the condition. Thus as with any energy treatment it's important to do this treatment a few times. At each treatment the energy that you are communicating to the person's energy field will imprint more and more. You and your client will be the judges of how many times this needs to happen. I usually only need to give three treatments.

Quite often as energy starts moving through the discomfort or disease that the person has come to you with, there can be the sensation that things are getting worse after the treatment. This is normal. As healing energy starts working it moves things around, and the additional feelings or sensations associated with this may seem to be a worsening of the condition. You must reassure your client that this is normal, and that it is in fact a good sign that your work has begun to produce results.

So to recapitulate, here are the steps to help you remember the pre-treatment evaluation sequence:

1. Prepare the space.
2. Center yourself and offer prayer.
3. Visualize roots of light grounding your feet with the energy of the earth.
4. Visualize a dome of clear or amethyst light around you and your patient.
5. Energize your hands by rubbing them together vigorously and evaluate the etheric web of the person by moving your palms across the

surface of the etheric web. Adjust the etheric web to obtain a consistent depth.

6. Consult with your client for feedback on possible problems related to what you are feeling with your hands.

Here is a summary of the healing treatment:

1. Center yourself again and open the energy field and the client's energy centers by placing your crystal's C face on the spiritual plexus, forehead, and top of the head. Pull an invisible string toward the sky to complete this step.

2. Perform a crystal bath by smoothing out the field and balancing it, using long, caressing movements with the crystal's side that leads to the C face parallel to the body, at the surface of the etheric web.

3. Purify the crystal a few moments by gently moving it around in saltwater and then wipe it dry.

4. Assess the client's openness to learning the centering exercise.

5. Program the crystal with the appropriate intentions and color.

6. Holding the crystal's C face toward the top of the head, have the person visualize the color by guiding them verbally through that visualization from head to feet.

7. One by one, work on all those areas where you felt problems by starting a spiral movement outside the etheric web and moving in smaller and smaller circles until your energy cone is right up close to the body. Pull at the small hook you feel at the end of this spiral cone until it reaches well away from the body. When you've addressed all the locations and feel the treatment is complete, verify this with your other hand.

8. Wash all the specific treatment zones with a localized crystal bath.

9. Close the energy field.

At the conclusion of the treatment put your crystal in saltwater and put your hands under cool running water. Share verbally with the patient on what was experienced.

Be precise. Take time to determine the best intentions. Know that your crystal will help you but can only channel what you put into it. With that in mind you can assist those who come to you for help. Remember to put your crystal to rest in its red cloth and bag and to periodically refresh and renew it in running water. When putting it in the bag, ask it to rest, and when taking it out to use, press on it and ask it to awaken. A simple thought is sufficient.

DISTANCE HEALING

Healing at a distance has been practiced by many different cultures throughout the world. The power of thought can travel light years in an instant. This has been scientifically proven by electricity and other modes of communication that already exist on earth. We will describe a few of these techniques here, but it must be understood that these are more advanced healing modalities and should only be attempted by the most advanced practitioners. Of course, we must always be respectful of the permission needed to perform healing on another person. There must be a request made to you personally to receive the healing from you before you attempt it, the only exception to this being your immediate family and animals that you wish to help.

The simplest of all healing at a distance modalities is prayer. Praying for another person is easy, simple, and effective. The power of a focused, concentrated beam of prayer has been highly underestimated. As our current educational systems do not train people in the higher levels of human consciousness, this is widely ignored. Yet there are demonstrations of this power throughout the world, the most well known being in highly charged spiritual places where people have gone to pray as a part of their spiritual beliefs. In some of these places we see hundreds of crutches, prosthesis, and wheelchairs that people once needed to be able to walk and that were left there because those people found instant healing in these places. This is because of many reasons, but one of the main ones is the power of prayer. Many people praying in the same place will create a great vortex of energy, beneficial energy that beings can call on to heal.

There are many other such instances of what we call *prayer circles*. The most common format for such a circle is where the one to be healed sits on a chair surrounded by a circle of people who pray while one of them administers some form of healing on them. This method can also be done at a distance. As I have a trained circle of advanced practitioners, when one of our community is ill and we have no access to that person, I will perform a distance healing on them while the other practitioners are praying to help the process. We have great results with this. An important element in using this type of energy healing with several people is that the people praying must send their energy to the healer and not to the one being healed. Sending the energy to the one in need of healing, when there are several people involved, can be very confusing. Each person in the group might have different intentions and might not direct the energy in the same way and they could therefore cancel one another out. When they send it only to the healer they will channel one specific, precise energy and intention with the added energy of others, thus making it a lot stronger.

You can use distance healing with people from your family or people who have requested help simply by sitting at your altar or meditation space and praying for them. If you wish to amplify this process, program your clear quartz crystal with an intention that is specific to this person and hold it while praying.

How you pray or what type of prayer you use is not important. What is important is the faith of the person praying, their concentration and focus. The regular practice of prayer is an essential part of your training as a crystal practitioner. It will purify and nourish the soul, which is your eternal, spiritual being. Prayer creates a channel of energy along which the frequency of help and healing can be carried. Distance and time are no obstacles. As far as the energy of healing and thought are concerned, distance does not exist.

In our ancient traditions there are many different ceremonies to conduct distance healing. As they involve powerful techniques that can be misused, they are only given to advanced practitioners through direct contact with a teacher and are therefore beyond the scope of this book.

We can also do healing in the dreamtime. Advanced practitioners can awaken in the dream, in what is called *lucid dreaming*. When you are consciously awake but dreaming you can travel to another person and do a healing on them. In all cultures dreams have had great import for many different aspects of community life, yet nowadays many parents disregard the importance of dreams and teach their children to ignore them, as in saying, "It's only a dream."

Our spiritual evolution involves becoming more and more conscious and aware. Ultimately that's what enlightenment means. To be completely conscious and aware in the present moment is to be enlightened. We do not cease to exist because we go to sleep. There is a part of us that is very active during dreamtime. We all remember some dreams. What is actually happening is a very intricate and interdimensional process of renewal, manifestation, and learning. There are many different levels in the dreamtime. Thus it's a good thing to be aware of this and try to bring more consciousness and awareness to your existence during the dreamtime.

The first step is to remember your dreams. As you prepare for sleep, do some purification of the room where you sleep so that the energies are favorable for deep relaxation. Then offer a short prayer, reviewing your day and giving thanks for what you've experienced. It's the same process that you use to remember dreams. As you look back at your day, start from the most recent events and go back to when you awoke in the morning. This is similar to what you will do when you remember a dream. As you travel through your day in your mind, if you see instances where you have not behaved appropriately or well, you can change this in your mind by reviewing the event and visualizing yourself acting in a more appropriate manner. This does two things. First, it will eliminate part of the karma that's related to this event because your consciousness has had active remorse around the issue and has offered correction. Second, you won't have to go back to that event in your dreams, which allows you to go to more positive and interesting aspects of your inner world.

Then, as you drift off to sleep, count from 9 to 1 as you repeat to yourself *I will remember my dreams.* When you awaken in the morning, try not to move. As you're drifting between the sleeping state and your waking state, that's when you can best remember your dreams. Hold them firmly in your consciousness as you become fully awake, after which it's a good idea to write them down. You will notice that although you remember a dream very well upon awakening, a few hours later you don't remember anything anymore. This is because it's a very different level of consciousness, and when in a daytime mode you are not at all in the same space. Thus it's more difficult to remember your dreams. But if they've been written down in your dream journal, you can come back to them.

In time, as you read back on this, you will understand many things. This is a very good practice. At this point advanced practitioners can move on to lucid dreaming; then to looking at their hands in the dream; and then to traveling in the dream to specific places. When you have accomplished all of this, only then will you be ready to start healing in the dreamtime.

The Herkimer diamond, which will be presented in the next part of the book, is the best stone to use for working the dreamtime. After you have purified, energized, and established a relationship with this crystal, you can begin sleeping with it. It will travel with you into the dreamtime, protect you, and help you remember your dreams. Programming your Herkimer before you sleep with it will make it more effective. As with all things, this needs practice. The first time you sit at a piano you won't be a virtuoso. You need practice. The same here.

Part 5

The Stones and Their Properties

There are a variety of stones that we use in the Native American tradition of crystal healing, but not as many as you would likely find in most books on this subject, as we Native peoples were limited historically to what we found in North America with limited mining technology. I have added a few other stones to this section, as I have a long experience with crystal healing and I have experimented for many years with stones that come from other traditions as well. However, the only stones and crystals you will read about in this book are those that have been extensively researched and experienced and that have proven their effectiveness over time with my many clients. This is the advantage we have when calling on ancient tradition. Generation after generation of healers have added their experience to the body of knowledge and have passed this on to the next generation. The most important stones are those of the quartz family, and we will soon explain why.

What creates this world is Spirit. All energy that comes into our world and manifests as matter does so through specific light frequencies. These light frequencies are produced by the creative mental emissions of those souls who assist Creator mind in the creation of worlds. As the first manifestations of Spirit come out of the void, they have geometrical shapes. These geometrical shapes are also vibration, and vibration, as it dances into the world, densifies and becomes matter, substance, atoms, and then molecules, which organize themselves according to their various geometrical shapes. As matter and substance evolve into higher and higher vibrations, it becomes sound, and then at an even higher vibration it becomes light of different colors. The color red is the slowest vibration, thus the densest; violet is the highest vibration, the fastest. From there it goes on to X-rays and gamma rays and cosmic rays and still higher vibrations as the light of creation continues to shine through creation.

One of the most important things to understand is that it's the color of the stone that influences its energy the most. Thus even the same kind of mineral substance will have different effects depending on its color. Any pure substance like pure corundum or pure beryl or pure quartz will be clear, translucent, with no color. It's the different impurities in a mineral substance, called *inclusions* in gemology, that give it its color. For example, if you have magnesium as an inclusion in quartz it will give it a violet color and we call it *amethyst*. In the same way, if you have certain inclusions in corundum it is called *sapphire*, and with other inclusions it is called *ruby*. Although they are the same mineral substance, corundum, these two stones have completely different energy. The same thing with beryl: with certain inclusions it's called *emerald* and with other inclusions it's called *aquamarine*. Thus, the color also changes the name of the stone as well as its primary function in crystal therapy.

We will examine the different types of crystals according to their color. Some of the crystals mentioned in this book have two or more colors. When they have more than one color they are organized according to their predominant color. Otherwise such stones are found under the section "Multicolored Crystals."

Clear Light Crystals

The notion of clear light, clear crystal, is very important. Clear indicates that it can transmit and transform all energies. It is neutral. You need this neutrality to be able to work well with people. Thus the clear, transparent to translucent quartz crystal can be programmed with anything as it is neutral and clear. It is the only crystal that you can bring through the whole energy field of another person from head to feet. Doing this with any other crystal, especially colored crystals, can be harmful. The natural, clear, transparent quartz crystal is beneficial for the etheric web of all humans. It can be used in agriculture and in many other ways as well. In fact, this is the material used to make computer chips. It's everywhere!

The clear quartz crystal is the most important crystal you will ever work with. It applies to all types of healing. The etheric web that surrounds a crystal and that also surrounds the human body have the same structure. They are knitted together in hexagons, the same weave that you will see in the lattices of a beehive. The wax hexagon lattices where bees store their honey and hatch other bees is similar to your etheric web and similar to the molecular structure of a quartz crystal. The element with which quartz is made, silica, is the most common mineral on the planet. Combine it with oxygen and you have quartz. When these two flower, manifesting as a specific crystal, we have a personality.

Thus, when you begin working with crystals you must begin with a clear quartz crystal. The size of the crystal is not important at this stage. It can be small or large, as size does not affect the energy it emits. What is important is that it is a single crystal and not a cluster. Clusters are important, of course; clusters are the kind of crystal you want to put on your altar. But as you begin working with crystals you will want to begin sharpening your perception of the specific life and personality of that crystal. Yes, every crystal has a specific personality! In a cluster there are so many crystals all joined together that you cannot make out any specifics. Because you are beginning to establish a specific relationship with the mineral world you need to be able to access your perception of a crystal's personality, and this is only possible with a single crystal. This is, of course, true for all crystals.

CLEAR QUARTZ CRYSTAL

A clear quartz crystal vibrates at a very high frequency. It's a being of light and fire that is especially well-suited to help us evolve and heal. Through our harmonic resonance with quartz we are led to evolve into higher energies and clearer perceptions. Change is guaranteed, but sometimes lots of change can be difficult. Our resistance to change can create difficult circumstances, lessons, and challenges in life. Be careful and slow in your work with crystals.

Energies, emotions, or entities that are thick, heavy, wicked, or hurtful cannot pass through a clear quartz crystal because that which is pure light is contrary to darkness. Likewise, all that is hatred, jealousy, envy, anger, and so on cannot pass through a clear quartz crystal. The light of the crystal entity thus constitutes a form of protection that repels any psychic attack, aberration, negative emotion, energy, or force that is harmful and/or contrary to your electromagnetic field. For this reason we use clear crystal quartz for protection. It is the best stone to help us repel other people's stray or discordant energies.

This is especially important once you start walking the spiritual path. In the beginning of training with crystals we cannot control our energy very well and our etheric web is not always tight and firm. Thus as we work on cultivating empathy in order to better feel the energy of crystals and the energy of other people we're trying to help, we often receive impressions and energies that we do not want. Empathy is perfect when working with a client, but a hindrance when walking down the street. Beginners sometimes pick up a passerby's headache or nausea without knowing what happened. As a healing practitioner working with energy you are very susceptible to picking up all kinds of energy.

To protect against these problems we use a quartz crystal. We wear the crystal at what is called the spiritual plexus. This is at the point of the sternum where the sternum ends, between the heart plexus and the solar plexus, just above the stomach. This area is also called the *point of vulnerability*. This is where we receive many impressions and energies. If you have someone coming toward you with anger, you might feel this center tightening up and clenching. This is our most sensitive area when it comes to perceiving energies on a physical level. This is where that clear quartz crystal will be useful in protecting you from outside influences, especially in the first years of spiritual practice as you become more sensitive to the energy of others and more perceptive, more empathic. At this stage you have not yet learned how to turn this ability off. Thus wearing a quartz crystal as protection is advisable. This should be a natural, uncut, clear quartz crystal with one point aiming toward the ground and the other extremity open. By other extremity open we mean that the way the crystal is mounted on the piece of jewelry does not obstruct the other end of the crystal, the one opposed to the point (see plate 4). This is so that the crystal can breathe through its whole length. It will ground the energy into the earth if something comes through that is not appropriate for your energy field, and it will take in fresh energy from the unobstructed other end. If you wear a crystal with the point upward, it will tend to accumulate energy in your throat center. You will feel your throat dry up and sometimes have difficulty speaking. Moreover, you will tend to retain undesirable energies, as they can no longer easily anchor into the ground, where their effects are neutralized. Thus both ends of the crystal must be kept open. The attachment must be around the length of the crystal; in this way the crystal will be able to breathe properly.

Another way that a clear quartz protects us is that it produces light, and light always repels darkness. It also amplifies your etheric energy, thus repelling everything contrary to your electromagnetic field. One of the characteristics of clear quartz crystal is its light refraction index, which is 1.55, meaning that as light travels through the crystal it is bent at an angle of 1.55. Thus the crystal will be more effective when worn outside one's clothing rather than beneath the clothing. It works with light and refracts light, thus this is added protection for your etheric web and your sensitivity.

Teaching Story

Many years ago I was assisted at a large wellness expo by one of our beginning students. As usual in these events there were many people stopping by our booth to look at our wares—our crystals, books, and music. After a few hours this person became overwhelmed by the energies of so many people passing in front of the booth. She had to go outside to renew herself. As time went on, she had to go outside more frequently. This was annoying, and so I decided to help her by taking a crystal pendant from the booth and putting it around her neck. From that time on she was able to go for several hours without a break throughout the weekend. I could take a break and leave her at our booth without worrying that she would lose her focus. As her etheric web was amplified by the quartz pendant, it allowed for more comfort, as she was now more impervious to any negative energies emanating from the crowd.

You will also notice, if you find an appropriate quartz pendant, that this protection feels good when working with people you don't know. It will allow you to feel more relaxed and comfortable. This is especially true if you are a naturally sensitive person. If you're in public places all day, you will feel less exhausted. Your etheric web, amplified by the quartz, will immediately repel that which is contrary to your energy patterns and help reduce the stress we sometimes feel in public places.

One of the qualities of a quartz crystal is its ability to attract positive ions and release beneficial negative ions. After a time its energy field can become saturated with positive ions and it will need a saltwater bath to be able to continue doing its work. Passing it through saltwater for a few seconds will sufficiently clear its energy field for it to continue to attract positive ions and release negative ions.

The crystal you wear for protection must be purified at the end of the day, every day, for at least twenty minutes. You must also try to prevent other people from touching it. Curious people might be attracted and want to look at it closer. When they do this out of curiosity, their hand will transmit a positive ion charge onto the crystal. This will saturate its electromagnetic field and make it less effective. If this happens, purify it for a few seconds by moving it through saltwater.

Faults or cracks within certain crystals may create the appearance of rainbows. These rainbows are very beautiful and are also said to augment the crystal's capacity for amplifying intention. Rainbows have a very special significance in Native American lore. They often come when we do ceremony in a proper manner. This is nature saying that it has heard our prayers. One clear light shining on a cloud of water crystals creates rainbows in the sky. Such beauty reflects the order and harmony of the universe. Thus, when rainbows appear in crystals, we say that they amplify the innate perfection of the intentions programmed into the crystal.

Another benefit of working with quartz crystals is their ability to mend tears and holes in our etheric web. The etheric web is our first line of defense against harmful energies as well as infections of viruses and bacteria. Many things can create disharmony—tears, holes, and other negative influence—in our etheric web. Drugs, traumatic experiences, smoking, alcohol, being intentionally evil, electromagnetic pollution, and so forth—all of these can create problems in one's etheric web. There are many imbalances a person might have in their electromagnetic field. Some places in the web may be denser, others thinner. The etheric web can even be upside-down or off to the side, not aligned with the physical body. In this case the person will feel ill at ease and unbalanced. As a quartz crystal has the same molecular energetic structure as our etheric web, it will automatically begin to heal the problems that may appear in the etheric web. Just carrying a quartz crystal around in your pocket or wearing it will begin this process. There are, of course, many other ways to amplify this process when you are working with crystals; in chapter 13 we saw a powerful way to do so with the laying-on of hands.

All clear quartz crystals vibrate to their own specific tone or frequency. This may not be in harmony with your own basic tone, as we each vibrate at a precise frequency. One of the ways you can find your basic tone is to sing the first note that comes to you when you wake up in the morning and write it down. Repeat this experiment every morning for a week. You will find that the same note reoccurs. This is your fundamental tone. Each quartz crystal also sings a specific frequency. When she was young, one of my elders had to find a crystal that had been buried in the woods as part of her training. She would listen for the sound and would find the crystal in the woods. You can also learn to hear crystals sing! They each give out a beauteous sound that is a prayer that enhances creation. Nevertheless, it sometimes happens that your basic, fundamental tone and that of the crystal strike a dissonant chord. If you vibrate on the note C and your quartz crystal vibrates on F sharp, this interval is dissonant. This dissonance between you and the crystal can cause unease, nausea, or even dizziness. This does not mean that the crystal has bad energy. There is only incompatibility. If this occurs you can give the crystal to another person who may be more in tune with it. You could also use it in a way in which you are not in its immediate vicinity.

You should never pass a colored crystal through someone's entire electromagnetic field unless you really know what you're doing. Only clear quartz crystals can be passed right through another person's entire electromagnetic field. We call this a *crystal bath,* since it clears the person's field of positive ions and supplies beneficial negative ions. Certain other crystals can be used locally at precise points on the body, but it is only with a clear quartz crystal that you can work in complete safety through the whole etheric web, from head to toe.

When a clear quartz crystal is larger than your two fists put together it is called a *generator.* It's too big to be a handheld healing crystal, but it can be put to work amplifying intentions and thought forms as it sits in its special resting place.

So let's review this very important information on the clear quartz crystal: Clear quartz is the crystal best adapted to our human energy. Surrounding us is an electromagnetic energy field called the *etheric web,* the first energy field around our body. This field has a hexagonal molecular structure like bees' alveolus, that is, each molecule of this energy body has six sides. The quartz crystal's electromagnetic field and its molecules are also hexagonal. For this reason it is well-adapted to the human body. Also, it's no coincidence that clear quartz is the one crystal most frequently found on our planet. About 65 percent of the mineral substance of which the earth is composed is silica. The quartz molecule is 2 atoms of oxygen for 1 atom of silica. Thus, the clear quartz crystal is the most important crystal for our crystal healing modalities.

DIAMOND

Of all the crystals and stones, diamond is at the summit (see plate 5). It has attained a high level of evolution and as such is a potent symbol of eternity, immortality, fidelity, the source of all life, the one, the primordial intelligence that governs the world. What makes this stone so special is that it's the only crystal made of only one substance, which is carbon. Its crystalline molecular structure is cubic, a very stable and balanced form. It is also the hardest of all the stones, a 10 on the Mohs scale. The clear diamond will reflect all the colors of the rainbow. We find different colors in diamonds: steel gray, white, blue, yellow, orange, red, green, pink, as well as purple, brown, and black.

Diamond is a very powerful amplifier. I've noticed that instinctively women will wear their diamond engagement ring only on special occasions, while the rest of the time they will wear their wedding band, which is a plainer ornament. This intuition is correct. Diamond should only be worn for special occasions—for ceremony, meditation, and at those times when our energy and focus are strong and pure. We want the diamond to amplify only the good things, and to wear one daily would not be a judicious use of its powerful amplifying energy.

And then, of course, there's the diamond as a symbol. This is why diamonds are on wedding rings—because they symbolize the eternal bond and fidelity that two lovers vow to each other. It is a fact that many couples find themselves together over and over again, from lifetime to lifetime. We know when we've found our soul mate; this is the person with whom we have had an eternal relationship. Thus, the diamond.

As diamonds are very expensive stones, I've rarely seen them used for anything other than jewelry. I personally have never used diamond in crystal therapy.

Clear diamonds are often used in conjunction with other stones. For example, tiny diamonds arranged around an emerald will amplify the work the emerald is going to do. This is true of any other stone as long as the diamond is clear. Otherwise, for colored diamonds, consult the section on what colored stones can be used together ("Simple Practices for Crystal Healing" in chapter 11).

HERKIMER DIAMOND

The Herkimer, often called the *Herkimer diamond* because of Herkimer County, in New York State, where they are found, is not a diamond but is in the quartz family. It's a clear, sometimes a bit smoky quartz crystal with two points that are opposed to each other (see plate 6). When a crystal has two points opposed to each other at 180 degrees this is called a *bitermination*. However, unlike other biterminated quartz crystals, the Herkimer is slightly stockier and harder. Quartz crystals have a hardness of 7, while the Herkimer has on some faces a hardness of 7.5.

Herkimer is the best stone for those who wish to do dreamwork, an important practice in many traditions. Dreams are considered real and important in the everyday life of indigenous cultures all over the planet. Herkimer does several things in this respect:

- It helps us remember our dreams.
- We become more conscious of our dream state and can enter into a lucid dreaming state more easily.
- If we are in right relationship with the Herkimer it will travel with us and protect us in the dreamtime.
- It harmonizes our energy field, making the transition from sleeping, dreaming, and being awake easier.
- At the beginning of using it the Herkimer might send us to the antipodes of our habits while in the dream world; in other words, those who dream a lot will dream little, and those who dream little will dream a lot. Thereafter, this phenomenon will fade away.

The Herkimer favors transitions. It can be used, for example, during childbirth. The birthing mother will hold two Herkimers, one in each hand, making it easier to let go of the child she has held for nine months. It also helps with the ultimate transition, the passage of death. Some people cling to their life when it is obviously over or have a fear of death, thus undergoing unnecessary suffering. Just having a Herkimer on the bed close to the person is usually sufficient. Of course, there are many ceremonies to help someone in these moments of evolution and transition to the luminous world. Yet modern society is ignorant of them, and the major religions have lost the magic that makes these rituals effective. Thus communing with a crystal that has seen millennia can be useful in these circumstances.

Those who wish to travel out of body will find Herkimer useful. It's used in shamanic journeying and what is incorrectly called *astral traveling*. The right way to describe this is to say you are traveling in your body of light.

Herkimer is not a stone to carry around with you, since it tends to make us vaporous, lightheaded, and distracted. It can even be really dangerous in certain circumstances, such as when we drive a car. No jewelry made of this stone should be worn daily, except for sleep, for work with life transitions, or for meditation. It is also possible to overdose on Herkimer essence, so be careful! The side effects could cause you to walk around in a daze and be in the wrong place at the wrong time.

Crystals of the Red Ray

The red ray is stimulating and energizing and corresponds to the first energy center at the base of the spine. Red is the color of passion, love, and vital life-force energy. Red stimulates and strengthens the constructive energies of the body. It can also give instantaneous energy. Because it is such a strong color, always harmonize with green or blue after having a session with the color red.

GARNET

There are several kinds of garnet, but this only refers to garnets of the red ray. Garnet is a very special stone as it needs to be cut and polished to liberate its energy (see plate 7). As far as I know it's the only stone that must be cut and polished before it liberates its energy. Stones that have been tumbled and beaded to make necklaces also work well. They gain even better color and energy when they are cut as gems. Garnet is a deep, dark red and works in a softer way than ruby. We most often work with garnet before going to ruby as a gentler approach to the red ray. Garnet is helpful when working with the endocrine system, anemia, mononucleosis, and similar diseases.

According to OhShinnàh Fastwolf, garnet is also a mystery stone. In the Apache tradition of the warrior shamans, garnet was used to work the time-between. The time-between is a special light that happens at dawn before the sun rises and at dusk after the sun has set but there is still light in the sky. This is the "time-between," sometimes called twilight, when the crack between the worlds is open. It is a very special time when shamans of her tradition would practice interdimensional travel. This is interesting as it explains how for many years the very well-known, well-documented Apache shaman-warrior Geronimo could attack and evade five thousand American troops, three thousand Mexican soldiers, and thirty-six Indian scouts and never be caught or lose a battle—and all this with fewer than thirty-five warriors. OhShinnàh, who followed the same shaman-warrior training, mentioned that the stone used to teleport during the time-between was red garnet.

I'd like to take this opportunity to stress the fact that when people live close to nature and gather their sustenance directly from nature they develop incredible gifts that don't seem to emerge in civilized life. This is very telling and well-documented. Vine Deloria Jr., that great Native American thinker and author, wrote a book on the incredible feats the European colonizers observed when they first encountered and shared with First Nations peoples.* They could not understand what they were seeing, as it went against all they knew, yet they did document it for posterity. I've seen this also, as I've shared and trained with shamans all of my adult life. Yet it's nothing compared to what people in traditional indigenous communities living in nature in earlier times

---

*Vine Deloria Jr., *The World We Used to Live In: Remembering the Powers of the Medicine Men*. Golden, Co.: Fulcrum Publishing, 2006.

developed. I explain and demonstrate the reasons for this in my book *The Philosophy of Nature*. To put it simply: Nature is Great Spirit's school, where there are no lies and the fundamentals of the universe are all there for our understanding. When living in unity and harmony with nature, we develop a lot more than is possible in an artificial, civilized lifestyle. The reasons for this are easy to understand—just think about it. Compare the amount of sensory stimuli a developing child will experience in nature as opposed to what one encounters in a classroom.

RED CORAL

Red coral participates in three different natural kingdoms. It grows through the contributions of the small critters that create it; it looks and breathes like a plant or a small tree; and what remains after it's been created is very much like a mineral substance (see plate 8). We consider it a spirit that combines all three natural families, animal, plant, and mineral, to build a viable, strong ecosystem. As such it's a unique life form and should be strongly protected. It will help with our own ecosystem. For Native American peoples and also for the Tibetan people whom we consider close relatives to our race, red coral symbolizes the vital life force. It is used as a symbol of the vital force in jewelry and is most often combined with a blue-green stone like turquoise. Although there is a canceling out of colors here, this is not a problem for two reasons. First, turquoise and coral do not act as crystals do, as their internal structure is not crystalline. They act as symbols, a completely different approach that is quite effective.

Red coral can be used to stimulate the regrowth of bone cells. To do this, swing a piece of red coral in a back-and-forth movement in the electromagnetic field, following the length of the bone where the reformation of bone mass needs to occur. Do this for two to five minutes, repeating two to four times times a day. This method is used with the complement of azurite, which is used after using red coral to reduce inflammation. If there is pain, we can begin with azurite and then go to red coral, coming back to azurite afterward.

I once healed a bad fracture in my arm, and what happened is a good illustration of what we can do with red coral. I had a really bad fall that needed two metal pins to hold the bones of my forearm in the right place for the time it needed to heal. Knowing that I could accelerate the healing with red coral, I tried to convince the doctor who saw me to schedule my return and evaluation to remove the pins at three weeks rather than the six weeks he prescribed. He was very adamant about it, but I finally succeeded in getting an evaluation at four weeks, but it came too late. The X-ray showed complete healing. In fact, the healing was so thorough that when they removed the cast they discovered that the skin had grown over the edges of the pins. That surprised them. They had to cut open the skin, but when they tried pulling on the pins, the bones had grown so firmly around them that they couldn't get them out. They had to go to another department to get a bigger set of pliers, and it took two people to pull the pins out! Doctors often think they know it all. On this occasion I proved them wrong!

Red coral is also used for bone cancer and osteomyelitis. Always use red coral to promote the growth of healthy bone cells and azurite to control the pain. We once had a complete recovery, within five weeks, of a young girl with severe osteomyelitis. Her doctors, after three operations in which they had tried scraping the inflammation off the bone in her left leg without results, were considering amputation. She came for healing five times, once a week, and on the third meeting she was walking without her crutches and had this really wonderful smile that completely lit up the room. One of the treatments I recommended that she administer to herself several times a day during that month was the red coral and azurite treatment for rebuilding bones described above.

ROSE QUARTZ

This stone is a microcrystalline pink-colored quartz. Some clusters of tiny rose quartz crystals do exist but are rare. Most are microcrystalline and are most often tumbled or cut and polished in different forms. The egg shape or heart shape are favorites (see plate 9). Rose quartz is associated with the heart center and the red ray. Rose is a mix of red and white; this is why rose quartz is considerably softer and easier to use than other red stones. It's symbolic of compassion, unconditional universal love, empathy, and understanding. It's prescribed for all heart problems (whether physical or emotional), heartbreak, or heart attack. It will help calm, console, appease, and nurture the heart.

As such rose quartz has proven useful countless times with babies who seem to have no end to their crying. It often calms them and restores their sense of security and well-being. Of course, we are careful to give them a polished piece that is too big to swallow, as all babies instinctively put everything in their mouths. We have also had good results in calming hyperactive children with rose quartz.

This is one of most useful stones for our modern age. Our emotions are being denied by a hard, asphalt-paved world full of institutionalized bullies, corruption, injustice, and inequalities. Rose quartz does a lot to make it easier for those who are too sensitive to the everyday onslaught of emotional challenges experienced today.

RUBY

Ruby is both the king and the queen of the red ray.* It is a brighter red than what we find in garnet. It too is a corundum and a very hard stone, 9 on the Mohs scale. Ruby gives instantaneous energy.

We use ruby to rebuild, to give primordial vital energy needed to strengthen and fortify the body. As such it's also very useful for all degenerative diseases, including cancer, multiple sclerosis, Parkinson's disease, and so forth. Even the cheaper, opaque varieties of ruby are useful and powerful (see plate 10). We use them to purify the blood of toxins and

---

*There are orientations to the spirals in crystal lattices. We say if turning clockwise, it is solar, thus masculine. If turning counterclockwise, it is terrestrial, thus feminine. Some stones, such as ruby, have both.

negative emotions. Ruby can be used to strengthen the blood when a person is afflicted with anemia and similar diseases. For all these long-term treatments it's better to start with garnet and then go to ruby.

As with garnet, we always want to rebalance a ruby treatment with a blue or green stone. The red ray is very powerful and calls on the energies of the body, on its inner reserves. Thus the need to balance out with green or blue after treatment. Let's take the example of anemia. You might begin with garnet for a week and then go to ruby for a few weeks or until you get good results. When the person comes back to a healthy body, then do a week on emerald.

Ruby symbolizes unconditional universal love, a love that gives itself freely without thought for oneself. A powerful demonstration of this in First Nations traditions is the Sun Dance ceremony, where the men give their blood and suffering so the people can be healthy and live long and happy lives. Jesus's dying on the cross to absolve the sins of the world is another example. As we're in the Christian world we can also mention that the Pope wears a ruby ring as a symbol of his service to the people.

It is said that since ruby symbolizes universal, unconditional love and compassion, it will react negatively to people who are egoistic and selfish; the karmic return will be amplified by the ruby. On the opposite spectrum, ruby will help a person to be of service to others, to be generous, to be helpful, and to offer love, compassion, and understanding to others and oneself.

Ruby essence is used to remain awake on long drives or when we need to sustain our attention and concentration when tired. We must be careful, though, as it can be overdosed, as it calls on the body's reserves.

Crystals of the Orange Ray

Orange revitalizes and stimulates; it's a warm, harmonizing color associated with the second energy center or chakra. This color works with the digestive system and recharges the etheric web. It also has an impact on the throat center because of that center's correspondence with the second chakra.

CARNELIAN

This beautiful orange member of the agate family is very useful and really affordable, making it a stone we use a lot (see plate 11).

Carnelian is very useful for all speech impediments when these problems originate in the energy center located at the throat. Stuttering, difficulty expressing oneself, the inability to say important things when the time is right for them to be said, and similar problems in self-expression will be alleviated when carnelian is worn close to the throat center. This is a unique trait of carnelian—that it needs to be worn close to the afflicted area, namely, the throat center. Most crystals and gems can be worn or carried anywhere on the body and the etheric web will transmit the energy where it needs to go. Carnelian needs to be worn close to the throat or around the neck. A string of round beads is the perfect piece of jewelry for this and is beautiful and pleasant to wear.

One of carnelian's most important contributions is recharging the etheric web. There are a great many problems today with the balancing of the etheric web. Because of the proliferation of electromagnetic pollution, artificial lifestyles far from nature, and sheer stress, our modern world has a huge negative impact on the etheric web. Traumatic events and addictions can also cause imbalances, tears, and holes in the etheric web. Carnelian will recharge the etheric web, while quartz crystal will help rebalance and mend tears and holes.

When you feel a person's etheric web around their physical body with your hands, you'll often notice that it is not uniform in size all around the body as it should be. This is very revealing and indicates many things to the advanced practitioner. The first step in all energy treatments is to rebalance this energy field (see chapter 12, "Preparing for Hands-On Energy Healing," for this technique). Carnelian is the first stone one would try when treating low energy, great fatigue, and depression. If not sufficient, then go to the red stones.

CITRINE

Let's now take a look at this member of the quartz family and analyze its properties in order to learn how to work with it properly. First we must distinguish between the two types of citrine: Madeira citrine and golden citrine (see plate 12). Madeira citrine is orangish brown and belongs to the orange ray. It helps with the digestive system. Golden citrine has a yellow color and belongs to the yellow ray. It regulates the nervous system.

Citrine is also called *coyote stone*. In Native American mythology, the coyote is a beast who plays tricks on us, forcing us to learn despite our bitter resistance. This outrageous trickster has countless stories of his misadventures in trying to impose his egocentric desires on all who come within his reach, only to find himself (and those around him!) under a pile of shit. Great fun, yet powerful teachings for all in the community.

Citrine is used for those who are the most resistant to treatment, as well as for people who are stubborn and have fixed realities. Indeed, the person who comes in contact with the vibrations of citrine tends to open up to higher vibrations, to spiritual realities that he or she is not normally used to recognizing. To the businessman struggling with a fixed reality, I suggest his wife offer him a tiepin decorated with citrine that he can wear. It's not necessary to tell him why; her intention, amplified by the crystal, will be enough to bring about a change. She will have played a little coyote trick on him.

There was a time when I began teaching crystal healing a long time ago when these traditional healing methods were still very much under the radar and not well known, when several women students bought small citrine clusters from me. They were encountering fierce resistance from their husbands, who thought all this crystal healing stuff to be hogwash! They programmed the clusters for their husbands and put them on the bedside table to appear as decorations. They were all very happy with the results. One student told me her husband sold his business and was now working at the alternative health center they created together. The women played coyote tricks on their husbands, and it worked wonders!

This stone stimulates the mental and spiritual bodies and eliminates toxins in the lower energy centers. It helps open us to higher realities on the spiritual level. In addition, it clears the energy field of densities that may exist there. We can sometimes see brownish areas in people's electromagnetic field, reflecting traumatic relationships that the person has experienced in their lifetime. Citrine can disperse these densities. Most so-called psychosomatic illnesses have these symptoms. Asthma is a good example of a psychosomatic illness that responds very well to the use of citrine.

Citrine is also used for trauma in general. Let's take the case of a man who has been in a car accident and who experienced the death of his wife and child in that accident. He absolutely must come in contact with his grief, with everything he has just lost. He must feel it and express it. Yet the shock is sometimes so terrible that all expression is blocked. The experience becomes repressed, buried in the depths of consciousness because it is too painful. In this case, if no release of grief takes place, the man will keep this in his electromagnetic field. This trauma will later express itself in an inopportune moment or will promote the development of various pathologies. It is important that the affected person be able to cry, to scream, to express what he feels, otherwise he will accumulate pain, and without any purification this can be very harmful. It would be good for such a person to hold a piece of citrine in his hand. You can help them by visualizing the light of the citrine and emitting it. In cases of severe trauma, citrine is an excellent stone to release the accumulation of negative emotions in the etheric body. It helps dispel the dark, heavy energies in the etheric web and helps with the expression of heavy emotions, whether recent or ancient.

It should be remembered that all negative emotions have a positive aspect. Hate will reveal love and compassion; grief will reveal courage; anger will reveal integrative wisdom; angst will reveal consideration for others; fear will reveal ageless understanding. To reveal that other aspect of the negative emotion, we call on the energy of water. Emotions have to flow. Flowing in this case means expressing them—crying, screaming, laughing, singing, groaning, etc. Otherwise they get stuck in the negative aspect and can create emotional problems, and in time, physical pathologies. This is why they are sometimes called *psychosomatic* diseases.

When working with citrine, always begin with Madeira citrine, the orange ray. When the person has evolved and the treatment is well underway, then you go to golden citrine, to the yellow ray. This is the best way to work with these wonderful crystals.

Crystal of the Yellow Ray

Yellow is the fastest vibration in the warm color spectrum, and an even higher vibrancy is the color gold. Yellow gives energy like the other warm colors, but on a higher, more subtle vibratory level. This ray corresponds to the solar plexus and works with the nervous system and the brain.

TOPAZ

There are several kinds of topaz, a beryl in mineral classification. There are blue, smoky, yellow, and golden beryls, which are all called topaz. But as our tradition has only the memory of working with yellow and golden topaz (see plate 13), the following information concerns only these varieties.

This stone makes a connection with the sun. The sun is a god for members of the mineral world, and thus this stone is said to be of the gods. It works with the intellect and the higher senses as a strengthening ray that boosts the higher frequencies of emotional and mental expression. It's conducive to all projects and activities that benefit beings. Singers, artists, writers, and other creative people will enjoy the inspiration it gives them. It's an energy that fills the bones with the high vibration that illuminates one's vital energy. It reveals truth that comes from reality.

Reality and Truth

It's a given in the Native way that Creator spirit, the ultimate God, speaks to us constantly through his creations. We only need learn to read the great book of nature, and it takes a lifetime to do so. This is because to read this important book we need more than a mental, intellectual understanding; we need a synchronization of physical, emotional, mental, and spiritual knowing. This unity is a given when you are born in nature. As civilized beings, however, we need to learn it anew. A good way to start the journey of reading the natural world around us is to begin with the mineral kingdom. We have here a potential of knowing that comes from direct experience with a mineral, which can in turn foster a relationship and thus some form of emotional attachment. Such a relationship can bring a knowledge of Spirit through physical contact with the crystal as well as an appreciation of its energy. Thus all aspects of our being come into play when we work with the members of the mineral kingdom. This can be a happy journey, as it will lead to a better understanding of the world we live in. This is an example of the kinds of thoughts topaz can inspire. Being a complete atheist would make it impossible to train in this discipline of crystal healing, as Spirit is one of the natural dimensions of human existence. To live without it is to ignore the part of our being that belongs to Creator. Not advisable!

It's a given that yellow topaz is a magical stone. Program it to be invisible and hold it in your left hand, and you'll be surprised. Many incredible stories have been told over the years of how under impossible circumstances people have gone past dangerous situations without being noticed. It is beneficial to feel awe and wonderment. These are happy feelings that transcend daily life. Topaz is helpful in fostering these emotions. There are many stories that I've heard about the effectiveness of going unseen in difficult situations by using topaz. I mention here a well-known doctor in Quebec: a few months after he took my seminar on crystal healing he thanked me, as he could now finally go grocery shopping without being stopped every other aisle by people wanting to shake his hand.

We must explain why we have faith in these magical uses of certain stones. It may appear to be superstition, but we have repeatedly manifested the same feats time and time again. The indigenous worldview is not Cartesian; it is not considered logical or "scientific." We understand that a person's thoughts influence the world around him. In fact, quantum physics has come to the same conclusion. We find it much more interesting and real to live in a universe where magic and the mysterious are common occurrences. I would hate to live in a world that refuses the ideas of magic, of the marvelous, where the mysterious workings of nature are absent. I have with my own eyes seen extraordinary, inexplicable occurrences. On some occasions I have witnessed ordinary civilized people faced with extraordinary occurrences because of our ceremonies, but completely oblivious to what was happening. This is due to a worldview that does not account for magic. As these people cannot comprehend such things, they cannot see it—a form of cognitive blindness that might find some relief with lots of citrine and then topaz . . .

How sad to live in a world where magic no longer lives. Please understand that magic does exist, that it's a good thing to marvel at the strange, marvelous beauty and extraordinary diversity of the fabulous earth on which we live. The creation of the world and its continuation are a part of our psyche, and we can be active co-creators of these wondrous events. Allow yourself to participate in the mysteries of creation!

And to close, let us thank golden and yellow topaz, which have inspired these thoughts!

Crystals of the Green Ray

Green is the color of health and corresponds with the natural world and the heart center. A neutral color, it is stimulating yet relaxing.

When you don't know what color to use, go to green. Health is a state of balance, thus green has that vibration.

Green Stones for Stress

It's important to understand that too much stress can cause a great many health problems. A certain amount of stress is useful in situations where you need to be at peak performance, but continuous stress is very harmful. It has been found that modern people have 1500 percent more stress than generations at the beginning of the twentieth century. Our lifestyles are often equated with progress, but as far as my observations go, modern life has our health, emotional equilibrium, and mental abilities considerably decreased compared to the people living prior to industrialization. One of the foremost French ecologists, Pierre Rabhi, has said that you'll never see farmers running through their work. They are slow and relaxed in everything they do. The same is true in all aboriginal nations. Ninety-nine percent of all daily activities are conducted by Native peoples in a relaxed, happy, and gentle way. Even strenuous chores are not performed in a stressful manner. As modern life has us striving to make ends meet and depends on a constant source of money, which can disappear in an instant, we are often stressed-out. Thus, reducing stress needs to be at the forefront of research into how to better live our lives. Practicing relaxation and meditation are excellent ways to reduce stress. Having the appropriate colored crystals (green, blue, and indigo) programmed in specific places where we see them often is also very helpful.

AMAZONITE

This soft green stone is also microcrystalline. It's very calming, the stone of choice to reduce stress (see plate 14). It's also beautiful as a decoration in a natural environment or to give the sentiment of nature to indoor settings. It's not an expensive stone, at least not in the Quebec province close to where it's mined. We have several on the property where they are the most useful, close to where we work and walk, and one on the kitchen windowsill where we can look at it when doing the dishes.

BLOODSTONE/HELIOTROPE

Known by both names, this microcrystalline stone is dark green with blood-red dots and splotches on it, thus the name *bloodstone* (see plate 15). There are ancient legends in Native American lore that refer to this stone that essentially speak of a great evil force that was transformed into doing good things for the people. What was left of the wendigo monster after being transformed was bloodstone. We use it to stop bleeding. To stop the flow of blood, apply the stone directly to the wound and press firmly. It's also used for cleansing the blood of poisons. To purify poisoning, apply it to the affected part of the body. As well, it has proven its effectiveness again and again in treating venomous snake and insect bites when applied directly to the body. Bloodstone can also be used in a similar way for liver problems. Apply it to the skin above the liver.

CHRYSOCOLLA, MALACHITE, AND TURQUOISE

These stones are cyan, light blue to dark green. They work in similar ways in some repects so we will consider them together (see plates 16–18). Malachite and turquoise are not crystalline. Their structure is mostly amorphous. They don't hold intention as well as crystals do, yet they are associated with silica (the main ingredient in quartz), especially chrysocolla.

Chrysocolla and malachite will help in diluting fear accumulated in the diaphragm and solar plexus, and can actually, if you do the work of facing your fears, help them disappear altogether, including any residual physical effects. They are also effective in collaboration with other healing methods for ailments of the stomach, spleen, and pancreas complex.

They generally help with balance and equilibrium of the emotional body. They have a very reassuring and stabilizing energy.

Malachite has the particular quality of being able to communicate its energy very well through touch. Feeling this stone communicates its energy better than wearing it. It's not a very hard stone either, so it's much better to have different shapes that you can hold. Malachite beads are very nice to wear and effective when they touch the skin. One of the best shapes to be considered when working with malachite is an egg shape, which is very comfortable to hold.

Turquoise is a very spiritual stone. Although it does not have a crystalline structure, it has been used it since ancient times by many indigenous peoples to symbolize one's relationship with the sky and spirituality. It has been used extensively by Native Americans of the Southwest and by Tibetan people, who are very close in their ways to Native American peoples. As all stones are, like us, in a constant flux of evolution, there are some (also like us) that are devolving rather than evolving. Turquoise is one of the stones that does not have the same energy as it used to have.

In the traditions of the Tibetan and Native American peoples, when we receive a turquoise as a gift, especially from a friend or a family member, this communicates a very strong protection energy. Any old jewelry that you may have received as a gift will still have this vibration. We are more inclined today to go toward chrysocolla than turquoise to find the attributes that were once communicated by turquoise. The advantage of chrysocolla is that it does have a microcrystalline structure. Although some chrysocolla specimens are very soft, 2 to 3 on the Mohs scale, we are finding harder and harder deposits that go up to 6, making it hard enough for jewelry. It has a beautiful deep blue-green color. It is often mistaken for turquoise, but its energy puts it on a different level. I suspect this stone will continue to evolve in eons to come.

Chrysocolla and malachite can be used to dispel the physical effects of fear that have lodged in the solar plexus. One must not react to fear. When you see fear, don't identify with it; simply affirm "I am not this fear" and leave it to follow its own course. Consider that it does not belong to you, thus there is no need to identify with it. (More teachings on fear when we speak of aquamarine.)

Malachite is very harmonious in family settings. It brings harmony and peace to the household. Although crystals should not be used for talking circles* the way talking sticks or feathers are used, an exception can be made for family talking circles using a malachite egg, as it is not crystalline.

CHRYSOPRASE

Chrysoprase is a wonderful microcrystalline stone, soft and almost dreamlike (see plate 19). It's a light green, the color of a green apple, often containing different shades of green. It has a generous, amicable feeling and is used mostly for anchoring the mental body to reality. To do this it works through the optic nerve, thus to obtain this effect we need to look at it. So a pendant won't be very helpful; we rather use it as a ring or a bracelet, or have it sitting on a desk or someplace where we can look at it often.

Mental problems that have improved with this stone are neurosis, psychosis, schizophrenia, and all illusions of the mind that display a distorted sense of reality.

EMERALD

The king and queen of the green stones, emerald, is also one of the most expensive (see plate 20). Like the other green stones, emerald will help with balance and equilibrium. It works with the heart and circulatory system. We use it to improve one's equanimity on an emotional level and for when there is a need for harmony in our relationships. It is known to help shamans with their communication with devas and other nature spirits. It is excellent for rebalancing after using ruby or garnet or other stones of the red ray in therapy.

Emerald will inspire you and fill you with a feeling of unconditional

---

*I write more about talking circles in my book *Le Cercle de Toutes nos Relations* (written in French). Quebec: Éditions Le Dauphin Blanc, 2017.

appreciation for the gift of life in all its diversity. Its vibration is beneficial for tired nerves and when you are in a general state of fatigue. It helps balance the level of glucose in the blood. Emerald is a very beneficial stone for all those who work as caregivers or healers. Health is a state of balance. Healers seek to help those who consult them attain this balance in their lives.

Balance is an act whereby we have time for rest, sleep, exercise, work, quiet time, and for joyful and meaningful relationships. In our current busy, stressful lifestyles, where it's often difficult to make ends meet, this is a challenge. It's good to call on emerald's soothing and energizing rays.

GREEN JASPER

Green jasper is the best stone for those who wish to harmonize with nature (see plate 21). Being at one with the world we live in is very important. When understanding the damage caused by our artificial, synthetic way of life, we see a great benefit from having a piece of green jasper with us. It's a very pleasant stone that attracts strong telluric energy. Some people find it useful for grounding.

GREEN TOURMALINE

This stone harmonizes, equalizes, balances, and soothes (see plate 22). It's used for problems of the heart and for blood circulation. It assists in dissolving blood clots and can be used to treat both low and high blood pressure. It has a very high energy and frequency. Some people use it to amplify clairvoyance, intuition, and other gifts of Spirit. It's such a beautiful stone, often found in crystal form—one of my favorite crystals.

JADE

The word *jade* commonly refers to two different minerals: nephrite, a silicate of calcium and magnesium, and jadeite, a silicate of sodium and aluminum (see plate 23). Jadeite is very expensive, while nephrite is less expensive. You will find jade in all shades of green, from clear to olive and dark green; it also comes in clear brown, opalescent, orange, milky white, yellow lavender, white, black, and gray. Some varieties combine two, and some three colors. Yet it's the pale green color that is most commonly thought of when we think of jade. In Asian culture, each hue of jade has a different meaning. There are not as many uses or meanings in our culture, and we mostly work with nephrite, a close cousin of jadeite.

Jade is a very hard stone, from 6.5 to 7 in Mohs hardness. Nephrite is from 6 to 6.5. Both are very resistant and tough stones, easy to work with as jewelry.

Jade is commonly associated with spirituality in Asia, yet many other cultures also consider it a sacred mineral. Among these are the Maori people of New Zealand. Many sacred ornaments carved from jade are used by the Maori, and these ornaments acquire more and more energy as they are handed down from one generation to the next.

Jade is symbolic of eternity, everlasting beauty, steadfastness, resilience, meditation, and spirituality. Because of this symbolism, jade is the stone of choice for those who work in palliative care.

At some point in their lives all people on a spiritual path are called to accompany people leaving this physical world behind. The soul and spirit are immortal and eternal, thus this is the aspect of being that we invoke when helping people go into their final transition with serenity. Thus, when helping people who are dying, it is helpful to wear jadeite or have a piece of jadeite for them to hold. It speaks of the immortality of the soul, and its very compact crystalline mineral structure makes it an excellent accumulator of sacred energy. It is also a good stone for integrating one's spiritual path into ordinary life. It has frequently been associated with royalty and wealth, particularly in the form of jadeite, whose translucent green qualities are prized, making it very expensive.

PERIDOT

Peridot is a very special stone as it's one of those rare gems that holds two colors. Two rays, yellow and green, are present in this lime-colored crystal (see plate 24). Due to the special influence of two colors, peridot is quite versatile and has been used in the treatment of influenza, depression, obesity, constipation, ulcers, diabetes, and prostate problems. Peridot is also one of the magical stones. It has been used since ancient times, and not only in North America but in other cultures as well, to counteract evil energies. In Europe, the exorcists of early days would have peridot mounted on gold jewelry that they would wear when helping people who were under the influence of maleficent entities. We have used it many times with children who have nightmares, with immediate results. We only need to have a peridot in the bed somewhere with the child and the bad dreams go away.

Crystals of the Blue Ray

The blue ray is electric, soothing, and relaxing. Any condition that needs to cool down, such as fever or infection, calls for blue. It is also useful for unwinding and relaxing. Blue corresponds to the throat center.

AQUAMARINE

Truth be told, with the information we have today* and in my experience of having often been called on to do this kind of work, possession of a person by an evil entity is literally impossible. Whenever someone comes to me or has been referred to me to be liberated from possession, I've found that the problem was within the psyche of that person and not from some entity. The soul takes a long time, months and years,

---

*See the books and research by Michael Newton, PhD, and the ongoing findings by the Newton Institute, www.newtoninstitute.org.

to adjust to a human body and brain. There's no room or possibility of another entity being able to remove that soul or relegate it to some corner of the mind. Yet aquamarine has been very helpful in these cases for another reason entirely: This gemstone vibrates to the frequency of truth (see plate 25). It will incite one to reveal the truth and put light on any situation where obsessions, aberrations of thought, delusions, and suchlike have clouded the psyche. Aquamarine is also very effective for reconciliation and for human relationships in general.

Over the centuries, the emphasis on evil, devils, monsters, and the the rest of the general misinformation presented by religions that try to control their flock with the fear of hell and Lucifer's evil cohorts has created an extensive imagery of maleficent beings. There are many difficult conditions of life on earth today: the extreme violence of modern bureaucratic society enforced by oppressive authorities; "justice" manipulated to serve the elite; police brutality; repression by military bodies; widespread poverty and homelessness, which is rampant in most countries today; and the general ravaging of the earth. There is a concurrent degradation of ethics, as society's values and morals are now determined by technocrats and governments, the new gods. This leads to a life perspective in which there is no life after death, perpetuating the idea that we have to take what's available now for our pleasure, as it will all be over one day. These dire conditions create traumas that impact our psyches. People are sometimes overwhelmed with fear and anxiety and need to put a name on it, hence the sense that some evil entity has taken control of our lives. This is completely illogical, yet the direct consequence of global misinformation coming from both science and religion.

The only devil here is one's fear. Of all the negative human emotions, fear is the one that causes the most harm in today's world. On a global scale it has contributed to the escalation of nuclear stockpiles that could obliterate the planet. On a personal level it prevents us from seeing with clarity the real issues in our lives and the omnipresence of the basic human qualities that are the foundation of our emotional well-being: love, peace, and joy.

Most fears are illusions. They are not based in reality. In our tradition we speak of two real fears. There is the fear of falling: We are in a very high place, on a roof, close to the edge, close to the edge of a cliff. We feel a strong need to cling to something and feel jittery all over. This is a completely natural and healthy response. Then there is the fear evoked by a sudden noise: gunshots; sirens; loud, sudden disturbances. With this there is a physiological response—we want to throw ourself down and hug the ground. This too is natural and healthy.

Our tales and teachings say that all other fears are creations of the psyche, that they don't actually exist. If you consider your soul to be an immortal, eternal entity, as all traditional spiritual wisdom schools have held since the beginning of time, nothing should cause you to fear anything or anyone. Prior to the coming of European colonizers, young warriors of the tribes would test themselves in this understanding by going to spar with the warriors of neighboring tribes. They would steal horses or go counting coup. To succeed in counting coup was the highest honor. It consisted of touching the enemy with a coup stick, a long, slender pole that did not inflict any harm, and come back unscathed. This was quite different from the warfare inflicted on Native peoples by the Europeans, who went about a genocidal campaign, killing children, women, and elders.

Fear is the worst emotion in that it hampers your evolution and attracts that which you fear. As our souls and minds have the power of creation (and invention), producing thoughts supported by this powerful emotion will nourish an energy form that can eventually attract the manifestation of that thought. Fear attracts that which you are afraid of. If you are afraid of thieves, they will come. If you fear fire, you will be a victim of it. If you are frightened of the devil, he will show himself to you in one of his myriad guises. That is because your thoughts are creative. Humans are endowed with the gift of creative thought. We have the ability to manifest many things, many inventions. All things begin as thoughts and from that point on those thoughts will attract the energies and means that will eventually manifest those thoughts.

The current "civilized" world teaches and trains people using fear as punishment for not complying, which is the mainstream way of trying to get people to do what society thinks is right. We live in a world full of fear, so it's important to learn how to dispel fear.

First, we must consider all fears other than the fear of falling and the fear of loud noises to be illusions. Then we must confront our fears. The fear beast is a real coward. If you run away from it, it will follow you like your shadow. Yet if you turn around and face it, it will run away, as it's a very fearful creature. You must look it in the face, go head-on, looking directly at it in an effort to understand where it comes from. Where did it come from? Why do I have this fear? If we look at it long enough, as it's ultimately an illusion, it will dissipate.

Teaching Story

I once had a very sympathetic man who followed one of my crystal courses. About a year later I got a phone call from him. A few months after the crystal course he was involved in a very bad accident on the Quebec Bridge leading from the north to the south shore. He spent three months in the hospital and then a month of rehabilitation at home. Lots of physiotherapy. After that he took his car and went back to work as a traveling salesman. But when he tried to go over the bridge at the same spot where he had his accident, a great fear overtook him. He hit the brakes and stopped in the middle of the bridge. This caused a great big traffic jam that took hours to dissipate. They towed his car away. The next day he tried the same thing, but with his wife beside him in the passenger seat. When he got to that exact same spot, fear overtook him again, and they had to trade places and come back home. So he called me to find out how he could overcome this fear, as he needed to go over that bridge often as part of his work. I told him that he needed to go to that bridge and walk across it on the pedestrian alley. He was to go right up to the place where he had his accident and stay there a few moments and look over the bridge, down at the water below. This second part is important, I told him, as the fear of heights is a real fear. Then, I told him, he should look at the bridge itself, at all the traffic lanes, and at his fear that came from the memory of his accident. I told him to do this seven days in a row.

A few years later, I met him by chance in a shopping mall. Happy to see him, I asked how his bridge experience went. He told me that the first time on the bridge he shook like a leaf. The next day the shaking wasn't so bad. The third day it was even less. The fourth day he hardly felt anything. He continued all the way up to seven times, finally not feeling anything on his last pedestrian stroll across the Quebec Bridge. The fear had so dissipated that the first time he took his car over the bridge he only remembered after he had gone over the bridge that he had once had a fear of that bridge. The fear had completely dissipated.

Here is another story illustrating the same principle. I had a woman come to me who was afraid of spiders. It was quite bad, as in the summertime she felt apprehensive when thinking that there were maybe spiders on the walls outside the house. Finding a spider in the house, she had to call a neighbor to get it out of the house. This is quite another type of fear, as it goes very deep into the collective unconscious, to symbols that are very profound in the primal mind. However, Europeans and Native Americans have a very different perspective on spiders. Most civilized cultures are afraid of insects, especially spiders. Native Americans consider spiders to be very important and powerful entities that work with the accumulation of knowledge and the spirit of strong, powerful, feminine energies. Thus, I could not work with this woman using live spiders. It would not have been respectful of spider mind. I had to find a different approach.

I had a room prepared where there was absolutely no light, where it was completely dark. We sat on the floor in opposite corners. I guided this woman through a visualization in which in the opposite corner of that room, close to the ceiling, there was a very small, harmless spider. The second time I had the woman visualize a slightly bigger spider who was slightly closer to her. The third time this spider was now weaving a web. And so on and so forth. On the seventh day I had her visualize big, hairy tarantulas crawling all over her body and even entering her mouth.

Afterward the woman no longer has any fear of spiders. Now, if she finds one in her house, she gathers it up on her hand and takes it outside. She has learned to respect these very important creatures of the animal world.

Aquamarine vibrates to the frequency of truth, thus in that it leads to understanding what is true and real, it will dispel fears. A therapist can use this vibration to dissipate a person's obsession with the object of her or his fear. In so doing, the reality that the person's fear is an illusion will become clear and thus will be much easier to dispel. We must learn to look at fear, not run away from it, but go toward it so that we may master it. Once we have integrated our understanding that fear is but an illusion, it will simply fall away, and we will be able to move on with life.

As our whole world has been educated with fear, we have many problems related to the illusion of fear. This makes aquamarine one of the most important stones to work with. With the help of this mineral we can help others look at their fears and liberate them from its ghastly spells. Remember, the only true fears are those of falling from a great height or a sudden intense noise. These are physical fears that are legitimate and useful. All other fears can be dissipated and cleared.

Aquamarine also carries the vibration of the element of water as its name suggests. It's a cooling stone that can be used to alleviate fevers. It can also be helpful in addressing all conditions involving the liquids in the body. It helps with relaxation and can relieve stress. It's a very beautiful gemstone that can be carried easily and will dissipate tension and nervousness.

AZURITE

Azurite is a blue, sometimes deep blue or indigo mineral that comes in many different forms, sometimes aggregate, sometimes microcrystalline (see plate 26), other times in crystal clusters.

The prime use of azurite is to relieve structural stress on the organism by facilitating movement. All pain in the bones, tendons, and ligaments is first treated with azurite. It seems to free a special energy for the human structure when passed along bones and tendons in the etheric web. Without actually touching the body we do a back-and-forth movement along the length of the specific bone or articulation affected. Usually a minute or two will suffice to reduce pain. Repeat as many times as necessary. A great many cases of tendinitis have completely disappeared within a relatively short time with this type of treatment.

Due to the porosity of certain types of azurite that leak sulphur when placed in water, we don't recommend making essences with azurite.

CELESTITE

This beautiful pale blue crystal, often found in clusters (see plate 27), is effective in treating migraines and headaches, especially when used as an essence (see "Crystal Essences," pages 151–53). As essences are completely nontoxic, containing only water, you can use them as often as you wish. Take a spoonful under the tongue and apply to the forehead and temples as well. If you have chronic migraines, consider keeping a celestite cluster near your bed. Celestite is also effective in reducing inflammation and combating infection and fevers.

DIOPTASE

Dioptase is a deep blue, often indigo, with tints of emerald green often found in small crystal clusters (see plate 28). It's useful for treating high and low blood pressure. It has also been used to help treat Parkinson's disease. It has special spiritual attributes that make it a good tool for meditation. This mineral has a hardness of 5 and three good cleavage angles. These attributes make it fragile and not the best for jewelry. Dioptase has been used extensively as a pigment, as the color is very striking and beautiful. It is a rare mineral that can be used as an ornament on meditation surfaces, altars, and healing shrines.

Crystal of the Indigo Ray

Indigo relates to self-knowledge, intuition, and wisdom. Whereas blue relaxes, indigo brings an even deeper relaxation conducive to sleep. It's used to go into deep levels of meditation, contemplation, and divination. Indigo is associated with the sixth energy center, the forehead/third eye. It's good for all the openings in your head—sinuses, ears, nose, eyes, and anything related to the lungs.

SAPPHIRE

There are several types of corundum; those that are blue and deep blue or indigo are called *sapphire* (see plate 29). Its use has been documented in Native culture, and it was also used by the oracles of ancient Greece.

Sapphire is conducive to deep states of meditation and reflection. Its color induces deep relaxation and sleep. For all introspective research, intense prayer, divination, devotional practices, and similar spiritual pursuits, sapphire is the stone of choice. It enhances all activities of a ceremonial nature and the energies of the fifth energy center at the throat. I have a silver bolo of an eagle in which the eye is a sapphire. This piece of jewelry thus invokes the energy of my totem animal, the eagle, and stimulates my ability to do my work and perform my spiritual music. This illustrates a way of using a gemstone that might give you inspiration for your own needs.

Sapphire is used to help with all afflictions of the openings in the head, thus the eyes, ears, nose, and sinuses, and closely associated with the sinuses, the lungs. Sapphire essence has been known to restore failing eyesight. Sapphire essence, like all essences (see "Crystal Essences," pages 151–53) must be made with sterile, purified water and the drops put directly in the eyes. Sapphire essence is also useful for treating insomnia. Other essences that might help with insomnia are Herkimer and celestite.

Crystal of the Violet Ray

Violet, associated with the crown center, stimulates the higher faculties of the human mind and spirit and has a calming effect on the lower energy centers. Use violet for that which needs transformation. Other uses are for helping and healing stress, nervousness, high blood pressure, epilepsy, neuralgia, and mental disorders that are not hallucinatory or schizophrenic.

AMETHYST

The amethyst crystal is the stone flower of transformation. It's associated with high spirituality and evolved beings. This stone is a quartz crystal with magnesium inclusions, which give it its violet color (see plate 30). In amethyst, the magnesium inclusions create an ultraviolet spectrum, symbolizing alchemic processes and transmutation on both the physical and spiritual levels. Thus the amethyst is sometimes known as the "flame of transmutation." It's the color of spirituality in general—not any kind of spirituality, but that of the highest evolved beings.

Amethyst is not a comfortable stone to be around if you are delving into low energies, and there are some people who just can't stand amethyst. Anyone who constantly needs grounding should not move toward this stone. This is why we avoid using amethyst with the following conditions: hyperactivity, autism, schizophrenia, and retardation. Amethyst should not be used for those who are closed-minded, fixed-reality people. By fixed reality I mean someone who has a very narrow view of reality or a closed mind. An example is the businessman who refuses to see anything outside of his vision of a materialistic world. In such cases, amethyst cannot help. It will clash with the person's vision of the world as it seeks to awaken their spirituality, and can consequently throw them off-balance. Use citrine instead. Those who are well-established in their spiritual practice and who seek to move to a higher vibrational level of perception will benefit from amethyst. It will relax or scale down the energy in the lower energy centers and boost the energy of the upper energy centers. In fact, some overeaters can use it to lower their appetite.

Amethyst is also a stone that can be used for protection when traveling. As such, it's good to program one for safe traveling and keep it in the car.

Amethyst is the stone of choice when we want to transform dependencies and addictions. One of the ways we can do this is by placing a small polished piece of amethyst under the tongue whenever we get the desire to indulge in a harmful substance. What amethyst does as the stone of transformation is to communicate to the body the message *transmute*. This will interact with the body's physiology, setting forth an impulse that will make it easier for us to take the energy that we would have given over to our addiction and replace it with a more positive activity or consumption. We use it to treat alcoholism, drug addiction, gambling, and similar problems.

It's important to understand addictions, as it's a very widespread problem today. Most people today suffer from some kind of dependency, although not everyone shows signs of losing control over their life because of them. Many will skip from one dependency to another to avoid any one of them becoming too much of a problem.

One of the reasons the problem of addiction exists is because we live in a very artificial world, far from the cycles and primary activities we would have if we were living an indigenous, close-to-nature lifestyle. We live in a world that is very repressive, where we must conform to a great many social standards that have no real beneficial qualities to them. For example, working nine to five, five days a week, all year round, does not respect the natural cycles of nature. Modern society rejects those who do not conform to this idea of reality by putting them in prisons or in psychiatric hospitals, while homeless people unable to find work or a place to live are segregated in many different ways. In truth, everyone is unique, and this should in fact be welcomed as there are infinite gifts in these unique potentials. But because of the potential for rejection and isolation if we are different, something that is felt as soon as we start our first year in school, we often perceive our unique potential as dangerous. Thus the fear of being isolated in society because we are different. When the energy to manifest our potential arises in us, especially when it runs contrary to the norms established by society, we sometimes channel it into activities that will reduce the vitality of our bodies on both the physical and emotional levels. In doing this, the energy to manifest our unique potential disappears for a time. The fear of being different, even if it's on a subconscious level, disappears. We start to relax and feel elated—that is, until our energy rebuilds and the inner urge to develop our potential arises anew. We then decide to develop or to react to our subconscious fear by trying to suppress it. Overeating, drinking alcohol, gambling, compulsive smoking, recreational drug use, binging on video games or TV, and so on are examples of the many kinds of activities that are detrimental to our health. They reduce one's vital energy and allow us to avoid difficult emotions. Traumatic events that have left scars and unresolved issues in our emotional body crave resolution. They will be constantly knocking on the door of our consciousness to be addressed. Yet we don't always have the tools to resolve them, especially in this so-called scientific world that negates the importance of human emotions and has very limited resources to resolve emotional issues. Psychology and psychiatry are very recent sciences that don't take into account the spiritual aspect of our being that is always at the heart of our evolutionary experiences. Compared to the traditional healing methods of Native peoples around the world, these disciplines are but stumbling toddlers, often causing as much harm as good in that they prescribe medications for problems of the heart and mind. Thus we often camouflage and repress difficult emotions that are screaming to be healed. This is another reason why we have so many dependency issues. When these addictive behaviors that reduce one's vitality become a way of camouflaging all these inner problems, we become dependent on certain substances and behaviors. Over time, the body gets used to this kind of "relief" and looks for it, and we slowly lose control. This is when what was a habit becomes an addiction.

The energy toward self-realization that allows us to deal with our issues is a good energy, a necessary impulse that helps us evolve. We must recognize our cravings for what they are—beneficial energies seeking a way to express themselves. This is why a small amethyst piece under the tongue is so efficient. It helps us take that energy, transform the habitual tendency, and channel it into beneficial activities. Interestingly, an essence won't work as well as the stone in this case, even if the energy is similar. It is the physical sensation here—which relates to the person's first years and the tendency to put everything in the mouth in order to know it—that has a reprogramming effect.

Teaching Story

Here is the story of a woman who cured her alcoholic husband with amethyst. Since the man was in denial and far too advanced in his addiction to use a small piece of amethyst under his tongue—he was drinking almost two liters of whisky a day—she programmed an amethyst crystal, which she then put inside his bottle. He drank all the whisky without noticing the amethyst. She then took the crystal out of the bottle, purified it and programmed it again, and put it back in the next bottle. She continued in this way, doing this for several days. Then she noticed that her husband had replaced whisky with wine. This time she put the amethyst in the wine bottle, taking care to purify and reprogram the crystal after each bottle. After that he went on to beer, and she continued with the same treatment. In the end, her husband joined Alcoholics Anonymous and began treatment. He stopped drinking. It was only some years later that she told him what she had done.

This story illustrates an innovative use of amethyst. It's important to know that the only people on whom we can attempt healing without their permission are our immediate family members. You do not have permission to work on anyone who is not immediate family, and you must not work on friends, even if very close, who have not requested or given you permission to receive your healing energies. This is standard protocol for all healers, as doing healing without gaining permission interferes with a person's life path and will adversely affect your own karma (the law of cause and effect).

Another common reason for addictions is that expressing our emotions is not acceptable in our society. A child won't feel comfortable crying on his teacher's shoulder even if he or she feels the need for comforting. The same is true in the workplace—can you see yourself crying on your boss's shoulder? Thus we suppress. With time it gets really difficult, and often we don't know why. The pressure of unexpressed emotion builds, and then, well, we just eat our emotions! We get fatter and fatter, or we drink or get stoned.

Instead we might just want to find a confidant or a talking circle, where we can let it all out . . .

Alcoholism, drugs, and other addictions represent an illness of the soul whose progression can be stopped by a spiritual program of reorientation and rehabilitation. In some cases using an amethyst will not be sufficient. A spiritual program like the one used by the Twelve Step program that addresses various types of addiction can be very helpful for healing the soul. There are a great many of these types of fellowships (Alcoholics Anonymous, Narcotics Anonymous, etc.). Participation is free of charge, and the help of other people who have the same problem has a very high success rate.

Amethyst can also be used as a protection crystal (see plate 31). It is in fact a more protective crystal than clear quartz. The violet color has a repelling quality. You do not want to use amethyst if you are fairly comfortable around people. Only use it as a protection crystal if you are very sensitive to being around people and want to remain in your own bubble most of the time. As with clear quartz, when used for protection, always place amethyst over your spiritual plexus, at the base of the sternum.

Meditating with amethyst is very helpful. One of the many beneficial uses of this mineral is for addressing issues involving sexual differentiation. If someone is confused about their sexual orientation, it can be very useful to meditate with amethyst to make one's inclination clear. In our Native cultures we have always honored those we call "two spirits."

They have the two polarities and are just as comfortable loving their own sex as the opposite sex. They find their place quite easily in our traditional societies. This is not the case in the current world societies that have been heavily influenced by religions that exert control over people, especially over their sexual behavior. As making love is one of the strongest ways to attain unity with the Divine, it would be counterproductive to religious institutions to allow people to have sex freely, as they would no longer need religion to give them some understanding of divine will. Thus the Church has put in place a lot of conditioning and programming around sexual behavior. Control a person's sex life and you control them. They then become dependent on religion. This results in a lot of discrimination against those who go against the norm. But it is very important for people who are two spirits to honor who they truly are.

One of OhShinnàh's students had married and had many children, but she was very unsatisfied with her life. She was getting to a place where the difficult emotions that she was experiencing had led her into alcoholism. Upon meeting OhShinnàh, who saw clearly who she was and recommended meditating with amethyst, she discovered that in fact she was more comfortable loving women. This turned her whole life around, and she became an excellent healer and a very strong practitioner of our Native tradition.

It's important to understand that this same-sex orientation is inscribed in one's genes, that homosexuality is a physiological disposition. In Native American culture, the grandmothers would be able to discern this at a very young age, before the child was five. Thus these special children would not be segregated, but in fact were encouraged in the discovery of their unique orientation.

White Crystals

White represents the presence of all the colors of the spectrum. Unlike clear light, which reveals the seven colors of the rainbow, white light is more opaque than clear. White shines out its frequency, so if you want to shine, to teach, to perform, to display, wear white.

MOONSTONE

Moonstone is a microcrystalline stone that is most often a soft, shimmering white color with a yellow to bluish white sheen (see plate 32). It's associated with the Great Mother Goddess in her many manifestations, as all cultures have some representation of this deity. This is the stone most often used by women for many reasons. Its association with the moon makes it the stone of choice when rebalancing a woman's monthly cycle, which should be in sync with the phases of the moon. One of the problems that stem from our artificial lifestyle is that many women are no longer on regular moon-time cycles. Other environmental conditions that interfere with the moon's energy, such as electromagnetic pollution, have created premenstrual pains, acute menstrual discomfort, and excessive bleeding. Moonstone can help a woman harmonize her monthly cycle. Putting the purified moonstone in moonlight so that it takes on lunar energy and then wearing or keeping that moonstone close can be one way of using it to regulate the monthly cycle. Moonstone is also helpful for increasing fertility for couples who have not been fruitful in their endeavors to conceive a child.

Men can also benefit from moonstone. We carry both feminine and masculine polarities within us. Our current incarnation and sex in this lifetime is an indication of our current tendency and preference, yet we hold the potential to incarnate as either a man or a woman when our soul is in the spirit world. This choice is dictated by preference as well as by the circumstances that will best lead to our evolution along the spiritual ascent toward higher levels of manifestation. Macho men displaying a misogynistic attitude are often unconsciously afraid or uncomfortable with their inner female aspect. This is where moonstone can help, as it allows such men to tune in harmoniously to that feminine aspect of their being and hopefully transform their macho attitude. Usually moonstone will be brought to such men by those who know them, as they are often unwilling to recognize that they have these shortcomings or that their macho attitude is not conducive to harmonious relationships. In the same way, moonstone can also help women connect with their feminine identity.

The customs and consideration given to a women's cycle in indigenous culture are very different from those of modern civilization. It's generally understood among most Native American people that women acquire more power and maturity than men naturally because of their moon time. A man has to work harder to attain this level of maturity and self-knowledge, which is imparted through coming-of-age rituals and men's circles. But the natural rhythm all women experience by the grace of their biological clock allows them to understand who they are. It is a monthly initiation into the female mysteries and gives women the potential for innate communion with the energies of the Divine Holy Mother, who produces all life in the universe. Rather than call it menstruation, or a woman's period, it's called a woman's moon time, the sacred days when women are in direct contact with the flow of the Great Mother Goddess's wisdom stream. Native nations have a special place called the moon lodge, where a woman can go to pray and meditate during her moon time. Honoring this natural rhythm in a woman's life is not only a precious source of wisdom and information for the community, as many visions and dreams originate in the moon lodge that have helped and even saved the people from attacks by white soldiers; time spent in the moon lodge also prevents common societal female problems. Our current modern society has seen many women experiencing much discomfort, pain, excessive blood loss, mood swings, and other negative experiences that come from not honoring or even understanding the profound significance of the female moon time. It has been reduced to a medical condition that needs to be covered up and ignored as much as possible. Can a working woman call in to work and say, "It's my moon time, see you in a few days"? Not hardly.

In Native culture when a woman is on her moon, with the energy of the Great Goddess flowing through her, it's considered that she has a very powerful energy that men or even other women who are not on their moon don't have. It's said that they can inadvertently sap the energy of others without even realizing it. Being stronger, this woman attracts the vital force of other people. This is one of the reasons why traditional women would leave their families to go to the moon lodge and enjoy some quiet time and commune with the spirit of the Great Mother Goddess flowing through them. It's also the reason why in Native communities most medicine women do not perform healing when on their moon.

It's not always possible to do that today, so if a woman needs to perform a healing act and is on her moon time, she can put a piece of moonstone in her navel, maybe put a small BandAid over it so it stays there, and keep it there during the time of the treatment. The reason this is done is so that the energy can only move from the healer to the patient and not the other way around. Always remove the moonstone as soon as you have completed the treatment. OhShinnàh has said that she would hear a little hissing noise when she removed the moonstone. This is probably an indication that the moonstone was blocking the secondary energy center in a certain way and that the energy started circulating again when the moonstone was removed.

OPAL

Opal is in a category by itself, as it has a white color yet it is the reflection of different hues of the rainbow within it that acts as the catalyst of its healing energy (see plate 33). We could have included this stone with the multicolored stones, yet its predominant color is white. Opal is a very special stone, as it contains water. Thus it's used for all healing where we need to work with the kidneys, urinal tract, lymphatic system, etc. Do not use fire opal when you want to work with the blue ray or with the water element in the body. Use it for the emotional body and to promote more energy in the emotional body that is related to the mind.

All opals are used for amplifying the feminine nature of being. They have an energy similar to moonstone, only on a more active and creative frequency. They sometimes need to be coated with oil so they retain their sheen, as some have a tendency to lose their water. Opal refracts light and will then display many colors of the rainbow because of the water content. They are emitters of rainbows! They do have crystalline structure, although it's considered to be a lot less structured than most microcrystalline minerals. Thus they do not retain programming and intention at the same level as other crystals. Forget permanently programming these crystals, and instead work with short-term programming.

PEARL

Pearl is the feminine gem par excellence! The fact is you will rarely see men wearing pearls.

Pearls are not crystals. They are the hardened secretions of oysters that protect themselves against grains of sand that have infiltrated their shell by coating them with layers of secretions that make them soft to the touch (see plate 34). The energies of the moon and water are contained within pearl. They offer protection to beautiful women from the inappropriate thought forms emitted by some men upon seeing them. Pearl deflects these thought forms and clears the woman's energy field of any residual energy imprints these thought forms may have left. This is a good example of one of the laws of the universe called *harmonic resonance,* or the law of harmony. As the pearl is the way the oyster protects itself from abrasive elements that have lodged in its gentle flesh, it's this frequency that is activated when wearing pearls in a conscious way.

As most pearls come from the sea, there is no need to purify them in the same way as other crystals. Yet we do need to purify them when they have been used as protection. Just run them through saltwater for a few moments, holding them in one hand and running them through with the other so that the movement is also energizing them and purifying the energy field around them, which is sufficient. They do not need to be purified a whole week as other crystals do.

Black Crystals

Like white, the color black also contains all the colors of the spectrum, but unlike white, which shines out, black is discreet and low-profile. If you want to keep your energy to yourself in a more protective mode, wear or use black stones.

BLACK TOURMALINE

Black tourmaline (see plate 35) is very powerful as an absorbent of negative vibrations and frequencies. It can hold a lot, helping us through evil places and energies by assimilating these energies. It also needs to be purified frequently when it's been programmed to do this kind of work.

This stone is also helpful in meditation as a means of calming the mind and opening up to Spirit by letting go of our ordinary, mundane thoughts.

OBSIDIAN

Obsidian is a shiny black stone that is found in many different forms all over the planet. It's in fact volcanic lava that has cooled very quickly and did not have time to crystallize. Thus obsidian is amorphous, it has no crystalline structure. It is more akin to glass than to crystal. It's this very state of amorphous emptiness vibrating in this stone that dictates its use. We use it as a divination tool, to empty our thoughts and have a shiny, mirrorlike surface that we can gaze upon (see plate 36). As the emptiness of the void gives rise to form, our availability (mirror gaze) that falls upon the vacuity in obsidian will allow the visions and answers we seek to emerge from our own innate wisdom. In the Snow White fable, when the evil queen asks her magic mirror, "Mirror, mirror on the wall, who is fairest of them all?" that mirror is an obsidian mirror.

It is the inert, static quality of obsidian that makes it useful as a clair-voyant tool. This highly amorphous quality, combined with the appearance of solid stone, calms the mind, giving us access to higher levels of perception. I find obsidian useful for grounding and have always been attracted to this mineral. Some small, roundish obsidian stones found in the American Southwest, known as Apache tears, are used for protection and in ritual amulets. Obsidian is found in many places throughout the world and has been used extensively as cutting tools, arrowheads, and weapons, as it can be chipped to a very sharp edge, as cutting as glass is.

SMOKY QUARTZ

The antidote to Herkimer's tendency to dreaminess is smoky quartz. It will bring back to reality anyone who has misused or overdosed on Herkimer. It favors anchoring and grounding oneself in reality.

Smoky quartz helps you get back in touch with reality and promotes a more concrete, down-to-earth lifestyle. People who always tend to make great plans, who talk a lot about it but do not achieve much, those who live in their dreams or those who are always undecided, never getting anywhere, should use smoky quartz. It's important that our life and our spirituality be down-to-earth, with practical applications.

We have a physical body. Inhabiting one's body and manifesting one's potential as a human being is a source of profound joy. It is good to be in the reality of things and have discernment. Our world and media are full of innumerable illusions. Smoky quartz helps us manifest this more practical, down-to-earth, grounded spirit, without losing the awe and wonder we have for the beauty of life.

Some quartz crystals have been irradiated, becoming completely black. We should not use these, as they don't have the same vibration as a true smoky quartz. There are genuine smoky quartz crystals that are completely black, much like irradiated quartz, but it's impossible to tell the difference, so I would err on the side of safety and only use smoky quartz that retains some translucency (see plate 37).

Multicolored Crystals

Diverse colors present in a single crystal often enhance the beneficial effects the stone can offer. This is akin to what we say of the rainbow people, those who have several different ethnic ancestors, from the white, red, yellow, and/or black races of humanity. We call these people two feathers, three feathers, or four feathers, and each of their different racial ancestors gives them special gifts. Multicolored stones will have special attributes that are unique because of the presence of several colors.

AGATE

This microcrystalline stone is very common and is found in many places all over the world. It usually presents itself in many different layers of crystallization, with different hues and colors (see plate 38). This is symbolic of the different aspects of our manifestation here on earth. These different facets of our being are the physical body, the emotional body, the mental body, and the spiritual body. There can be conflictual tendencies between these different bodies. For example, if your mind knows that chocolate is not good for you but your emotions crave it to the point of binging on it, then there will be great discomfort and inner strife. This is when the spiritual body should intervene to help you make the right decision. We mention this because agate can be used to help integrate and unite these different facets of our body. As such, this is an excellent stone for traveling, for when we are far from our Native grounds, from our home, when we may be destabilized and have more difficulty remaining whole and united within ourselves. Agate will be helpful in these circumstances.

The moss agate variety is very helpful for those working in agriculture.

Agate contains a lot of quartz, so it's quite comfortable for a person's energy field and is easily programmed.

LABRADORITE

This black and gray stone has green, blue, violet, and white sheen and reflections (see plate 39); it also contains its fair share of unknowns and mysteries. Labradorite assesses levels of subtle clairvoyance while allowing us to remain grounded and in contact with the physical world. It readily activates one's psychic abilities. If the use of labradorite is motivated by dubious intentions, it can create illusions. One must always remain vigilant when working with crystals, even more so with labradorite. It makes very beautiful jewelry that enhances the light in one's aura. Be a shining person today and splash some light on your family and friends!

WATERMELON TOURMALINE

This wonderful stone has a deep red core and surrounding green exterior, hence its name (see plate 40). It helps with balancing our polarities, the yin and yang, feminine and masculine, the lunar and solar aspects of our psyche and body. It will help the physical body eliminate excessive radioactivity. It's a great stone to wear when traveling by plane, as it can help you adjust to jet lag. It is also used to foster an understanding of our multidimensionality as human beings.

Other Stones

AMBER

Amber is not actually a crystal, but a fossil, the fossilized remains of resin from long-ago evergreen trees (see plate 41). The most precious pieces of amber have insects that were caught in the resin. It has proven to be invaluable in removing the pain young children suffer when teething. It also balances yin and yang (feminine and masculine) energies in both men and women. Artists are fond of it as amber encourages imagination and the recall of interior landscapes. For some people it represents vital energy and is used to promote regeneration.

FOOL'S GOLD/PYRITE

The symmetrical beauty of this stone is pleasing to the eye (see plate 42). It can be a useful support in your visualization and inner imaging process, for fortifying the blood in cases of anemia and iron deficiency, and for rebuilding the bones at a cellular level, since it takes strong blood to make good bones. Pyrite also helps with management of financial assets, investments, and material wealth despite its funny common name, which comes from the comical story of people thinking it was gold. Its color, reminiscent of a copper-colored gold, puts it as a stone of several colors. Like opal, pyrite can reflect several other colors depending on the light. Red is the predominant color, a reflection of the large quantity of iron it holds. So, not for jewelry. It's also a bit too soft to be used as a gemstone.

⌃

There is no need to be ambitious in the field of crystal healing. We don't need many crystals. If we have understood that they are true friends on our path, we also know that just a few *real* friends are needed in our lives; we don't need many, only the truly significant ones, those who feel magical to us.

Shamanism is the path to Spirit, and Spirit manifests everywhere. A true shaman sees life in everything except technology. There are in indigenous communities certain technologies that are alive, that is possible. But modern technology is a direct path to death for all life on Planet Earth. That's why only magic and firm, true intention can be successful in healing a humanity that's lost its way.

We can reverse this tendency. That's why the ancient secrets of crystals are revealed here and now. Crystals are always striving for perfection. That is their nature. They also seek harmony for the earth and all her beings. May they help you and yours, always . . .

Conclusion

Elders of the Native American temple-builder nations have given us valuable insights into healing with crystals. These methods, techniques, and principles, combined with a lifetime of practice and experiences with the flowers of the mineral kingdom, have blossomed into the insights offered in this book.

All healing is at its core a spiritual endeavor. Thus the importance of keeping a regular spiritual discipline, giving time and energy to purification practices, breathing and stretching exercises, meditation, and prayer. This will awaken and amplify your ability to help and to heal those who come to you. We have no need to push ahead or rush on the spiritual path. Slow and steady is the way to go. It's better to give a short time every day to practice than to go for many hours and then become tired and skip days of practice. True learning takes time. As we are eternal souls, we have all the time we need.

We are immortal spirits learning hard and powerful lessons about ourselves as we experience life on earth. This planetary classroom has many beings in it, mineral, plant, animal, elemental, and invisible. All are important messengers of the One Light, the One Source that creates all. They all carry teachings and they are all doing the work that Creator has asked them to do. Thus they deserve respect, and when they receive this consideration they reveal great gifts of knowledge, wisdom, and health.

Being connected with the land and spending time in nature will give you a feeling for the interconnectedness of all things. This understanding is important, as crystals come from Mother Earth. The planetary energies and influences are a part of the energy work that you'll need to integrate into your healing practice at some point along the path. Being a conscious member of the ecological system is what being human entails. This will help you understand the power crystals have. Thus treating them with respect, purifying and energizing them and seeking communication and right relationship with them will allow you to gain valuable healing friends. We have given you here a specific methodology that is logical and verifiable. You can test this for yourself so that you can work with the conviction of experience rather than with blind faith.

Remember the three fundamental laws of healing: unconditional love, nonattachment, and intention. The philosophical foundations that countless elders have passed down through the generations have great validity. We must meditate on them so that we tread on solid ground, protecting ourselves and others with insight and wisdom.

I hope you will find this book useful in your healing practice. I wish you peace, light, and much joy as you discover the beauty and power of the crystals as wonderful healing friends and companions on your evolutionary path.

May beauty be all around!

WITH LOVE,
LUKE BLUE EAGLE

Index

Numbers in *italics* preceded by *pl.* refer to color insert plate numbers.

addiction and dependency, 225–29
agate, 74, 88, 236, *pl. 38*
air, pure, 29
amazonite, 210–11, *pl. 14*
amber, 237, *pl. 41*
amethyst
  about, 224–29
  addiction and dependency and,
    225–29
  illustrated, *pl. 30, pl. 31*
  inclusions and, 189
  light, 174, 180
  as protection crystal, 225, 228
  purification and, 127
  use of, 99, 225–28
  west and, 53
anger, 83, 89, 191, 206
animal totems, 47, 49, 52
aquamarine
  about, 216–21
  essence, 153
  fear and, 217–21
  hexagonal structure and, 76
  illustrated, *pl. 25*
  inclusions and, 189
  vibration frequency, 217, 221
  water element and, 93, 98, 221
artificial stones, 38
astral field, 159

astral traveling, 198
azurite, 76, 98, 152, 200–201, 221–22,
  pl. 26

bad behavior, correcting, 9
balance, 53–54, 63–65, 72, 214
bitermination, 34, 197
black, 100, 234
black crystals, 234–37
black tourmaline, 234, *pl. 35*
blessing ceremony, 132–33
bloodstone/heliotrope, 84, 211, *pl. 15*
blue ray, 98, 216
blue ray crystals, 98, 216–22
body. *See* care of the body
bone cells, red coral and, 200–201
brain, hemispheres of, 41, 42–43
breathing, 88–89, 110

Canadian cedar, 59
care of the body. *See also* spiritual
  practice
  about, 26–27
  exercise and, 29
  food and, 27–28
  keys to, 27
  life mission and, 30–31
  pure air and, 29
  pure water and, 28–29

sleep and, 30
sunshine and, 30
vital energy and, 26–27
carnelian, 50, 88, 97, 153, *pl. 11*
celestite, 93, 222, 223, *pl. 27*
center, wisdom of, 53–54
centering
    about, 40–41
    benefits of, 43, 44
    brain hemispheres and, 41, 42–43
    brain waves before/after, 44
    defined, 1, 41
    exercise, 43, 44, 177
    mechanics behind, 41–42
    observations, 43
    practicing, 168, 174, 175
ceremonies, 6, 11, 36–37, 113, 183–84,
    198
C face, 178–79
chakras, 107–8
Chiiyaam, 61–62, 122
chrysocolla, 152, 211–13, *pl. 16*
chrysoprase, 213, *pl. 19*
citrine
    about, 205–7
    cognitive blindness and, 209
    as coyote stone, 49, 205
    earth element and, 88
    fixed reality people and, 205, 224
    illustrated, *pl. 12*
    south and, 49
    use of, 206
    working with, 207
clay, 87–88
clear light crystals, 189–98. *See also*
    specific crystals
clear quartz crystal
    breathing through length, 192
    calming kundalini with, 106
    C face, 173, 175–76, 178–79
    dissonance, 194–95

frequency vibration, 190, 194
healing treatment using, 175–82
illustrated, *pl. 1, pl. 2, pl. 3, pl. 4*
importance of, 189–90
light and, 192
in mending tears and holes, 194
molecular structure, 136
north and, 48
one-pointed, 173
positive and negative ions and, 193
pretreatment evaluation using,
    174–75, 180–81
programming to another stone,
    149–50
protection with, 191–92
purifying before use, 174
purifying energy centers with,
    108–9
rainbows, 193
sacred sound and, 83–84
colors
    about, 94–95
    black, 100, 234
    blue, 98, 216
    choosing, 100
    combinations of, 99–100
    as crystal attribute, 94
    east, 49
    green, 97–98, 209–10
    indigo, 98–99, 223
    jewelry, 148–49
    north, 48
    orange, 96–97, 203–4
    primary, 95
    red, 96, 198
    south, 50
    violet, 99, 224
    west, 53
    white, 100, 229
    yellow, 97, 207
coming-of-age ceremonies, 63–64

communication
    with crystals, 34–36
    with Four Grandfathers, 54–56
    with Mother Earth, 37
compassion, 67–68, 69–70, 82
consecration ceremony, 144–45
contemplation, 82
context, Native American teachings, 1, 16
corn flour, 104
crying, 90
crystal (artificial), 38
crystal bath, 176
crystal essences, 151–53. *See also specific crystals*
crystal families, 76–77
crystal healing
    distance, 182–85
    intention, determining, 169–70
    with jewelry, 147–49
    path of, 3–4
    in pouch or pocket, 149
    programming in, 149–50
    with quartz crystal, 175–82
    simple practices for, 146–51
    spiritual preparation for, 20–33
    as step-by-step process, 15
    visualization, 150
crystal home, 130
crystals. *See also specific types of crystals*
    as alive, 33–36
    as amplifiers, 2, 3, 21–22, 100, 196
    blessing, 132–33
    care and maintenance of, 128–32
    communication with, 34–36, 37
    consecrating, 144–45
    early interest in (author), 5–6
    energizing technique, 128–29
    hands-on, preparing for, 158–65
    hardness of, 75
    minerals as, 74–75
    Mother Earth and, 36–39

as multidimensional beings, 34
in Native American training, 4, 5
programming, 145–46, 177–78, 185
purifying, 126–28
right relationship with, 134–42
sacred sound and, 83–84
structures of, 76–77
things to avoid, 131–32
turtle altar, 103
working with, preliminaries to, 20–33
wrapping, 130
cubic structure, 77

dance, 23, 26–27, 54–55
Dance of the Four Directions, 54–55
death process, serving, 215
Deloria, Vine, Jr., 199
diamonds, 75, 77, 130, 195–96, *pl. 5*
digestion, 27, 84, 87, 97, 164, 203
dioptase, 98, 152, 222, *pl. 28*
directions, 44–56. *See also* Four Grandfathers
disharmony, 33, 107, 194
distance healing, 182–85
dreams, remembering, 184–85

earth, 86–88. *See also* elements, five
east, 48–49
elements, five, 79–80. *See also specific elements*
emerald
    about, 213–14
    balance and, 214
    as colored stone, 148
    essence, 153
    illustrated, *pl. 20*
    inclusions, 189
    in jewelry, 196
    visualizing, 15
emotions, 86, 91, 202, 206–7, 208

energetic hands, 160–62
energizing crystals, 128–29
energy
    crystals and, 21
    divine, 94
    etheric web, 48, 148
    modulation of, 21–22
    spiritual, 17
    thought and, 143
    vital, 26–27, 162–65
energy centers, working with, 106–9
energy field, working with, 60, 122,
    133, 136, 162, 179
energy fields, human body, 158–60
etheric web
    about, 48, 148
    feeling, with hands, 168, 204
    hands-on healing and, 158–59
    hexagon lattices, 190
    mending tears and holes in, 170, 194
    problems with, 168–69
    reassessing, 169
    recharging, 203, 204
    sensing, 161
exercise, 27, 29, 110
eye of the hand, 160–62

fear, 93, 197, 207, 211–13, 217–21, 226
feminine, the, 230–33
fire, 84–86, 103. See also elements, five
food, 27–28, 163–65
Four Grandfathers
    about, 44–46
    center and, 53–54, 56
    communicating with, 54–56
    east, 48–49
    north, 46–48
    south, 49–50
    symbols and traditions of, 45
    west, 50–53
free will, 31–32

garnet, 86, 96, 98, 151, 198–200, 203,
    pl. 7
Garrett, J. T., 16
geometrical forms, 77
gratitude, 23, 24, 110–11
Great Mother Goddess, 60, 129, 230, 232
green jasper, 84, 98, 214, pl. 21
green ray, 97–98
green ray crystals, 98, 209–16
green tourmaline, 84, 98, 214, pl. 22
grounding, 38, 140, 171, 214, 224, 235

hands
    energizing, 168
    energizing crystals with, 175
    washing away residual energies from,
        171
hands-on healing
    energetic hands and, 160–62
    human body energy fields and,
        158–60
    laying-on of hands and, 166–72
    preparing for, 158–65
    vital energy cultivation and, 162–65
happiness, seeking of, 68
hard-core shamanism, 17–18
hardness of stones and crystals, 75
harmonic resonance, 105–6, 233
healing. See also crystal healing
    balance and, 18–19
    distance, 182–85
    fundamental laws of, 66–72, 240
    holistic understanding of, 14–19
    listening and, 15
    love and, 66–70
    nonattachment and, 70–71
    physical body and, 14, 15
    right intention and, 71–72
    seeking of happiness and, 68
    shamanism and, 17–18
    spirituality and, 15, 239

heart, fourth energy center, 107
Heart Meditation
about, 121–22
healing and, 69
prayer, 122–23
progressing from, 153–54
uniting and, 122, 124–25
Herkimer diamond, 17, 185, 197–98, *pl. 6*
hexagonal structure, 76
heyokas (contraries), 8
higher mental field, 159
holistic healing, 16
humor, 8, 9

illness, 15, 70–72, 95, 206, 228
inclusions, 189
indigo ray, 98–99, 223
indigo ray crystals, 99, 223
initiations, shamanic, 17, 52
insomnia, crystals for, 223
intention, right, 71–72
Inuit, 51–52

jade, 214–15, *pl. 23*
jewelry, crystal, 127, 147–49
juniper, 59

Krieger, Dolores, 166–67
kundalini, 106–7

labradorite, 35, 76, 84, 99, 237, *pl. 39*
laughter, 8, 9, 49–50
law of harmony, 136
laying-on of hands
about, 166–67
administration of, 167
defined, 166
methodology, 168
practicing, 171–72
summary of steps, 172
life mission, cultivating, 30–31

lifestyle, 16
light, 43, 54–55, 94–95, 100, 105, 109,
188, 192
listening and healing, 15
liver, 81–82, 83–84
love, 66–70, 72
lower mental field, 159
lucid dreaming, 184, 185

malachite, 75, 98, 128, 152, 211–13,
pl. 17
masculine/feminine balance, 63–65
matrix stone, 80
medicine, 10–11, 16
Medicine Wheels
about, 117–18
creating, 118–21
as place, 121
stones and, 120–21
Medicine Wheel teachings, 53
meditation
about, 24–26
compassion and, 68
crystals for, 228–29
Heart Meditation and, 121–25,
153–54
north and, 46
sapphire and, 223
Three Suns Meditation and, 154–56
mental body, 14
metals, jewelry, 148
mind
disease and, 16
intention and, 10
meditation and, 24–25
spiritual practice and, 32
universal, 108
mindfulness, 25, 26. *See also* meditation
minerals, as crystals, 74–75
monoclinic structure, 76
moonstone, 90, 230–32, *pl. 32*

Mother Earth
  communication with, 37
  respect for, 36–39
  turtle symbol, 102
  uniting with Father Sky, 124
  we as part of, 25
multicolored crystals, 236–37
music, active listening to, 44

Native American teachings
  about, 40
  centering, 40–44
  context, 1
  elders and, 4, 6–7
  foundational, 40–65
  Four Grandfathers (cardinal
    directions), 44–56
  masculine/feminine balance, 63–65
  oral, 1–2
  smudging, 56–62
natural world, reading, 208
nature
  in balance with, 19
  center and, 56
  ceremonies and teachings in, 36–37
  communion with, 83
  destruction of, 2
  as Great Spirit's school, 200
  laws of, 114
  respect for, 36–39
  wisdom and resources of, 10
nature spirits, 111–12
negative ions, 57, 193
nonattachment, 70–71
north, 46–48

obsidian, 75, 234–35, *pl. 36*
offerings
  how we live our lives, 112
  prayer, 23–24, 110–11
  reciprocity and, 117

right relationship and, 113–14
smoke, 60–61
as testimony to gratitude, 111
turtle altar, 105–6
OhShinnàh Fastwolf, 4, 56–57, 68, 129,
  166, 199, 229, 232
opal, 86, 90, 93, 232–33, *pl. 33*
oral teachings, 1–2
orange ray, 96–97, 203–4
orange ray crystals, 97, 204–7
orneida, 26
orthorhombic structure, 76
oversoul, 18, 159

pearl, 60, 90, 233, *pl. 34*
peridot, 148, 216, *pl. 24*
Philosophy of Nature, The, 10
platonic solids, 77–78
point of vulnerability, 191–92
positive ions, 177, 193
prana, 26
prayer circles, 183
prayers
  about, 22–23
  distance healing and, 182–83
  of gratitude, 110–17
  offerings and, 23–24
priestcraft tradition, 6
programming crystals, 145–46,
  177–78, 185
protection, crystals for, 128, 191–92
psychosomatic diseases, 207
purification of crystals, 126–28, 173
purification of space, 174
pyrite (fool's gold), 238, *pl. 42*

quartz crystal, 190. *See also* clear quartz
  crystal; rose quartz; smoky quartz

rainbows, in crystals, 193
Rainbow Warriors, 7

rattles, 104
red coral, 128, 200–201, *pl. 8*
red ray, 96, 198
red ray crystals, 98, 198–203. *See also*
   specific crystals
Red Road, 4
rhombohedral structure, 76–77
right intention, 71–72
right relationship, 113–14
rose quartz, 96, 201–2, *pl. 9*
ruby
   about, 202–3
   essence, 151, 203
   fire element and, 86
   garnet versus, 199
   illustrated, *pl. 10*
   inclusions, 189
   lasers and, 21
   south and, 50
   triangular structure, 77
   use of, 96, 202–3

sacred sound (ether). *See also* elements,
   five
   about, 80–81
   crystals and, 83–84
   liver and, 81–82, 83–84
   nature observation and, 83
   telepathy and, 82
sacred space
   about, 3
   creating, 102–25
   energy centers and, 106–9
   Medicine Wheel and, 117–21
   offerings and, 109–17
   turtle altar and, 102–6
sage, 59, 121–22
saltwater, 57, 128, 131, 136, 144, 179,
   193
sapphire, 77, 98–99, 149, 189, 223,
   pl. 29

sea salt, 104
serpent fire, 106
sex and sexuality, 64–65
shamanic journeying
   about, 137–38
   to a crystal cave, 139–42
   to meet crystals, 137–42
   shadow body and, 138, 139
   shamanic power and, 138–39
shamanism, 16–18, 238
shamans, 17–18, 36, 51–52, 199
shells, 104
sleep, 30, 134–35, 223
smoke offerings, 60–61
smoky quartz, 140, 197, 234, *pl. 37*
smudging
   benefits of, 57
   burning of herbs and, 59–60
   Chiiyaam and, 61–62
   defined, 56
   effects of, 56–57
   herbs for, 59
   opening windows during, 57–58
   smoke offerings and, 60–61
solar plexus, 8, 97, 107–9, 175, 207,
   211–12
song, 23, 89
south, 49–50
Spirit, 4, 46–48, 64, 72, 238
spiritual body, 14, 159
spiritual practice
   about, 6, 22
   amplification through, 21–22
   care of the vehicle and, 26–31
   following original instructions and,
      31–33
   free will and, 31–32
   meditation and, 10, 24–26
   mind and, 32
   prayer and offerings and, 22–24
   relationships and, 32

Temple Builders, 20–21
tests and trials of, 33
visualizations and, 26
vital energy and, 163
working with crystals and, 20–33
stones. *See* crystals
stress relief, 204, 210, 221
subtle vision, 129
Sun Bear, 16, 32, 117–19
sunshine, 30
sweetgrass, 59
symbols, 10, 45, 116–17, 170

teaching stories
crystals as alive, 35
dependency and addiction, 227
fear, 219–21
harmonizing human relationships,
150–51
mindfulness, 25
offerings, 114–16
prayers, 110–11
protection with crystals, 192–93
summer solstice ceremony, 50
vital energy of food, 164–65
techniques, 7, 20, 66, 72, 85, 130, 142,
158
Temple Builders, 6, 17–18, 20–21
tetragonal structure, 76
third brain, 107
Three Suns Meditation, 154–56
throat, 107, 127, 204
topaz, 49, 76, 97, 207–9, *pl. 13*
totems, 18, 137–42. *See also* animal
totems

triclinic structure, 76
turquoise, 75, 152, 200, 211–13, *pl. 18*
turtle altar
about, 102–3
blessing, 104–5
as divine light symbol, 105
elements of, 103–4
offerings, 105–6
twilight, 199

violet ray, 99, 224
violet ray crystals, 99, 224–29
visualizations, 26, 71–72, 150, 174
vital energy, 26–27, 162–65
voice, 89–90

water, pure, 28–29
water element, 91–93, 103. *See also*
elements, five
watermelon tourmaline, 237, *pl. 40*
west, 50–53
white crystals, 229–33
white light, 100, 229
wind, 88–90. *See also* elements, five
wisdom
of balance, 53–54
of east, 48–49
of love, 67
of north, 46
of south, 49
of water, 91–92
of west, 50–51

yellow ray, 97, 207
yellow ray crystals, 97, 207–9